PRIEST

where is thy Mass?

MASS

where is thy Priest?

THE SEMINARY INTERVIEWS

ANGELUS PRESS

2915 FOREST AVENUE,
KANSAS CITY, MISSOURI 64109

Library of Congress Cataloging-in-Publication Data

Priest, where is thy Mass? Mass, where is thy priest? : seventeen priests tell why they celebrate the Latin Mass.-- 2nd ed.
    p. cm.
  ISBN 1-892331-26-8 (alk. paper)
  1. Mass. 2. Catholic traditionalist movement. 3. Catholic Church. Ordo Missae (Pre-Vatican II) 4. Catholic Church--Clergy--Interviews. 5. Priests--Interviews

  BX2230.3.P75 2004
  264'.02036--dc22

                                                                    2004006837

ANGELUS PRESS
2915 FOREST AVENUE
KANSAS CITY, MISSOURI 64109
PHONE (816) 753-3150
FAX (816) 753-3557
ORDER LINE 1-800-966-7337
WWW.ANGELUSPRESS.ORG

ISBN 1-892331-26-8
Second Edition—April 2004

Printed in the United States of America

CONTENTS

FOREWORD 1

FR. RONALD CONRAD 5

FR. CHRISTOPHER DANEL 13

FR. VINCENT MICHAEL 35

FR. FRANCIS LE BLANC 43

FR. PAUL GREUTER 49

FR. BRIAN HAWKER 57

FR. EUGENE HEIDT 65

FR. HARRY MARCHOSKY 77

FR. VIDKO PODRŽAJ 83

FR. CLEMENT PROCOPIO, O.F.M. 89

FR. CARL PULVERMACHER, O.F.M. CAP. 101

FR. RONALD RINGROSE 109

REV. MSGR. RAYMOND RUSCITTO 121

FR. GRAHAM WALTERS 141

FR. PAUL WICKENS 151

FR. WILLIAM YOUNG 167

FR. STEPHEN ZIGRANG 187

These interviews were conducted as an apostolate to Roman Catholic priests by St. Thomas Aquinas Seminary (Winona, Minnesota) of the Society of Saint Pius X. The intention of this apostolate was to record common areas of concern between the priests interviewed and other priests who are struggling with living their Catholic priesthood in today's Church and world. It is difficult for many priests to do so, torn as they are between belief and action.

The interviews, granted between May, 2002 and September, 2003, reveal that the crises of conscience faced by these seventeen priests became extreme enough that they took extreme action–to leave the celebration of the New Mass and to celebrate exclusively the traditional Mass.

The priests whose interviews are published here are normal, sound, and clear-thinking. None are member-priests of the Society of Saint Pius X. Strictly doctrinal theses are good and necessary, especially in this time of crisis, but these interviews put a human face to it.–*Ed.*

FOREWORD

In this book, seventeen Roman Catholic priests tell their stories of why they celebrate the Latin Mass and not the New Mass. It is a matter of conscience.

Some of these priests, ordained before the Second Vatican Council, never celebrated the New Mass. Others said the New Mass when it arrived in 1969, but eventually moved away from it. Others, trained in postconciliar seminaries and ordained after 1970, abandoned the New Rite for the Latin Mass.

The crisis of conscience that the new liturgy would impose on Catholics was predicted over thirty years ago.

In 1969, Alfredo Cardinal Ottaviani, the Prefect of the Vatican's Holy Office, wrote a letter to Pope Paul VI warning against the New Mass. He said it represented "...both in whole and in its details a striking departure from the theology of the Mass as it was formulated by Session XXII of the Council of Trent." His letter, also signed by Antonio Cardinal Bacci, accompanied a *Short Critical Study of the New Order of Mass* by a group of Roman theologians, better known as *The Ottaviani Intervention.* The intervention critiqued the original Latin text of the New Mass. It critiqued the New Mass "at its best"! It cited the Protestantized nature of the New Mass, its omissions, ambiguities, and subversion of Catholic teaching. The *Critical Study* said:

> It is obvious that the New Order of Mass has no intention of presenting the Faith taught by the Council of Trent. But it is to this Faith that the Catholic conscience is bound forever. Thus, with the promulgation of the New Order of Mass, the true Catholic is faced with a tragic need to choose.

Here are seventeen priests who sided with the "Faith that the Catholic conscience is bound to forever":

- a priest who, when he expressed desire to return to traditional Catholic worship, was told by his bishop to see a counselor;
- a clergyman whose bishop told him that "transubstantiation" was a long and difficult term that isn't used anymore;
- a young cleric who says traditional devotions were refused by his seminary's hierarchy;
- a diocesan priest who says his young bishop died of a broken heart because of the changes in the Church after the Second Vatican Council;
- a priest who admonished his eucharistic ministers for joking at the credence table during Mass, only for them to write angry letters about him to his bishop;

- a seminarian at a Benedictine monastery where for years invalid Masses were celebrated because the monks made their own hosts with elements that annul the Sacrament;
- a New Jersey pastor who, because he publicly opposed a perverse classroom sex-education course, was suspended by his bishop and evicted from his rectory.

Then there is the Monsignor who challenged his bishop's decree that the Tridentine Mass is forbidden, explaining that no Vatican document expressly outlaws the Old Latin Liturgy. When the bishop wrote to the Vatican and the Apostolic Delegate asking if the old Mass was abrogated, the bishop received either round-about answers, or no answer at all.

This is because the Tridentine Mass was never forbidden, as admitted by the Vatican's Alfons Cardinal Stickler.

In 1986, Pope John Paul II appointed a Commission of nine Cardinals to examine the legal status of the Latin Mass which included Cardinals Ratzinger, Mayer, Oddi, Stickler, Casaroli, Gantin, Innocenti, Palazzin and Tomko. It was instructed to examine two questions:

1) Did Pope Paul VI authorize the bishops to forbid the celebration of the traditional Mass?

2) Does the priest have the right to celebrate the traditional Mass in public and in private without restriction, even against the will of his bishop?

The Commission unanimously determined that Pope Paul VI never gave the bishops the authority to forbid priests from celebrating the traditional rite of Mass.

Regarding the second question: The Commission stated that priests cannot be obliged to celebrate the New Mass; the bishops cannot forbid or place restrictions on the celebration of the traditional rite of Mass whether in public or in private.

This report was contested by the Vatican's *Ecclesia Dei* Commission, but Alfons Cardinal Stickler removed all doubt of the report's authenticity. On May 20, 1995, at a *Christi Fidelis* conference in Fort Lee, New Jersey, Cardinal Stickler gave an address entitled "The Theological Attractiveness of the Tridentine Mass." His Eminence was asked about the Nine Cardinal Commission of 1986.

The Cardinal recounted the story of the former head of *Una Voce* in Europe asking explicitly if the Latin Mass had ever been forbidden. Cardinal Benelli never replied yes or no. Cardinal Stickler explained:

> Binelli couldn't say, "Yes, the Pope forbade it." He can't forbid a Mass that has been used not only for centuries, but has been the Mass of thousands and thousands of saints and faithful. The difficulty was that the Pope *could not* forbid it,

but at the same time, he wanted the New Mass to be said, to be accepted. And so he could only say, "I *want* the New Mass to be said."

Cardinal Stickler reported: "Pope John Paul II asked a commission of nine Cardinals in 1986 two questions. The *first* was, 'Did Pope Paul VI or any other competent authority legally forbid the widespread celebration of the Tridentine Mass in the present day?'" The Cardinal said "I can answer because I was one of the Cardinals....No, the Mass of St. Pius V [*i.e.*, the Latin Mass] has never been suppressed." The *second* question was, "Can any bishop forbid any priest in good standing from celebrating the Tridentine Mass?" Cardinal Stickler replied, "The nine Cardinals unanimously agreed that no bishop may forbid a Catholic priest from saying the Tridentine Mass."

These priests adhere to the Latin Mass in accord with centuries of Catholic doctrine and devotion. Theirs are stories of courage, faithfulness, persecution, and relief when they celebrate the rite which fully expresses their Catholic priesthood.

These priests reveal their background, place and year of ordination, the circumstances that led them to adopt, or not abandon, the Tridentine Mass. Some tell of outstanding Scholastic formations, others of unwieldy, even heterodox seminary formations. They discuss the questions: How does a priest who celebrates the Latin Mass maintain a livelihood? Is learning or re-learning the Latin Mass difficult?

I applaud these priests and those of the world over who refuse to collaborate with the ecumenical Liturgical Revolution that has been a disaster for the Church. How could this revolution be anything but disastrous when, according to the *Ottaviani Intervention,* the New Mass "has much to gladden the heart of the most modernist Protestant"?

Because of traditional priests, Catholics worldwide are instructed in the traditional Faith, nourished by the traditional Sacraments, brought into an atmosphere of supreme reverence, and take part in a sacred action that is–without ambiguity or apology–a true re-presentation of Our Lord's Passion and Death on Calvary. I thank these seventeen for telling their stories.

John Vennari
Editor, *Catholic Family News*
December 12, 2003
Feast of Our Lady of Guadalupe

FR. RONALD CONRAD*

EDITED TRANSCRIPT

When were you ordained, Father?

FR. CONRAD: In 1987. I studied at the most conservative seminary I could find. I had been with the Navy almost fourteen years, and after that, I spent seven years as a government hunter with the US Fish and Wildlife Service.

What was the basis of your late vocation?

I always wanted to become a priest since I was a kid. I was even in the minor seminary, but when Vatican II came it changed everything. I said, To heck with it, and just went into the Navy in the early sixties.

What did they teach you about the priesthood in minor seminary?

FR. C.: They taught us that there would be service involved and that there would be great demands upon us. I remember when the bishop said, "If you don't want to work hard and you think that you can convert all the Indians, then this isn't the diocese for you. If you want to work for about twenty years and convert one Indian, then I'll consider you to have done a great job."

Well, at least he did teach you that the priesthood was about conversion and not just social work!

FR. C.: Oh yes, social work was the furthest notion. In fact, we were instructed that, when we became social workers, the priesthood was over.

What were you taught about the priesthood after Vatican II?

FR. C.: Well, I was pretty fortunate. I had conservative priests who protected and defended me. I never went through what a lot of the young men have to endure to get through the seminary today. I remember that one year they brought a nun in who tried to give me an assignment called "Ministry." My professor of Dogma went up to her, and he said, "Pardon me, absolutely not. This man is graduating, and he's already had all his ministries, and that's the end of it." I never had any contact with the modern stuff because we used all the traditional books then.

---

* "Fr. Ronald Conrad" is a pseudonym used at the request of the priest.–*Ed.*

What was the atmosphere like in the seminary?

FR. C.: Not too shabby. We said the Divine Office together. We attended Mass together, prayed Rosary together, and everything was pretty good. It was the last semester when changes started to take place. For example, you could say your Office in private, and so on.

What happened after ordination?

FR. C.: They made me pick up a master's degree and another degree in philosophy. Before I finishd I was thrown out of the diocese for refusing to study liberation theology. When I was accepted in another diocese, I was appointed Assistant Vicar at the cathedral. Everything went well except when my sermons were too conservative. They wanted an end to those kind of sermons, especially those on Confession, Sin, Hell, and Judgment.

They would rather hear something "uplifting"?

FR. C.: Yes. I remember they ordered me to say a charismatic Mass. By then, the parish Masses were full of charismatics who would give talks and all that. At the end of one Mass, I said, "The Mass is over," and one of them came up to me and said, "No, no, there is still stuff that has to go on," and I just walked off. That's when I got in trouble, and I received another assignment. It just kept on going like that until I was in the furthest district of my diocese. I even had to travel to another state to have my confession heard because my confessor was that far away from me.

When did you start saying the traditional Mass?

FR. C.: Well, I always said it. I said it on my day off when there was no one there, but I was "turned in," so to speak, and I received a letter saying that if I were caught doing it again I would be suspended. Finally, the bishop and I went our separate ways. I just tossed around from diocese to diocese.

What year was that?

FR. C.: It was either 1989 or 1990.

So you had been a priest for just three years. It didn't take them long to get rid of you. But from the time you were ordained, you were saying the traditional Mass privately?

FR. C.: Yes. I had learned most of it when I was in the minor seminary, and then a traditional priest helped me along. He sent me a video, and I kept working on that. I had Latin in college, and I got most of that, too. But, needless to say, I love the traditional Mass. I just can't see myself ever saying the *Novus Ordo Missae* again. I'm not saying it's not valid, but I'm saying it's not Catholic. That's the way I feel about it. If my mother, God bless her, were still alive today and she were having her funeral across the street in the *Novus Ordo*, I wouldn't do it. I would say my own Latin Requiem Mass here for her.

What's the big thing that makes you say the *Novus Ordo* is "not Catholic"?

FR. C.: Well, I remember constantly being irritated. Every time I was finished with the Mass, I kept getting angrier and angrier. I never used Eucharistic ministers, and then one day two popped up. I asked what was going on, and they said, "We're your Eucharistic ministers." After Mass was over, I said, "If you ever do that again, I'll have to throw you out. There's not enough people to warrant it." They informed my superiors, and I got in trouble again. But I still didn't use them. In fact, they were afraid to come back. I just hated all the garbage that went on, all the touchy-feely phony baloney. Everything irritated me to the point that I just couldn't take the nonsense anymore. I was seriously thinking of leaving the priesthood.

But you were saying both the old and New Mass, so you must have seen the great contrast.

FR. C.: An absolute contrast! In fact, I even was publicly saying the New Mass in Latin, but then, again, I was stopped from doing that. The bishop didn't like it; he wanted "participation." I could never understand it–readers, servers, Eucharistic ministers, *etc.* That was his notion of "participation." I wondered if the other people in the pews who **weren't** doing any of these things were participating in the Mass. It just slowly irritated me until I was at the boiling point.

The traditional Mass had the opposite effect on you?

FR. C.: Oh, it sure did! It was very calming thing. I loved it. I just couldn't get enough of it. To this day I think I've missed celebrating only one or two daily Masses, not for reasons of sickness, but because I was flying to Europe.

Did you see other priests frequently miss saying Mass?

FR. C.: Well, yes, there was one priest who was missing consistently, but he was suffering from alcoholism. The vicar said his every day, and I said mine every day. I can't speak about the others since I wasn't with them. But I know that many of them didn't say the Divine Office.

Would you say that this is a reflection of the idea that the priesthood is a job?

FR. C.: Yes, it's becoming just a job, a way to retire, a comfortable living. We got good pay and good benefits, you know. I mean–a $250 gas allowance, a $250 car allowance, plus salary! We'd get to keep our Mass stipends. It was a pretty good-paying job. Plus they covered us completely from head to toe in medical and life insurance. So it was pretty good in that sense of the word. But the traditional notion of vocation is completely missing from the picture. In fact, priests wanted Sundays off and would have liked to see weekday Masses done away with.

Would you say that the New Mass is the reflection of a new religion?

FR. C.: That's what I think. I do not believe that the New Mass expresses anything that is Catholic. In fact, I even think Thomas Cranmer [apostate Archbishop of Canterbury (1489-1556) who implemented the reforms of Henry VIII and invented the Anglican liturgy–*Ed.*] would flip if he could see today's New Mass compared to his own reform.

Does the new priesthood fit the New Mass of the New Religion?

FR. C.: Well, there's no real discipline left in the seminary, so if they don't get the discipline in the beginning they're not going to have it in the end. When I was assigned to a Marine company, I had to go through the training. There was a certain discipline that we had to develop so that we could work for the whole and not just for the part. Well, that's missing in today's modern seminaries–at least, that's what I hear from those who know. The concept of the traditional priesthood is a thing of the past. Today, a priest is just one of the guys: "Just call me by my first name, and don't worry about calling me Father." The concept of the dignity of his office is missing. The priest has stepped off the platform and now he's standing at the level of the laity, so there's no more discipline or hierarchical structure. It's a horizontal thing, and that's the New Religion.

If the priest is still "another Christ," it's because Christ is his brother?

FR. C.: Yes, the emphasis is that He's our brother, and that's true. But the more essential notion of a Catholic priest acting *in persona Christi* seems to have faded away. As you might know, Catholic University did a survey a few years ago and found that more than 64% of the priests don't believe in transubstantiation. If it's just a communion service, who needs "another Christ"? Why bother?

What is the way out of this mess?

FR. C.: The only way out is re-indoctrination, the re-teaching of the Catholic Faith. Thank God for the Society of Saint Pius X, because I wouldn't be here if it weren't for it. I think the Society is fulfilling a mission so that when Christ returns someday, He will still find the Faith upon the earth. It may not be the big Catholic Church that we knew in the past; it may just be small groups of people here and there. But, nevertheless, I think–and I'm sincere about this–that while the Society is not *the* Catholic Church, it certainly is a very important *part* of Her. I really believe it is doing God's will to preserve the Catholic Faith. If I thought for one moment that what the Society was doing was wrong, I'd drop away from helping it just like that.

What option is there for younger priests (who have never had training in Latin and traditional theology) to restore or salvage their priesthood?

FR. C.: A lot of the young men I've met who have asked me about that seem to be conservative. Now for me, conservatism *per se* is not the proper direction to go in. Traditional Catholics go directly to the causes of the crisis. Conservatives are those who are willing to tolerate the disadvantages of the New Mass to win a little, meatless bone. I've met young men trying to study Latin, trying to understand the Faith. In fact, I met one who started wearing the cassock, told the people that there would be no more holding hands at the "Our Father," and insisted that the church be kept quiet. Maybe we're starting to see a small revolution among the younger men coming in, depending on the seminary, of course.

They're going to have to do a self-study course in Latin or go to a school that teaches it. They might even have to take a couple of years in the [Society of Saint Pius X's] seminary at Winona, Minnesota. In any case, they're going to have to get a hold on basic Catholic doctrine, or they'll just keep getting the wrong information. There's not much choice among places. Read the best books and desire to be a good priest.

I would also be concerned about how they will be able to overcome the infiltration of the homosexual community into the Church. It has a whole different agenda and model of what the Church is. It starts at the top–the pope and the bishops. Practically speaking, the bishops don't care about moral fiber any more; they're only interested in social causes. The destruction that's occurring in the Church can be blamed on the bishops. That's the bottom line. If the bishop is the captain of the ship, the priests beneath him are just first, second, and third mates, and they have to be obedient to the superior. And remember, the captain of the ship stands on the bridge *alone*. He makes the decisions. If his decisions are bad, then everyone suffers; if they're good, then everyone benefits.

What about the older priest who has left the traditional Mass and is spinning his wheels wondering what he can do to try to revive his priesthood? How would you assuage his fears that he will be suspended if he starts celebrating the traditional Mass?

FR. C.: You have to tell him that such a "suspension" is really canonical nonsense. He's trying to preserve the Catholic Faith that we've always had, and if a Churchman is going to suspend him for keeping the Faith, somebody is wrong, and it's not him. The Faith goes back to Christ Himself and the Church Fathers. A priest is duty-bound to preserve the same Faith in the present age. If Churchmen reject that, they're rejecting Christ. A priest who fears suspension for preserving the Church of Christ has to make a firm decision to do what's right. When I did, I lost my retirement, I lost my medical benefits, I lost most everything. But it was either that or lose my soul!

What about for the older priests who were ordained in the late sixties or seventies and who have never had a traditional formation? They say you can't teach an old dog new tricks: How would you respond?

FR. C.: That's nonsense. We're living, breathing, intellectual beings, and we make decisions every day of our lives. If a priest *realizes* the problem, he is equipped to *resolve* the problem and straighten himself out. Given the opportunity, I pray he will. A person with a deep and holy character wants to do God's will. Certainly, he may have to do some extra studying on the side so he can bring himself up to par.

Let the older priest understand that not everyone's going to be a pastor, and that he may have to be an assistant pastor for the remainder of his life. Let him be resigned just to live this way, and hopefully the younger priests around him will help him in all charity when he has difficulties. Now and then I still make some mistakes, and these young fellows correct me. I don't take any offense; it's just the way it is.

Any man who sincerely wants to be a priest will do everything in his power to make sure that he's doing God's will. He will invite good, concrete criticism and he will accept it. If he can't, then I guess it's not to be. All I can say is that I love the priesthood more than life itself. I can't see doing anything else. Prior to finding a refuge with the Latin Mass, I was on the verge of leaving the priesthood. So, I'm quite grateful because I just love the old Mass. I can't express it any better than that.

FR. CHRISTOPHER DANEL

EDITED TRANSCRIPT

Father, would you tell us a little bit about your seminary formation?

FR. DANEL: Certainly. I eventually completed my formation in Rome, but I started my training in Philadelphia. The seminary was fairly orthodox in its doctrine, for the upper years, though I only did two lower years of humanities there. The teaching was fairly orthodox. All the practices at the seminary were also very good, traditional in orientation for the most part.

Did you wear the cassock?

FR. D.: We did. The cassock was obligatory for anything that happened in chapel; a collar shirt, for anything other than that. But most of the seminarians wore the cassock all the time.

How were they perceived by the other clergy and seminarians of the area?

FR. D.: The seminary was perceived, locally and nationally, as kind of right-wing, the same reputation that St. John Vianney in New York had at that time. It is something of a regional seminary even though, per se, it's of the Archdiocese of Philadelphia. There was a Jesuit University down the street, St. Joseph's, which was very liberal and had an ecumenical chapel, not even a Catholic chapel. There was always a little bit of disdain on the part of most of the Jesuits for our seminary. Our own diocese underwent a transformation in seminary training after the departure of the former bishop. We used to send all the seminarians to either St. Charles Borromeo in Philadelphia, the North American College in Rome as well as the Roman diocesan seminary, or Mount St. Mary's in Emmetsburg–all pretty orthodox places. They cut all of the above except for the North American College, and are soon to quit using the Roman Seminary in Rome. In Philadelphia, we used to hear all the "horror stories" about St. Meinrad, Notre Dame in New Orleans, Mundelein, St. Mary's in Baltimore, and Boynton Beach. It's the "who's who" of liberal seminaries. That's where their seminarians are now going. The liberal monsignors in the curia of the diocese had been for a long time trying to get the seminarians out of the seminaries we were using and into the liberal seminaries. We had a vicar general who is now married. He married his secretary at the cathedral (he didn't marry her at the cathedral, but she was the secretary there!). Well, I was touring the curia with the bishop emeritus one time, and this vicar general was telling the bishop "how interesting it was that we now have a seminarian in the Roman Seminary, a seminarian in the diocese of Rome, interesting how this is going to play out when 'Rome' comes back to here." He was saying this to the bishop, and the bishop was nodding, "Oh yes, it is interesting and a good prospect." Then as soon as the bishop had turned around, the monsignor gave me a scowl that said, "Look out when you get back!"

So it's the unpardonable crime of being Roman.

FR. D.: That's right.

Tell us a little about your formation in Rome.

FR. D.: The seminary I went to is in the Lateran compound which also includes St. John Lateran Basilica and the Lateran University, which was originally the *athenaeum* of the seminary and separated in 1929. The seminary was moved from St. Apollinare at Piazza Navona by Pope St. Pius X, so that it would be closer to the cathedral, which is St. John Lateran. There were 180 of us, 100 were from the diocese of Rome, and of the other 80 there were probably 25 or 30 of us who were foreigners, and the others were from other Italian dioceses. So it was very much an Italian house.

The more conservative seminarians tended to be from Bergamo in the north or from Puglia in the south. But the Romans were very much reflective of their diocese, which is decidedly liberal. In fact, in the Vicariate [chancery] of the diocese, they had put up posters at one point. You know the old adage, "*Ubi Petrus, Ibi Ecclesia*"? Well, they put up these posters at the entryway to the Vicariate saying "*Ubi Christus, Ibi Ecclesia*" to further extend the notion of the mystical body to the Protestant sects. I suppose I should point out that I am a "traditionalist" despite my formation, which was perfectly and exactingly Conciliar. Some people assume that I am traditional because of the seminaries where I was formed, but that's not really the case.

What about the formation that you had in philosophy and theology; was it fairly sane?

FR. D.: Fairly sane, I would say, certainly the academic formation. I did my philosophy at the Pontifical Lateran University. I had done two years of humanities in Philadelphia, so when I went to Rome, I entered directly into the first year of their biennium of philosophy. Then I studied theology at the Pontifical Gregorian University, and it was pretty sane there. There were some professors who were off the wall, but in those cases we recognized what was going on and besides, going into it, we knew from the upper year seminarians who was liberal, who was giving the teaching of the Church and who was not, and so we went prepared with our own texts of Catholic authors. We would listen to the lectures and then go home and study real theology!

Sometimes, for the exam, we had to parrot back what the professor had said, but in some cases we could get away with bringing in some Catholic theology. But it wasn't the proverbial case of the disciple presuming to know more than the master. It's just that some heretical notions were obviously and objectively present. For one course in moral theology, for example, (that was actually a written exam, which was rare), the question was on "fundamental option," and so I gave the Catholic interpretation and then I put, "However, there is another interpretation which is followed by x, y and z," and I also included the professor's name in that list. So it showed how his position, which he had explained in class, was contrasting with the teaching of the Church!

That must have been quite a balancing act!
What was the philosophy they were teaching you?

FR. D.: At the Gregorian, they do a systematic approach with a heavy concentration of modern philosophy, unfortunately. Whereas at the Lateran, they give a Thomistic base on the principal questions, and then they give an historical *excursus* throughout the two years which explains how philosophy developed into modern and then contemporary philosophy. The emphasis is largely on the history of philosophy, more so than at the Gregorian.

So it was taught with a Thomistic base, but there was always the underlying assumption that what is newer is better?

FR. D.: That was not always evident at the Lateran, but at the Gregorian, that was certainly the case. It's not co-incidental that at the Gregorian in the philosophy department, the dean is German and a lot of the professors are German or at least German-trained.

So you have a heavy dose of Kant and Husserl,
whose philosophy seems to have taken over the Church now.

FR. D.: Certainly that is so at the Gregorian, but even at the Lateran the dean of philosophy was a lay professor who was a phenomenologist and very much fascinated by Husserl and by Edith Stein. There were specific electives on Stein.

So you moved on to theology then.
Were you taught anything more than the history of theology?
Was there any basis at all in Scholasticism?

FR. D.: No, in theology, the base wasn't so clear. Scholasticism was presented as a phase in the development of theology which reached its perfection in Vatican II. That was the main thrust. The first third to half of each course covered historical development including the Fathers and Scholasticism. Then you would come to a point where all was understood, the Church had been enlightened through Vatican II, even if they were explaining things that directly contradicted what they had taught before in the Scholastic tract, and talking about the "new understanding," the "enlightenment." These same phrases are still being kicked around there. Even today, coming out of Rome, there are references to the Eucharist as a "mystery of light" in which we "digest the 'secret' of the resurrection." It's all about enlightenment now. It's not far from Gnosis.

Do you think that it's fair to say that Vatican II is the new Pentecost, but a new Pentecost of a new religion? That is to say, Pentecost was the definitive birth of the Church, and the new Pentecost seems to be the birth of something else. Is that going too far?

FR. D.: No, I don't think that's going too far. I don't think the new theology is something that was thought up or invented *ex novo*, however. It's essentially the triumph of liberalism in the Church, and while the liberals and modernists had been condemned, their system was then allowed to rear its head again and flourish like never before. St. Pius X said that modernism is the "synthesis of all heresies." So, new religion, yes, in the sense that modernism is constituted as supposedly being the teaching of the Church, but it is certainly not new in itself.

Was there more than a passing nod to the modernist crisis and St. Pius X, the *Sodalitium Pianum*, and those sorts of things in your studies?

FR. D.: The only place that we touched on it was in the course on the history of the Church in the modern and contemporary era. In fact, I was asked those particular questions on my exam. A Jesuit professor from the Netherlands asked me specifically about that, and I think he was asking a good number of the Americans also from the American College about modernism because he knew that it's something that we take very seriously. In Europe it doesn't seem to be considered so much, not as much as we consider it.

Did you ever study *Pascendi* in any formal way?

Fr. D.: Only in that course.

Not even in philosophy? Blondel and the others are major figures in the history of modern philosophy.

Fr. D.: Only in the history course.

What was their opinion of Pius X or *Pascendi?* How did they react towards it? Did they care all about it, or did they just mention it in passing?

Fr. D.: Well, I would say it was not so much mentioned in passing, but it was taught impassively. There was no opinion expressed about it. This was in a history course. However, there was a professor while I was at the Lateran who was very keen on Blondel, and so he was the only one who really expressed any opinion. He was indignant that Blondel was even sanctioned. He said it very vaguely. He never would produce a text and say, "This is why he was condemned. Here it is in writing." He would just say that, "The bad guys were against him." That kind of thing! I'm simplifying it very much. That's not the language he would use in the lecture hall.

I believe you had a concentration in liturgy after your ordination. What areas did you focus on in this regard?

Fr. D.: There were three different areas: the history of liturgy, pastoral liturgy, and liturgical theology. Now I always maintained that people coming out of the program could be one of three things: either a rubricist, a pastoral liturgist, or a liturgical theologian. There were three from my residence who were in the liturgy concentration program and one was very much a liturgical theologian, and another was very much into pastoral liturgy. And because of his type of explanations of what we would do at the Institute, all three of us were ribbed from it. The other priests would kid us about making felt banners and such, which is very far from the truth, but it was all because of the interpretations of the pastoral liturgist.

So of the three possible bents, which are you?

Fr. D.: I came out of the Institute as a rubricist. Decidedly! So, it was frustrating and confusing to come back to the diocese and find such liturgical anarchy. I'd been told by the bishop that there was a need for a liturgical director in the diocese, that the diocese needed a trained liturgist. That's why I was doing these studies. But after I came back, any kind of advice or impression that I would give was completely discarded as being 'Romish' or behind the times.

For example, I was providing Mass coverage in one parish as a favor, and the church was built almost like an airplane hangar: it was completely square; you could've put the celebrant's chair anywhere, but they put it with its back facing directly to the tabernacle, which was diagonally off to the epistle side. So I moved the chair only slightly so that it would be more in the position of a sedilia and with the back not directly to the tabernacle, and I got calls from the chancery immediately–somebody had reported back–asking why I was moving 'furniture' around. So that was a little bit of an eye opener. And then, in some other assignments, other parishes, there were things going on which I had no say over. And it wasn't that I was looking to impose my will. I was just looking for the liturgy of the Church, even if it was the *Novus Ordo*. Some young priests joke about wanting an indult to celebrate the *Novus Ordo* because what is being celebrated in a lot of churches now is even beyond that. It doesn't even correspond.

The last parish I was in was fairly conservative, but the pastor still didn't use an altar cloth! It's something that we take as a given. But he would set a corporal which was completely ironed without any folds, almost as a place mat, and it would stay there. The rest of the altar was completely bare. It was like Good Friday every day.

But if they consider the Mass as a meal, shouldn't there be a table cloth?

FR. D.: You would think so, but in the States many people use place mats at meals, so I guess that's the new thing! But in doing that, the poor pastor was only mimicking the bad example set by the Cathedral.

On All Souls' Day, I celebrated the main Mass in the morning and then right after that I said what was supposed to be a private Mass, but there had been a few people who remained behind after Mass to make their thanksgiving. I came out of the sacristy, having taken off the violet vestments and having put on the black vestments, which I brought over from my quarters–we didn't have any in the sacristy–and I also brought an altar cloth with me and set that up and then quietly said on the high altar a *Novus Ordo* Mass in Latin for All Souls'. After that some of the faithful went to the pastor and said that they had seen the vicar set up an altar cloth on the high altar to say Mass, and why didn't we use an altar cloth any more on the new altar?... So monsignor brought out a green blanket type of thing. That was supposed to be the new altar cloth!

Anything besides that which looks ritualistic or smacks of triumphalism! You cannot call burlap triumphalistic!

FR. D.: And he would go both ways. For the midnight Mass of Christmas, he also set up a faldstool for himself right in the middle of the sanctuary and sat on that, and then some people complained that, because of its neo-classical design, it looked like the chair of some Roman god. So he got rid of that. That faldstool was used by the bishop for one ordination, and then the bishop refused to ever use it again because it looked too much like a faldstool. It was a constant inventing of whatever was new.

What about your earlier years; I believe that you are a convert. You were raised as a Protestant?

FR. D.: To some degree. When I was a child, we didn't have any religion whatsoever in the house. Before I became a Catholic, in my middle school years and early high school, we were going to a moderate Baptist church. That was kind of an interlude. Towards the end of high school, I received the sacraments in the Catholic parish in town. That was indirectly brought about through some Catholic friends in the high school. There was one friend of mine in particular who was doing a lot of spiritual reading at the time, and during class breaks we would discuss certain things; he was just exuberant about the things he was coming across in his spiritual readings. I started to see that there was a depth there that was completely missing in the Baptist Church. It is all so superficial, all based on appearance in the mainline Protestant groups.

Did you go through RCIA?

FR. D.: I did. Basically, I did my own theological studies. I was just in high school at the time so it wasn't anything greatly in-depth, just general catechism, but certainly more in-depth than what was provided.

When was your first inkling that there was such a thing as Vatican II that radically changed the face of the Church?

FR. D.: From the very first day in the seminary. Some of the seminarians were from the small mountain towns of Pennsylvania where the parishes had the same pastor for 40 years, so they maintained a lot of the traditional practices and had traditional devotions that we in the South didn't have that much. So, that was a little bit of an eye opener. And then, it always seemed to be a mystery to me why traditional devotion, however, at the official level in the seminary, was so frowned upon.

There was a group of us who would go up after the Mass and kneel on the steps of the high altar, which was behind a type of sedilia that they erected that separated the new altar from the old. We would say the Leonine prayers ourselves as a thanksgiving after Mass because, of course, they were suppressed for public use. But it was almost seen as something backwards, something clandestine. I started to see that there was a real contradiction there because for centuries, generations and generations of the faithful, and Saints, had been doing these things and now all of a sudden, it was banned, it was condemned, it was outlawed, it was evil. There was just a glaring contradiction.

When did you see your first traditional Mass, what we would call the Tridentine Mass?

FR. D.: I must have been in my second year of seminary. There was a conservative Jesuit priest, a professor of ours, who was delegated to celebrate the Tridentine Mass in a working class parish out on the edge of town, in one of the outlying neighborhoods. There were about three of us seminarians who went to this Mass and sat in the back. It was a low Mass and there were very few people there. It was interesting to see it for the first time. But it didn't captivate me the way other Masses would later.

Once I got to Rome, I saw some other Tridentine Masses: Cardinal Stickler had a Mass one time, and there is a Church on the Corso which has a Latin Mass every Sunday; there are two or three chapels that offer the Tridentine Mass. But seeing these things as a major seminarian, and understanding a little bit more, I guess, it was intriguing and captivating.At the same time, it was, unfortunately, a kind of a forbidden fruit. There's one church in Rome which is at the end of a blind alley; there's not even a little marker at the door saying what church this is, so it really is a secretive type of thing. There is also a bit of fear on the part of the seminarians going to these: "What if the superiors find out?" "What if the vice-rector comes in from your own seminary?"…

When you were in Philadelphia, was it the same sort of attitude? Were you afraid to talk about it afterwards?

FR. D.: We went clandestinely and we never talked about it openly. It would have caused problems, certainly, if we had said anything. Of course, there would have been the protection of the celebrant, one of our own professors.

How did you move on from the clandestine phase? You were studying liturgy after you were ordained. Did you ever risk trying to say the Tridentine Mass yourself at this time?

FR. D.: No, I didn't because I was still under the impression that there is no way that it can be said by a priest unless he has the indult. I hadn't really looked too deeply into the *canonical* question. There was a priest in our college who had the indult, he said, and he would celebrate the Mass on one of the altars of the private Mass chapel which was later dismantled. They turned it into a concelebration chapel with one altar, and then they made one other small room into a private Mass chapel, but it had only one altar. It would periodically close down for renovation, and when it would reopen, I could never tell what had been renovated; the pressure was on to concelebrate. But there were a number of us priests who would only say private Mass, essentially. So really, in that private chapel I could have said a Tridentine Mass, but I was under the impression that I couldn't do that without an indult and still be "faithful."

It was only after some further investigation into the whole of Tradition and into the events of the establishment of the *Novus Ordo*, that I started to see that, really, all priests can say the Tridentine Mass, that there is no need for a special indult because of the canonization of the Mass by Pope St. Pius V with *Quo Primum*–which is very clear–and also the situation of the Church. It is more faithful to the Catholic Faith to say the Tridentine Mass "illicitly" than, with all the faculties of the bishop, to say the *Novus Ordo*.

Even in Latin, in a very conservative form?

FR. D.: Yes. Even if it's in Latin, it's still devised as a half-way rite, half-way cult of God, half-way cult of man. You can't tell to which direction is the worship now, whether it is towards God or whether it is towards man. Everything about it, even if it is in Latin, is didactic. A lot of the references are taken out, of course, the external things–the genuflections, the signs of the cross, the reverence–most of that is gone. It can be celebrated in what can, for the most part, appear to be a conservative way, for example, as I found it at Montecassino, where I went on Easter break for three years. But even in those circumstances, if you look at the meaning of the texts, there is still something there that is not right.

How did you come to these conclusions? What made you really see the emperor's new clothes to be a bit lacking?

FR. D.: A good family I know. Many children, home schooling, very faithful. I had heard through the grapevine that they were not going to their old parish anymore, which had been my first assignment. Some time later I met them by chance and I asked them where they were going. It came out that they were going to the Society of Saint Pius X chapel in Charlotte, North Carolina. I wanted to respond to their case a little bit, kind of lead them in the right direction, so I started looking more into the claims of the Society. My knowledge of what the Society was about was not complete. I looked into things to help them out, so to speak, and I started to come to the conclusion which was, in a way kind of horrifying, that the Society was doing the right thing. It's much more comfortable to remain where you are, doing what you are doing, and think that the traditionalists have it all wrong, that the traditionalists are backwards, that they don't want to face that there is a new situation in the Church, even if there is a need, as some say, for a reform of the reform.

So you did a lot of reading on traditional "apologetics" as it were?

FR. D.: Right. I came across some discourses and declarations and so forth that led me to see that "traditionalists" are not just out there to start a polemic and to be divisive or to start a parallel church. They're out there clinging to the traditional Catholic Faith, and there is so much prayer offered up from these chapels, these communities, these convents, these seminaries, offered up for the restoration of the Catholic Faith, apart from any cosmetic reform of the reform that others are talking about.

We're looking for the Faith, essentially, in these places, and the prayer is there also for the Holy Father and for a strong papacy. The traditionalists aren't, I came to see, rebelling for the sake of rebellion. They're ready to be the first in line behind the Holy Father if he's the first in line behind his predecessors. But as long as he is the head of the train, so to speak, that's going off track, they're not going to follow. They'll wait, they'll pray, they'll cling to their Faith, hoping that he'll come back on track.

Incidentally, and continuing that analogy, some say that the track is wherever the engine leads, and that it's prideful to say otherwise. Some people have told me that. "You traditionalists are obstinate and proud!" they say. "You want to be more Catholic than the Pope!" That's not it at all. The Magisterium through the centuries, Sacred Tradition, the deposit of faith, has clearly determined and laid out the track, and right now, more often than not, the train's not on it. Any clear-minded *Christifidelis* can see the train wreck. It's more obstinate and prideful–hard-headed, really–to deny that objective reality and the gravity of the crisis.

Were there any particular things which you read, particular books especially which changed your outlook?

FR. D.: No, my reading was a little bit from here and there. It made for work; it made for a lot of angst. But after some research late one night, a long, terribly sleepless night as I remember, I started to understand that, after what I was discovering, there was no way that I could continue to lend my support to pushing this party line, which was so harmful to souls.

Did you know at that point what you were going to do about it?

FR. D.: No. I didn't.

That's the hard part, isn't it? So what did you do, concretely?

FR. D.: Well, concretely, I went to speak to a traditional priest. That was the first thing. He was the pastor of the parish where that family was going. I went to his Mass first of all. It was on a Sunday evening. I was in the pews. I didn't even go in clerical dress because I didn't want word to get back, even if this was in a different diocese. So I went as an anonymous observer. I was fascinated by seeing this Mass said in this way, in this setting.

Remember, I saw my first Tridentine Mass in Philadelphia. It was in a parish, but there were just a few people there, and I saw some occasional Masses in Rome, but it wasn't really a parish setting. It was different than going into a living, breathing parish in which this is the Mass and this is the Faith in which these people are bringing up their children, day in and day out and hearing this Mass every week, and it was very significant to see a priest who is one-hundred percent traditional. Before and after Mass, the priest was busy with confessions–there was such a line of confessions.

Must have been quite a surprise.

FR. D.: It was. He was busy with confessions after that Mass, so I went back home (I was visiting my parents at the time). I returned the next morning for Mass. That was another night I did not sleep too well, after seeing that Mass and seeing the Faith lived in that way. Then I went back in the morning, and I had the opportunity to speak with the priest at length. By that time, about halfway through that Monday morning Mass, I had realized that I really needed to take concrete steps. I spoke to the priest about what form or shape that could take.

Of course, that had to include, at some point, your learning how to say the traditional Mass. How did this happen?

Fr. D.: I went out to Kansas City to speak with the district superior of the Society. The sacristan of the church there, time-tested and true, was going to go through the Mass with me in the school chapel, but after a brief talk, we decided that instead of going through the rubrics while doing a dry Mass, I would just make the break and go ahead and say the traditional Mass even if it's a little choppy. That was my first traditional Mass. It was at the same time intimidating and exhilarating.

So you had been studying the rubrics?

Fr. D.: Concentrated *practice*, very little in fact. During my earlier seminary years I was looking personally at these rubrics in old hand missals and such. Then in the liturgical specialization, from only an academic point of view, we were specifically looking at the rubrical development of the Mass from the early Church, the age-old Mass which would later come to be called "Tridentine" in the Roman rite.

It was a very easy transition for you because you had been looking at the things all along, as a student. That first time is bound to be quite striking. As you say, it is a very different thing to look in books and then to actually offer the Mass. When was the first time you said the old Mass publicly.

Fr. D.: Publicly, it was a High Mass for "*Dominica in Albis*" in Richmond.

After you had made the break?

Fr. D.: Right. After that initial visit to the Society's district office and also to the seminary, I went back to my diocese for a period of six months, at my bishop's insistence. I used it as a time to tie up loose ends. That was the whole reason I was going back, and also as a time of preparation for making the break.

Did your bishop know you were leaving?

Fr. D.: No. I had asked for a leave of absence before my first trip to the district headquarters. And we went around and around about it. I couldn't tell him *explicitly* why I needed this leave–he wouldn't understand–but I told him that I wanted to take until Epiphany, which would have probably been about three months, for vocational discernment. I was between assignments anyway. But he was very unwelcoming of that kind of a prospect. I gave him every reassurance possible that I was not thinking of leaving the priesthood, I was only looking at how and in which way I should proceed, looking at which form my priestly ministry was going to take. Well, he wouldn't see any of it.

Was there always a certain *animus* ever since you came back to this new bishop after the first bishop was gone?

FR. D.: No, no, no. Not at all. Not at all. In fact, he showed every personal courtesy and kindness possible, and very much so. But, it's just this particular question, and I think there were some other priests of the diocese who were speaking in his ear about these things, so he was taking a little bit of a hard line against me. In one parish I had been in, the parish where I had just completed my assignment at that point, there was a temporary administrator, and this man was very, very liberal. Extremely so. He and I didn't get along, so this man and people like him were saying things to the bishop. So the bishop was taking a bit of a hard line. But when I was given an assignment and went back to the diocese for those six months, the issue was dropped and forgotten. He wanted me to be his MC, in fact, for the upper part of the diocese. So I was on for his Confirmations, and there was no tension there. But there was a little bit of tension with some of the liberal pastors. I was essentially there not only as the bishop's MC, but I was there to help things go smoothly for the parish. I was going to make the pastor look good to some degree. But since I was instructing the servers how to be diligent in respecting the sacred ceremonies, one pastor in particular was downright indignant. But I knew who these people were and what kind of theological positions they held, so it was no skin off my back. I understood. One develops thick skin through the years, I think.

So were you saying the traditional Mass on the sly during those six months?

FR. D.: Yes. As soon as I got into that six-month assignment, I erected an altar in my quarters, which were quite spacious. I made it after a visit to a lumber yard, but I made it right, with a footpace and everything. I was saying the traditional Mass there on days when I was not scheduled for Mass in the parish. Because of the Mass schedule–there were three priests–certain of us would have days off. The other priests wouldn't say Mass if they were not scheduled for a public Mass.

Did you often find this disposition of seeing the priesthood more or less as a job? Did you find that very widespread?

_FR. D.:_ Very much so. There were a few of the younger priests who, if they weren't scheduled to say Mass, would say one privately, but most of the older priests, those formed in the Conciliar and post-Conciliar years, don't see any reason for that. The Mass, as they see it, is offered for the 'gathered assembly'. If they're not scheduled, they see no reason to go into the church, although some of them will indulge the younger priests who would do that. I always said mine very much on the sly because nobody ever went into my quarters, except the cleaning lady, and I had the altar set up there. I would take the altar cards down and the missal, and put those away in the closet, so that there was no problem with that. But for six months I was saying the Tridentine Mass in that way, kind of clandestinely.

What were you doing for an Office? You were doing the *Novus Ordo* office?

_FR. D.:_ No, no, no. I was praying the traditional Breviary, and I made no bones about that. I started that shortly before that first visit to the district superior. Even when I would go into the parish for a scheduled Mass, even Sunday Mass, I would take my traditional Breviary. I'd leave it sitting right there on the sacristy table with the pastor coming through back and forth. They really don't care too much about whether or how you say the Office.

I get that impression. Do you know if many of your colleagues in the diocese said the Office at all?

_FR. D.:_ I do. There are priests who say the Office, certainly. There are plenty who don't say it at all, but certainly there are priests who say it daily.

That's an encouraging thing. So you just took up a Breviary, read through the rubrics, and that was that?

_FR. D.:_ Yes, and it was refreshing, very refreshing. It's so awkward saying the new Liturgy of the Hours because of certain…"prayers of the faithful" that are added, the invocations, the hymns… They have all sorts of Protestant hymns in the new Office. Actually, since the hymns are so absurd, there are a lot of priests who just skip the hymn. They go straight from the beginning into the psalms, the way the Roman Breviary goes, except they never recover the hymn after that. Of course, there are those intercessions at Lauds and Vespers which sometimes are just atrocious, worthy of Communist propaganda. Some readings of Matins also go on and on about workers' rights and solidarity.

During these six months, you are saying the traditional Mass in your quarters, you're saying the traditional Office.
When you have to say the New Mass publicly, what are your reactions, your dispositions of having to go through this?

FR. D.: It was a suffering. It was a suffering from two different points of view, or two different aspects. First of all, having to endure saying the Mass in its Protestantized form, having to sit there while the ladies come back and forth from the pulpit to read the readings or wave their hands around during the Gradual psalm. And then secondly, knowing that just by respecting the rubrics, you're saying it in such a way that the faithful are always coming up to you thanking you: "Thank you, Father, for the reverence you show"; "Thank you for a holy Mass." It's because some of the other priests conduct it like an auction or a social hall gathering. You have the faithful out there who show signs of just *thirsting* for some *reverence* during the Mass, and so it's a suffering to know that what they are getting is only a discounted, dime-store version. Some of the Collects, in particular, are not even second grade level.

The first form especially.
The alternate forms are sometimes very beautiful.

FR. D.: Oh, yes. Very often I would use the alternate prayer, but of course the conclusion there is wrong. They use a short conclusion for the Collect on the alternate prayers, so I would go back and forth. I'd have to use the alternate prayer and then use the long conclusion from the other prayer. We would have the usual practices: the women coming up to read, sometimes the children's Masses, with just no reverence whatsoever, and then the Eucharistic ministers. There were more rare events, like when a host was dropped and they just didn't know what to do. And it's not like they were too concerned. And then, there were always women Eucharistic ministers coming up to help at the tabernacle and "consolidating" the hosts into one ciborium. In the last parish where I was, they always used these kind of dish ciboria that would stack one on the other like Tupperware (whereas they had some magnificent old ciboria hidden away in the safe, unused). One time I was taking hosts out of one and putting them in another with my fingers and this poor lady very angrily dumped all the hosts from her little dish ciborium into the central one, and gave me a look like, "Stop wasting my time!" and then stormed back into the sacristy. Right in the middle of Mass. This happens all the time.

The sign of unity and charity...

_FR. D.:_ Right. Another time in another parish, the Eucharistic ministers were over at the credence table laughing, and I don't know if somebody told a joke or what, but they were supposed to be purifying the vessels, which is even banned in the *Novus Ordo* now, under the new rubrics. It wasn't under the old [1970]. After the Mass, in the sacristy, I told them quite charitably, "If there is anybody who should be exemplifying Eucharistic devotion in this parish, it's yourselves, but you were laughing and carrying on like it was a baseball game." Oh, what indignant letters went to the bishop! That I should dare call into question their devotion...rain on their parade, or whatever.

I could go on and on with the abuses that I've seen in different parishes. In Rome they like Offertory processions, and they'll bring up tennis shoes and soccer balls and all that and put them around the altar. There's any number of things that go on, and it really starts to take a toll on you, spiritually, whether you realize it or not at the time.

As you came towards the end of those six months, you must have been very anxious to leave and get away from all that, but on the other hand it must have been quite a trepidation to launch out into the deep, as it were.

_FR. D.:_ That's right. Because some of the connections and friendships that I had developed I knew would be changed, a few of them broken off, although true friends remain such, I've found. I have some very close friends who don't really understand why I've gone in this direction, but that doesn't change the friendship that's there. The whole relationship with the bishop and the priests of the diocese would be troubled. So there was some trepidation there. Then, really, doubts back and forth as to whether this was the right thing to do or not, in itself.

So what I tried to do was just go about my duties right to the last minute, going to visit some of the more conservative families, mostly the home-schoolers, to encourage them. I couldn't really tell them about the move I was going to make. So it came as a shock to some of them when I did leave because only a few days before I had been at their house and had never mentioned it! There was some angst about whether I was doing the right thing, but deep down there was peace, that I was starting to come to terms with it. Even the very last day, I made a last round of the homebound for confessions and Communion.

How did you overcome this mental hurdle about penalties and loss of faculties? Because this is bound to be one of the steepest hurdles to overcome for most priests who decide to leave the normal framework, let's put it that way.

FR. D.: Well, there are many in the traditionalist movement who have had to undergo sanctions and penalties, but it's endured with a real conviction that what you're doing is no different than what the Church has always done. If I were going off and doing something completely new and innovative, and the Church were putting sanctions on me, I would be worried. But I know that what I am doing is no different, no different, than what the holy priests of centuries past have done for generations. What I am doing is teaching and practicing the Catholic Faith. Does the Church legitimately penalize me for that? I don't think so. In fact, on a canonical level apart from faculties or no faculties, it is the Church herself who supplies jurisdiction in times like these.

St. Peter says that we must obey God rather than man.

FR. D.: Exactly. And regarding making the whole jump, I was also very keenly aware that I was not just leaving something behind, going off into some kind of mist or dark future, where who knows what's going to happen. I was actually going towards something. What I was leaving was not but a shadow of what I was going towards.

Do you find that to be the case now? What effect has the exclusive celebration of the traditional Mass had on your priesthood?

FR. D.: It certainly is the case. There is so much support and respect for priests in traditional parishes, and I can interact with the traditional faithful in a more fruitful way, for the sanctification of their souls and mine. It's like a family, the "household of Faith." As far as the effects of the Mass, it's indescribable! It's the devotion that is there, just inherently in the traditional Mass. Being able to plug yourself into this, as it were, has an incredible effect on your spirituality and on the way you are a priest. The nature of the priesthood is blurred and misunderstood in the *Novus Ordo*. And so when you are celebrating the *Novus Ordo* Mass, you really do feel like some kind of delegated president of the assembly. But that is never the case with the Tridentine Mass. You are so keenly aware that this is worship "in spirit and in truth," on a supernatural level.

So many features help to contribute to that, for instance the fact of facing east. Is there anything else that's striking to you about these sort of 'militant' features that help to bring out the centrality of the sacramental priesthood?

FR. D.: The speaking of some parts *sotto voce* such as for the Canon, and the other prayers. It's amazing how many priests in the *Novus Ordo* skip over those prayers or say them out loud, because they think, "Why would you say anything if the people can't hear it?" Because it's all about the people in the *Novus Ordo*. So, even saying the entire Canon and these other prayers *sotto voce*, you really understand that this is not about show, spectacle, what the people are going to see. It's not about appearance in any way. It's all about true worship of God. So, the use of *sotto voce*, facing east, the use of Gregorian chant, the way Communion is distributed.

The faithful, for their part, follow the Mass much more closely this way, and are engaged in a superior way. It's not 'active participation', but rather 'contemplative participation'. That all has a bearing on the way a priest experiences the Mass, spiritually, because he's not expected to be a 'liturgical animator', or to be 'dynamic'. What a heartbreak, to have to give out Communion the way it was before, in the *Novus Ordo*. There are all sorts of abuses in the distribution and reception of Communion in the *Novus Ordo*. So, to go where the faithful are receiving Communion so devoutly–using the Communion rail–is a big change.

I was in two missions last weekend. The High Mass on Sunday was something else! The Gregorian chant was executed flawlessly and even in the smaller of the two missions, the choir sang a polyphonic Mass. The altar boys were right on cue, even down to the torchbearers at the Communion. There were parishioners going all through the night to adoration of the Most Blessed Sacrament after the First Friday Mass and there was Benediction before the First Saturday Mass, all of which was very well attended. I heard in excess of four hours of Confessions while I was there. I examined the confirmandi, who were to be confirmed in a week's time and they knew their catechism by heart and were zealous for their Faith, all fervently Catholic. That's such a striking change from the way things generally go in the *Novus Ordo*, and I am starting to see that in traditional parishes, it's like that all the time. Something which is oftentimes left unsaid is the use of Confession. Obviously, in traditional parishes such as those missions, Confession is frequented more often and with more devotion, but I've also found that the quality of the confessions that I have heard in traditional circles is completely different. You really have no doubts why these people are on the other side of the screen. Some people in the *Novus Ordo* will come to confession so they learn to be a better person, but they have no idea of sin. Very rarely did I ever hear confessions without a screen, but on the occasions when I did, as is the standard practice for most other priests, it was just very bizarre.

For the priests that are sitting on the fence, trying to make a decision what to do, what advice would you give them?

FR. D.: Make contact with traditional priests. As long as Tradition remains as a type of mirage on the horizon, they will never understand it in its fullness. These priests who are on the fence, if they will sit down and talk with traditional priests, they will realize that these are not heretical or excommunicated monsters, as some have the impression. I would tell them, if you want to be edified in your own priesthood, go and talk to these men. They have a very clear understanding of what the priesthood is and of their own identity as a priest.

Make a visit, even if you have to do so clandestinely or anonymously, to a parish where the Mass is celebrated week in and week out, or daily in some cases, where that is the Mass and the Faith of the parish rather than relying on an occasional, once-in-a-while, special-event Tridentine Mass, as if it's a museum piece brought out and dusted off. Have some traditional families keep you in their prayers (then look out!). Take up the traditional Breviary as well. Leave the *Little Office of Vatican II* and take up the Breviary! To say the Breviary is an incredible help. It really is.

What about for those priests who don't understand Latin, what can they do?

FR. D.: I guess they could get some course books and brush up a little bit. Even if Latin is an obstacle right at the beginning, there are English and even bilingual editions of the Roman Breviary. They could start off with that. They could start off with that because, even in itself that's a big difference from the Liturgy of the Hours. But taking up a little bit of study each day, then they can start to come to a better knowledge of Latin. It's true, some have no understanding of the Latin. Better late than never!

It doesn't take a 300 IQ to learn Latin, or to learn theology, for that matter. A lot of the objections, would you say, can be overcome?

FR. D.: Yes, certainly. One thing that I was completely amazed by, was when I went back to that Monday morning Mass in Charlotte, the altar-boys knew their Latin just perfectly for the Mass. But that's not all. After that, they have the minor hour of Prime, in Latin. One of the boys read the Martyrology. I was just so taken by the fact that this kid, who couldn't have been more than ten years old, was chanting the Martyrology and all of them the Divine Office. These children didn't skip a beat, didn't skip a beat! If these kids can do it, anybody can. For centuries, small children have been learning the responses of the Mass, and learning them perfectly.

Some of the older priests, those ordained in the late sixties and early seventies, for instance, might object and say, "Well, you can't teach an old dog new tricks. How am I supposed to learn all this? Philosophy, Latin, start all over again?"

FR. D.: For the older priests, it doesn't take much for them to go back to what they had, if they remember it. Some of them authentically don't remember what they had. I was talking with a priest who was ordained over 50 years ago. And he was taking the liberal line, about the Mass being community, the gathering of the people and all that. And I asked him amicably, but straight out, "Is that what they taught you in the seminary back then? I'm just curious to know what was the emphasis of the teaching on the Mass when you were in seminary, Father." And he said, "Oh, yes. That was certainly it. The Community offering the Eucharistic sacrifice at the hand of the presider who was delegated." I think that he just didn't remember, maybe, what he had been taught before. The change agents of the reform were very, very effective. Then there are these priests that may be 25 or 30 years ordained, who went through the seminary during the crazy years. If they say, "You can't teach an old dog new tricks," well, certainly you can. There are a lot of priests their age and in their shoes who have done it. They wouldn't be the only ones. But also there has to be a conversion of heart. The priest can't just one day want to keep everything the same, but just tack on learning the traditional Mass or taking on the old Breviary. One must admit, "Okay, for most of my priesthood, I've been involved in this nonsense in the *Novus Ordo*." Many of the priests, during the initial years of the reform, probably were doing some crazy things in the parishes, these polka Masses and things that were starting up. Fine. Entrust all of that to the mercy of our Lord, and it's not too late to start doing it right.

Even just saying Mass in their quarters! This is a start. Trying to do the study, trying to make up for some of the nonsense.

FR. D.: And then also, you can take a look at some of the older priests who are dyed-in-the-wool liberals and convinced that the revolution was the right thing to do: these men, even with these convictions, are defeated men, and there is such a spirit of despair amongst them. That's not so among the priests who have remained true to the Faith, no matter what. So these priests that are 25, 30 years ordained, do they want to become older or retired priests who are defeated men because they never had the courage to be a priest the way Mother Church deserves to have her priests be? Or do they want to have that courage and step up to the plate?

That's the choice that's set before them, and each one has to make it for himself.

FR. D.: With God's grace, certainly, under the guidance of the Holy Ghost.

To contact Fr. Danel:

Rev. Fr. Christopher Danel
P.O. Box 1691
Roswell, GA 30077-1691

FR. VINCENT MICHAEL*

EDITED TRANSCRIPT

FR. VINCENT MICHAEL: I was ordained before Vatican II. I was a religious, but I've recently withdrawn from my religious order. I now have to seek either another order or a benevolent bishop who may permit me to continue priestly ministry.

You must have started your long formation back in the 1940's?

FR. M.: That's right, the forties. At that time my order was very, very orthodox–very traditional.

What did they teach you about the priesthood?

FR. M.: That the priest represents Christ at the altar. He acts in the Person of Christ in the sacrifice of the Mass. We were given the proper theological foundation for what the priest does sacramentally.

How would you describe the new idea of the priesthood?

FR. M.: Well, it all depends on how people define "priesthood"–I don't know what the modern thinking is on that. Do you want to suggest something to me?

Maybe you could describe what the new priesthood seems to be from the priests you've known. For instance, what do they say about the priesthood in the seminars you've been compelled to attend?

FR. M.: I was never compelled to go to any seminars where they pushed the so-called Vatican II updating of the priesthood. I was not required to go to those, so I didn't attend.

How did you escape these things?

FR. M.: I just simply didn't go!

So, is it fair to say that you've never been able to figure out what the new priesthood is?

FR. M.: I've heard comments about it: "The priesthood is for promoting community," and statements of that type. You know, it's the "social-worker" idea of the priest. But that's not what a priest should be doing! Other priests may be social-workers, but I'm not one. ***The idea of the priest as a presider***

* "Fr. Vincent Michael" is a pseudonym used at the request of the priest–*Ed.*

offends me, because the priest is not presiding over a meeting when he is saying Mass. But that's the term they use now, "presider." Instead of offering the sacrifice of the Mass, the priest is "presiding." Because of that idea in the new liturgy, the priests are being directed by the liturgical committees, and so on.

Do you think it's reasonable to say that the New Mass was concocted to reflect these ideas of the priest as presider and social-worker?

FR. M.: Yes, I imagine that the two are really one and the same thing.

Did you ever say the New Mass, Father?

FR. M.: Oh yes, *I said the New Mass for many years, because I was not tuned in to what was going on.* As a religious, I was schooled in the idea of obedience. It was made clear to us that various things were going to be changed and that we had to cooperate with the changes. Well, of course, I went along with that idea for a number of years, until I began to realize that the New Mass was not the Mass I wanted to be offering.

What made you realize that?

FR. M.: Well, it was the whole concept of the new liturgy, the prayers for example. What very much offended me was the substitution they made for the Offertory prayer. Instead of the old Offertory prayer, they put in a new one which is derived from a Jewish Seder ceremony–it is not Christian! When I realized that–I didn't know about that at the beginning, but I did a lot of reading–I realized that something was going wrong. I read, for instance, what Michael Davies had written on the New Mass, and I was very much intrigued by his thinking. I now know Michael Davies personally–he's a good scholar of the Mass.

When did you first start to doubt whether you should continue to say the New Mass?

FR. M.: Well, I'd say about ten years ago, in 1992. That's when I made the change and began to use the traditional rite of Mass.

How did your fellow priests react to your decision to begin saying the old Mass?

FR. M.: Well, of course, my contemporaries thought that I belonged on Noah's Ark! They said: "The Church is changing, and you have to change with it!" Obviously, I was criticized by the other priests, and they thought I was crazy to go back to the Latin Mass when the changes were already made.

I was not supported by most of the priests, but some did support me. Most of them thought I was a little strange to be saying the Latin Mass.

What were the reactions of your superiors when you started to say the traditional Mass?

FR. M.: I would say that the idea was objected to! It was not condoned by my superiors at all. They'd prefer it if I would just go back to saying the New Mass. One time, I was showing some new members around the community chapel, and I didn't plan to say Mass in that chapel, but my Superior came running in and said, "I hope you're not going to say the old Mass, are you?" When I told him that I had already offered Mass that day, he seemed greatly relieved and said he was sorry for making a rash judgment.

What was their objection to the old Mass?

FR. M.: I could never understand the objection of the bishops to the Mass. I never had an explanation given to me why they objected so much.

Was it a difficult transition for you to come back to the old Mass?

FR. M.: Not for me. No, I had no problems with the rubrics of the Latin Mass.

How is the old Mass different from the New Mass for the priest?

FR. M.: I think that the prayers of the old Mass are very much in keeping with the traditional theology of the Church–certainly with the theology of the Council of Trent. This is not exemplified very well in the New Mass. The Canon of the Mass, for example, was defined by the Council of Trent as being free from error. But we can't say the same thing about the New Mass. What I find objectionable about the new prayers is not so much that they're erroneous, but that they're ambiguous. If I said the New Mass privately, I would say it in Latin; I would not say it in the English form. The reason is that the English version has been mistranslated or paraphrased. This work of ICEL has been greatly criticized by Rome now, but the damage has been done.

Even in the Latin form of the New Mass, is it just the Offertory prayers which you object to, or is there something else?

FR. M.: Well, there is, for example, the omission of the "*Placeat*" before the final blessing. And the Last Gospel is omitted. I see no reason to abandon those, because they are very beautiful prayers, and they suggest what's going on in the Mass! Prayers like that express better what we were doing in the Mass—offering a sacrifice to God and doing it in a reverent manner. And I don't believe in dancing girls in the aisles, and everybody in the church shaking hands with everybody else, and things of that type.

Can the idea of the priest as a mediator be expressed in the New Mass?

FR. M.: Not very well. I don't think that it's emphasized at all. I think that the New Mass stems from the idea of developing the community, encouraging friendliness, which is good—I'm all for that—but it doesn't express what we are doing at Mass.

Archbishop Lefebvre said, when he was asked why he would not use the New Mass in his seminary, that he thought it was morally impossible to form a sacrificing priest in a seminary which used the New Mass. Would you agree?

FR. M.: Well, I would think that the old Mass would definitely emphasize the idea of the sacrificing priest more than the new theology would, so I would agree with him.

There are numerous young priests, some of whom have never seen the traditional Mass, who want to be good sacrificing priests, but their formation has been deficient. How would you advise such a young man to become a better priest?

FR. M.: Well, I think that the younger priests should realize that the Holy Father has given permission for the old Mass to be said, and that if they wish to avail themselves of that permission, there are avenues to do that. They can petition their bishops to allow them to do it. And I think they should be encouraged to do it, because we have a whole group of faithful out there who want the old Mass, and we have to have priests to replace my generation. They should be encouraged to seek the proper permission to say the old Mass and do it.

What about the case of the young priest who is in a diocese where the local bishop simply will not think of allowing the traditional Mass at all? What recourse is open to him?

FR. M.: Well, probably, the only thing he could do is to say Mass in private if he wanted to celebrate the old Mass on occasion. He could do that much. The bishop might restrict him as far as saying Mass for congregations in the diocese, but if he is able to travel and help out in a situation where a priest is needed to say the old Mass somewhere else, he can do that. But, of course, many priests have asked for and received permission from their bishops to say the traditional Mass, and that's been a happy situation. If their bishops refuse permission, the priests do have remedies available, but it's more difficult in those cases.

What about the commission of the nine Cardinals in 1986, who said, according to Cardinal Stickler, that the traditional Mass has never been abrogated or forbidden in any way? Would it be fair to say that a local bishop would be outside his competence to forbid the celebration of the old Mass?

FR. M.: I think I would have to refer to Bishop Timlin of Scranton, Pennsylvania, as one bishop who has set an example of generosity in applying the Indult. When he was asked the question "Why do you allow the old Mass in your diocese?" he said, "The Pope has told us to be 'generous' in granting this permission, and I understand what 'generous' means!"

What would you say is the cause of the lack of generosity of the bishops who won't allow the old Mass?

FR. M.: Well, that's exactly what I don't understand. I don't see any rational explanation for it. *I've heard the traditional Latin Mass objected to on the grounds of its "divisiveness," but, to me, it doesn't add up.* I just have no clear understanding of where they're coming from and why they have such an antipathy to the Latin Mass. I don't understand it at all.

The Church is diverse in many ways. We have the Eastern Rites, for example. The bishops have never complained about the diversity of the way Mass is celebrated according to the traditions of the Eastern Church, and the Latin Church has also contributed a variety of liturgies, all approved by the Holy See. We know that the New Mass is approved by the Holy See–that's quite clear. But the old Mass is still approved by the Holy See as well, so we have the possibility of having two rites in the Latin Church.

They *are* two different rites, because I don't see the present form of the Mass as flowing from the old Mass at all. *I can't see any natural development from the old Mass to the New Mass,* which is a very destructive, artificial, and man-made concoction. It's not based on anything that flows naturally and organically from the old Mass. Even though it's called the *Novus Ordo Missæ,* the new revision of the Roman rite, I would say it's a completely different rite. In the document of Vatican II, *Sacrosanctum Concilium* of 1963, or the Constitution on the Liturgy, clearly states that the changes in liturgy must flow naturally and organically from what went before and that changes should not be made unless the good of the Church requires them. As the eminent liturgist Klaus Gamber points out, the New Mass is a fabrication like something made in a workshop.

Could you point to some of the results of the New Mass which support the idea that it's destructive for the Church?

FR. M.: Well, I would say that there's much less reverence for the Blessed Sacrament. For example, when I was growing up, and when I was in the seminary, we always genuflected before the Blessed Sacrament when coming to and going from the church. Now, that is not done–people just take their place in the church without any genuflection. The lack of reverence is something quite striking, it seems to me, in the New Mass as opposed to the old Mass.

This is also evident in the fact that the tabernacle was removed, not only from the middle of the sanctuary, but sometimes it was removed from the church altogether. The "Adoration Chapel" separates the veneration of the Blessed Sacrament from the Mass, and the two are supposed to be unified. Pius XII wrote a wonderful encyclical in which he spoke about that in 1947– *Mediator Dei.* It would seem to me that, if the Council Fathers and the makers of the New Mass had studied that letter, they would have seen that some of the things they were introducing were in complete contradiction to the whole message of that encyclical, and that they were maybe even out of date!

For example, Pius XII spoke about a false antiquarianism, the desire to go back to the Mass of the first century. The desire to change the color of the vestments was mentioned as an example of this false antiquarianism. But things were quite different in the first centuries–there was a persecution, for instance! To go back to the ancient forms of the Mass for the sake of cutting out the traditional Mass denies the possibility that the Mass can grow organically and naturally over the course of the centuries!

Does the removal of the tabernacle merely represent a lack of reverence, or does it signify a change in Faith?

FR. M.: Well, it's a change in Faith as well, because the form of worship must correspond to the Faith. *The Faith and the way we celebrate the liturgy must go together, otherwise, either the liturgy or the Faith will become schizophrenic.*

I would go further and say that the New Mass, in many ways, has been the occasion of a *lack* of faith among some Catholics. As Michael Davies has pointed out, the New Mass resembles very much the Service of Cranmer, and Cranmer made the statement that "An altar is for sacrificing, but tables are for eating on." Now, we find in many churches a "butcher-block" type of arrangement instead of an altar, and that is only a table, made for eating on, and not for a sacrifice. That is very disturbing, because the Mass is fundamentally a sacrifice.

So, by over-emphasizing the "meal" aspect, the New Mass gets rid of the sacrificial aspect? Is this the crux of the problem?

FR. M.: That's right. You have to bring them both together, certainly, to receive the Body and Blood of Christ at Mass, and at the same time you have to offer the sacrifice of Christ to the Father, to renew the sacrifice of the Cross in an un-bloody manner. That is the traditional theology, but I think that the people today don't understand it. They just see Mass as a meal, and a community gathering, and so on. There is this sacrificial aspect of the Mass, which is essential to it. If the Mass is not a sacrifice, it doesn't have the meaning which the Catholic Faith has always given it.

What should be done in the case of priests who would like to begin saying the traditional Mass but think they can't because they don't know any Latin?

FR. M.: Well, Latin, of course, should be studied! That was one of the things that Pope John XXIII emphasized in his letter *Veterum Sapientia*. He underlined the necessity for all those studying for the priesthood to be familiar with the traditional language of the Church. Also, the universal language of the Church is officially still Latin. If a priest is unable to know anything about Latin, he certainly cannot translate the documents of the Church or use her language. If he were to find out what happened in the Church before the translations of the Latin texts into the vernacular, even those of the New Mass, it would be quite obvious to him that there are problems with the translations. If such a priest doesn't know Latin, he can only be a critic of the local translation, and not of the official Latin text. I think that the knowledge of Latin is important for all priests to have, whether they say the old Mass or the New Mass, it doesn't make any difference. It's simply the language of the Church–it's the universal language of the Roman Catholic Church!

The main difficulty we have now is that the Mass is said in hundreds of different languages, and the difficulty in translation is very great. Unless the translation is done faithfully, the people get a completely wrong idea of the official texts, of which the translations are supposed to convey the true meaning. The question of Latin is so very important that I hope seminarians listen to Pope John XXIII, when he urged that Latin be studied in the seminaries as one of the basic parts of the curriculum.

What is the way out of this crisis in the Church?

FR. M.: I would think that, for the time being, the Church should permit the two Masses, the two rites, to go on together, and to allow those who prefer one over the other to make that choice. If they let the Latin Mass be preserved by those who want it, I think that, in the course of time, more people will be able to understand that the Latin Mass is preferable. I would say that there should be permission both for the old Mass to be celebrated without any problem or criticism and for the New Mass to be celebrated *reverently* for those Catholics who want it. I think that they ought to be allowed side-by-side, because we have a diversity of liturgies in the Eastern Rite–the Roman Rite should have the same option.

Is there any satisfaction that you could point to, after these ten years, which confirms you in your decision to stop saying the New Mass?

FR. M.: When I say the Latin Mass for a congregation, they are very appreciative of my efforts. It takes a lot of sacrifice, because these days you have to travel to various places where a priest is needed, but I receive a lot of encouragement from the people whom I serve in this manner.

FR. FRANCIS LE BLANC

When did you enter the seminary, Father?

FR. LE BLANC: I entered the seminary of the Holy Cross Fathers in 1942, when they were still Catholic, and it was called St. Joseph University, in Nebrasso, Canada. I studied my Philosophy, Latin, and everything else. In 1946, I graduated with my Bachelor's degree in Theology. Then I entered Holy Hearts Seminary in Halifax, Nova Scotia. The fathers there were the cream of the crop! I was ordained in April of 1950, then I entered the ministry. Despite this new religion of Vatican II, I don't think we had any in my class that left the priesthood. (I'm talking about the two of us from my Archdiocese; I don't know about the others.) We are now both traditional-minded, celebrating the Tridentine Mass. I was always in the diocese, except when I entered the armed forces. I was a military chaplain for a while.

What did you learn about the priesthood in the seminary?

FR. LE B.: A priest is firstly a man of God, one who has a solid spiritual life, goes to confession often, recites the Breviary, prays the rosary, meditates daily, and makes his thanksgiving after Mass in front of the Blessed Sacrament. I had a visiting priest here not too long ago who did exactly that. He edified the people. The priest's life is not a life of only meetings and running around to visit parishioners. The priest's life is visiting the sick, hearing confessions, carrying on the ministry, not a life of becoming well liked by the people. No, the priest is to be a man of God, showing the best example to the people.

Well, I entered the seminary with those ideals in mind: to become a priest and to become a saint. I had very good spiritual direction, and I always read very serious books on the priesthood. I had as my first pastor a very good and solid monsignor, an ex-military chaplain. He always gave me the best example. My Archbishop needed a younger pastor who could speak fluent English at a Catholic high school. Everyone in my archdiocese spoke French, but since I spoke English, he placed me there. The example I received from the other priests was always very good.

How would you describe the modern idea of the priesthood?

FR. LE B.: The modern idea is that the priest is to be a highway commissioner. They're not even good social workers! They think the priesthood consists in running here and there. I had a case at a hospital–a poor man was dying, and the sister of the patient called her priest to give him the last rites. The priest approached her brother and said, "I expect he's gone, so we won't bother." So she called me, and I went and gave him the last rites. People want the true sacraments for their salvation.

Have you ever said the New Mass, Father?

FR. LE B.: Never! With Vatican II, things started to change. The vernacular started to come in. I didn't go along with any of the changes. My Archbishop was such a holy man. He was at the Council, but when he came back from Rome, he was devastated. He was so young, and yet he just couldn't take it. He died very young, completely broken-hearted because of the way the Church was going. So I didn't bother with the changes.

How did you have the foresight and courage to resist the changes?

FR. LE B.: It's not a question of foresight. In my eyes, my soul is so important that I'm not going to leave it in the hands of Tom, Dick, or Harry. I don't care who you are–I'm not going to throw away my eternal salvation to follow you on the wrong path! I'm the only one that can save my soul. Nobody else can. I was sure by a life of prayer that the Church's path at Vatican Council II was wrong. I've prayed all my life to the Blessed Virgin and in front of the Blessed Sacrament, asking for guidance to be kept on the right path. That's the only way to stay there.

What was the result of your resisting all these changes in the sixties? What did other people say? What did the Archdiocese do?

FR. LE B.: They never bothered me much. I was still in my parish all through the sixties and not making any of the changes. I wouldn't budge. Besides, when the New Mass came in 1969, I was already in the armed forces. There was nobody really to give me any problems in the military.

What was your assessment of the New Mass?

FR. LE B.: I was ashamed. The most horrible changes in the New Mass were the Canons, the reception of Communion, the disrespect towards the Body and Blood of Christ–if it truly is His Body and His Precious Blood! And the way the people dress! If you look at the whole thing, the New Mass is an abomination. Tradition is so important!

Is the New Mass any better if it's said reverently in Latin with vestments, with incense, with good music, and before reverent people?

FR. LE B.: I never saw anything like that! A priest in the diocese of Detroit came out and said the New Mass wearing a chasuble with the emblem of the professional hockey team called the "Detroit Red Wings." During the Mass, he would announce the scores. When I saw that in the newspapers, I was so mad. I told my parishioners to write to that priest and to his Cardinal. He got about a hundred letters. I do not know what was the result, but the priest answered one of my parishioners. He said that he did not see what was wrong wearing the Red Wings' emblem since it might prompt sports fans to come to Mass. He's not a good minister–he's not even being a good social worker!

Do you think that the current scandals among the priests are the result of the New Mass?

FR. LE B.: Yes. Because there are no graces coming from it–none! For example, one young priest was hunting to be made a bishop. When a scandal case was filed against him, he paid a large sum of money to prevent it from going to court. And then, the diocese paid another large sum because it too thought that it was a lot better to pay than go through a court case. Now, he's not being touched, and what did his bishop do? He made him a monsignor in February, and now he's a vicar general. The whole scandal came out in the newspaper. I think we are losing an awful lot of our Catholic laity, who, when they look at this whole mess, say, "To heck with it." Unfortunately, some priests give up as well. Sometimes they commit suicide. We had one here who hanged himself and another who shot himself. Well, there's one thing we have to say about the devil: He's not lazy. He's always on the job!

Is it possible for the priest to be a man of prayer if he says the New Mass?

FR. LE B.: I doubt that very much. The New Mass would drag him down.

How would you advise such a priest who is being dragged down by the New Mass?

FR. LE B.: I would advise him first to become a man of prayer and to begin to recite his Breviary. You know, most priests who say the New Mass don't recite the Breviary, much less the Rosary! Many of them, not all, do not make a meditation in front of the Blessed Sacrament, nor do they thank God after Mass. Archbishop Sheen used to spend an hour in front of the Blessed Sacrament every day! They have to become men of prayer. You cannot give what you haven't got. You cannot be the salt of the earth and the light of the world without a life of prayer. If they become men of prayer, they will change. But the problem is that most of them are so set in their way of doing things now, that they do not want to change.

I tell them that what is most important is to save their own souls. I ask, "What's important in your life, Father? Is it your soul, obedience to man, or obedience to God? Is it blind obedience?" If the bishop wants to go to hell, I am not going to follow him. I could be completely wrong, but in my opinion, you have thirty-five years of proof of the way many of our bishops have acted. I say, "So, are you going to continue following those bishops, or are you going to follow the right road? Many of those bishops are on the super-highway to hell, with no red lights. All the lights are green!"

Not long ago, you held a seminar for those interested in learning to celebrate the traditional Mass. Could you speak about that?

FR. LE B.: Yes. About three years ago, Fr. Perez, Fr. O'Connor (R.I.P.), and I lined up a seminar to teach priests how to say the Tridentine Mass. I freely furnished all the rooms, the food, everything. We had one priest and a seminarian who came from as far as Slovenia to attend this. I paid for the air fare of the Slovenians, and we gave the instructions here in our bookstore. We had a whole course. Then, I encouraged the Slovenian priest from Slovenia to contact the former superior general of the Society of St. Pius X, Fr. Franz Schmidberger. I told him, "From here on out, they should be able to lead you on your way." And my work was done.

Many priests seem to be afraid that, if they begin celebrating the traditional Mass, they will have nowhere to turn.
Have you ever heard of a priest who returned to Tradition going hungry or finding himself without a place to say Mass?

FR. LE B.: No. I know one priest who takes care of an alcoholic Romanian priest. He called me for help and mentioned that the priest had been drunk twice at the altar. I said, "Listen, I cannot expose my people to a priest like that. As a last resort, he can come here, but he will not say Mass in public, and will not be allowed liquor."

Do priests ever object to you that they cannot learn to say the old Mass because they've never learned any Latin?

FR. LE B.: No, never. I speak from experience, since we've had several who were able to pick up the Latin. One who does not know Latin can always learn it, and the Tridentine Mass is not that hard to learn. We could help him. We could breeze through theology. We have a whole library, a wonderful library, a Catholic library, with Canon Law and everything. But the problem is that human nature always finds excuses, such as, "Father, the *Novus Ordo* doesn't work, but I don't go to your Mass because I never studied Latin." Well, when they say that, I hand them a Missal. "Can you read English? You don't look too stupid to me. Here's the English, and here's the Latin. Can you read that [*pointing to the English translation*]? Don't give me that excuse!"

To contact Fr. Le Blanc:

Rev. Fr. Francis Le Blanc
12546 West Peoria Avenue
El Mirage, AZ 85335-3105
Phone: (623) 583-1027

FR. PAUL GREUTER

When were you ordained, Father?

FR. GREUTER: In 1954. I went to the minor seminary in Holland, and then I came to Canada for Philosophy and Theology. The seminaries were very orthodox, very good.

What did they teach you that the priest is?

FR. G.: They taught the real Catholic doctrine–the sacrificial priesthood.

So, you were ordained to offer the traditional Mass, and you said it more or less without adaptations for fifteen years before the New Mass came in?

FR. G.: The only alterations before 1969 were saying parts of the Mass in English, taking away genuflections and signs of the cross, and things like that. But I just didn't go along with any of those things.

Really? Did your refusal to budge cause any friction with your bishop?

FR. G.: Sure! I told him, "You can fire me, but I won't do it!" So he knew where I stood all along. The removal of those genuflections and signs of the cross took away from the sacredness of the Mass.

What was your reaction to the New Mass in 1969?

FR. G.: I never even touched it.

What happened then? Surely, the bishop couldn't just let that pass!

FR. G.: Oh, I told the bishop I was not going to go along, so he put me in as chaplain of a hospital, where I could do the least damage.

I'm sure the people in the hospital who had the Faith appreciated you very much.

FR. G.: I don't know. Some of them did, no doubt. But, after four years, especially in the last months, there was more and more frustration. Every day someone would say, "Oh, you are the nut that Father so-and-so was talking about!" So, I started to wonder if it did any good for me to be there any more. And I felt a nervous breakdown coming on. I knew that, after a nervous breakdown, I would be no good for anything else any more. The doctor told me to get away for a month. But when I got back, I felt the same. So I told the bishop, "I'm going to retire."

How old were you?

FR. G.: Forty-nine. I told the bishop that I was going to leave the Diocese.

The hostility of the others towards you, because of Tradition, must have been a great trial. Why do they have such hostility, if they're really liberals? If they're really for "freedom," why are they so hostile towards our freedom to be faithful to Tradition?

FR. G.: That is something that I never could understand, and I never got an answer to that question when I asked the bishop. *They tolerate Protestants, but they don't tolerate traditional Catholics!* I think it's because they have become more Protestant than Catholic themselves, so they're more hostile toward Tradition because it contradicts them.

Were there any attempts to re-educate you before you finally retired?

FR. G.: Oh, yes! The Jesuits came out with a ten-day study session for the priests. Even if a parish did not have a priest for Sunday Mass, that was all right! Half of the diocese went for ten days, and the other half went for the next ten days.

That study session was absolutely awful. It started on Wednesday night, and we were kind of taken to dinner. Then, on Thursday, we had some good arguments! Friday morning was just absurd, so I told the bishop I must go home. He was very angry.

What was so absurd about it?

FR. G.: Oh, it was just mad! Christ didn't know that he was God! All the miracles, they didn't exist, you know. They don't believe anything, you know, not a thing!

So you never went back to any more study sessions?

Fr. G.: No. Nothing could convince me that they were right. I had no faith in what they were saying or doing. If you look at Vatican II closely, you come to the conclusion that they used phrases that can be interpreted both in a Catholic sense and in a liberal sense. They undermined the coherence, the clearness of the Faith. Contrast that with all those dogmas of the Council of Trent: how clear Trent was in the expression of the Faith, and how vague they were at Vatican II. I have no faith in Vatican II at all.

So they just gave up trying to convince you because they saw that you were too stubborn?

Fr. G.: Oh yeah, they knew I was stubborn! I could see the other priests losing it when they went along. And, after that, I didn't even go to the retreats any more, because the "retreats" were held at a hotel, with tennis courts, a swimming pool, and everything. That, to me, was not a retreat! And I actually began to separate myself from the other priests, because we had nothing in common any more.

You were operating on two different wave-lengths. Do you credit your avoidance of the study sessions and the retreats with keeping you on the straight and narrow?

Fr. G.: Well, I was able to keep on track, mainly, because I kept up with my reading, and I kept to the traditional teachings.

Would you say that the current scandals of the clergy have any relation to this new idea of the priesthood, which your colleagues went along with?

Fr. G.: I don't know if the scandals are the result of that. *Personally, I think they are the result of a lack of basic spirituality.* Spirituality definitely went out the window when the changes came in. The priests whom I occasionally used to go back and visit after I left were so illogical! One priest, whom I have known since I was a kid of fourteen in the seminary in the old country, got sick and had to go to the hospital. He was not in my hospital, but he wanted me to bring him Communion in the hospital where he was, because the chaplain there was just carrying the Blessed Sacrament around in his pocket all the time, you know. (How did he dare to do that?) So, I would drive over there to bring him Communion, but, after he got better and became the chaplain of a hospital himself, he did exactly the same thing as the other priest–he carried the Blessed Sacrament around in his pocket!

The problem is basically a lack of spirituality, a lack of prayer. It is striking that the few lay people who go to the New Mass now hardly ever see a priest saying the Breviary. (I don't know their obligations–maybe they're not even obliged to say it any more!) But, if prayer is gone, the priest is gone–that is what we stressed in the seminary in the old country, year after year! *If a priest leaves out his prayers, he's gone!* Even when they still had the old Breviary, finally, Rome said that one of the Little Hours was enough. That's typical of the whole new attitude. As long as they prayed, they stayed pretty well in line, but when they stop praying, there's nothing to stop them from getting into all sorts of things.

Is this lack of prayer a result of the New Mass?

FR. G.: I personally think the New Mass is the basis of it. It is the root of the problems of the priests who left the priesthood–of several of them, anyway (I don't know them all that well). Some of the ones who left the priesthood, whom I did know, gave up the Breviary beforehand, and in the end of it all, they wouldn't even say Mass. "I never see you saying the Breviary," I said to one of the priests I was visiting. His answer was, "Oh, I've no time for it!" He had time to get married, but he had no time for his Breviary!

You claim, then, that the New Mass is the root of the loss of the spirit of prayer and, finally, the root of a lot of the lost vocations?

FR. G.: Exactly. Also, there is no challenge any more. As soon as they started changing all the rules, vocations plummeted because there was no challenge. People want a challenge, whether it's in marriage, or in the priesthood, or even in their jobs.

So, paradoxically, by trying to make things easier on the priests, the changes made it harder to persevere, because there was no longer any reason to try? Some priests won't say Mass on their "day off," because they see their priesthood as a job. Do you think that's a logical outcome of the New Mass?

FR. G.: I think that's a logical conclusion of the whole new attitude, which is basically the lack of a spirit of prayer.

What is the new priesthood?

FR. G.: I could never figure that out, really. Now the priest is just the president of the assembly. He just directs things, and very often the liturgical committee pretty well tells the priest what he has to do.

Is there any essential difference
between the priest and the faithful now?

FR. G.: In the New Mass, as far as I can see, there is no difference, because there's no sacrifice. What do they need a priest for? The "priesthood of the laity" is over-stressed.

Do you think that the New Mass was written to accommodate
this new vision of the priesthood, or do you think that the
new vision of the priesthood follows from the New Mass?

FR. G.: Well, I think the New Mass was set up to become something Protestant. Everything that was objectionable to Protestants had to be taken away, so what was left for the priest? ***They didn't leave him the sacrifice!*** It was very striking. After the Council, the "Normative Mass," which was pretty well the same as the New Mass, was proposed, and the bishops rejected it. Then, they changed it a little and just imposed it upon the bishops anyway.

You have always kept faithful to the Mass of your Ordination.
Have you ever doubted that you were right to take this stand?

FR. G.: I never had a doubt, ever!

What proof could you give that your refusal of the
new ways has been correct? How would you convince
a priest who doubts the wisdom of your stand for Tradition?

FR. G.: In the first place, the proof is all the Saints who have been formed by the two-thousand-year Tradition of the Church. The new way has yet to prove itself, and I've not seen anything good coming out of it yet! I've never really had any doubts about my refusal to change. When I wanted to go to the seminary, my Dad said to me, "I have no objection to your going to the seminary, but, if you want to go to the seminary and become a priest, you should make up your mind to be a good one, because we have enough of the other kind!"

He could say that even in the forties?
So, this crisis didn't start overnight in 1962!

FR. G.: No, it had already started before, especially in Europe, where there were so many priests that they didn't know what to do with them.

Is that why you came to Canada in the first place?

FR. G.: Yes. I couldn't get ordained in our diocese, because there were too many candidates for the priesthood. But I didn't want to be ordained in our diocese, anyway.

Was it too liberal already?

FR. G.: No, it was because of the attitude of the people towards the priests. The priests were of a class all to themselves. The dioceses of Europe were still very class-oriented. That was diminishing a little, but they were still class-oriented, and I liked what I heard from people about the Canadian soldiers who were staying in Holland during the War. The need for priests here was much greater than in Europe, and I liked the fact that the priests were respected here, but not put on a pedestal. That was what I wanted.

How would you advise a priest who is struggling, beating his head against the wall, because of trying to be a good priest in the new system?

FR. G.: First, he must reflect on the priesthood–what a priest *is* and not what he *does*–and work from there. Basically, a priest has to be another Christ. If you look over the history of the Church, the priests who really believed in the idea of the sacrificing priesthood all turned out to be pretty good priests!

Then, he must become a man of prayer. He has to pray! One thing really helped me to stay faithful. *I pictured myself dying and at the judgment seat of Christ, Who would ask me what I did with the priesthood that I had received.* It should make us shake in our boots when we see the powers, which belong to God, that are given to man in the priesthood! Those powers carry a responsibility with them, and we have to take that responsibility seriously.

Could you recommend a book or two which might be helpful for a priest who is trying to take his priesthood seriously?

FR. G.: Any of the old books on the priesthood which I read before 1962. Most of them were pretty good, most of them! I found that *The Rhine Flows into the Tiber* gives a good idea of the real operation of Vatican II. This put the Council in a different light for me.

How would you respond to the accusation that you have been disobedient by not going along with the changes?

_FR. G.:_ The Church herself set the rules which I follow, so I am obedient! I'm not going to break the rules of the Church, but if the authorities are going to change all the rules, where are we then? I hear, over and over again, from priests and from bishops, that even the dogmas of the Faith are not all true–they are true only for the time when they're made. The church with dogmas like that is not the Church of Christ! _So if you want to talk about disobedience, the ones who want obedience from us are not obedient to God!_ How can we be obedient to them? True obedience is due to the Church of God, not to the church of man!

How would you advise a priest who says, "That's all very well, and I'm ready to give up the New Mass and try and say a Mass which expresses the real priesthood, which I'm trying to live. But I don't know Latin, and I don't have any proper philosophical or theological formation, so what can I do?"

_FR. G.:_ I don't think there should be any objection. Okay, he might have to give up a year or two and take, you might say, a refresher course in Latin and in theology. I was talking to one priest who was trained in the new seminaries, and he never heard a word about transubstantiation in the whole course of theology! The Council of Trent was mentioned, but not one dogma of the Council of Trent was ever discussed.

Is it possible for them to do this, to take the time off to try and pick up a real formation?

_FR. G.:_ Yes. Financially speaking, I don't think there would be any objection. I'm sure they could go to a seminary and get some proper training, and they would not be left without some financial help. They would be kept alive.

Have you ever heard of a priest who was faithful to Tradition going without food, clothing, shelter, or a place to say Mass?

_FR. G.:_ Never. Our traditional people will gladly take care of a traditional priest. The objection I have heard is that the priests are afraid of losing their pension from the diocese and losing all their friends. As far as losing the pension from the diocese goes, they shouldn't worry about that, because it will be made up very well by the generosity of the people–they won't let a priest starve! As far as the loss of friends goes, let us take a good look at it. _Are_ *they fair-weather friends or are they real friends?* If they are real friends, they will respect your convictions. If they are fair-weather friends, well, they are not worthy to be called friends, anyway. You would make better friends among the other traditional clergy.

Several priests have told me that, at many of the deanery meetings, they don't want to open their mouths, because, no matter what they say, somebody is going to object to it. These meetings are usually either fighting sessions or socials where nothing substantial is discussed. There is no common language any more between the priests who stand for something of Tradition and the liberals. The priests in the dioceses normally have the best associations with each other on the golf course or the tennis court. But, as far as matters of the Church go, there is no common language. *When you come to associate yourself with traditional priests, at least you all speak the same language, you all share the same ideals, and that is a great relief in itself.*

I think that anyone who really wants to take his priesthood seriously will get the peace that we all need. The peace of God is very comforting, especially when you get old, you know, and you're checking on how far they've gotten in digging your grave! Then, you think about these things more and more.

What was it that one of the Cistercians said? "It's a hard bed to lie on, but it's an easy bed to die on!"

FR. G.: Yes, yes. In the priesthood, they say, the pay is lousy, but the pension is out of this world!

To contact Fr. Greuter:

Rev. Fr. Paul Greuter
4334 Jingle Pot Road
Nanaimo, BC V9T 5P4 (CANADA)
Phone: (250) 245-0508

FR. BRIAN HAWKER

EDITED TRANSCRIPT

When were you ordained, Father?

FR. HAWKER: In 1978. I entered the minor seminary in 1966, right after Vatican II. For the first year (or maybe two years), we still had the traditional Mass in the seminary. The minor seminary was a regular high school, and they actually did still emphasize Latin at that time. But, by the time I got to the major seminary, the new style of formation was fully in place.

When you entered the seminary, what was your idea of the priesthood?

FR. H.: Well, we had been taught to have very great respect for the priest, because he represented Christ. It was sort of drummed into us at home, and also by the nuns who taught us in grammar school, that the priest was the Man of God. That certainly changed by the time I got to the college level of the seminary. By that time, you know, things were really in revolution. The whole meaning of the priesthood, as portrayed to us there, was completely different from what I had always been taught.

What was the new idea of priesthood?

FR. H.: Well, the idea was that the priest is, in many ways, a social worker. The idea of the sacrificial nature of the priesthood in the Mass was completely thrown out, and I was kind of embarrassed by that. The priest was no longer meant to offer sacrifice–he was supposed to be just like everybody else and very much a part of the world. There was a kind of anti-clerical attitude, in the sense that it was always emphasized that we should have more contact with (and friendship with) lay-people rather than with the other priests. It was a very egalitarian idea of what the priesthood was all about. By the time I was ordained, or a little after that, there were many types of "non-ordained ministers": lay lectors, and so on.

Since the New Mass does not emphasize the idea of sacrifice, why would we need a priest to be an offerer of sacrifice? Obviously, I think, the New Mass has really contributed to the decline of vocations–to the priesthood and in general–for that reason.

What is the role of the priest in the New Mass?

FR. H.: In the New Mass, they all just gather together as an assembly to praise God, and the priest is supposed to be the presider, or the facilitator, of that gathering. They don't have any idea of the sacrificial aspect, which is clear in the old Mass.

How did you react when they were trying to form you to be a presider?

FR. H.: Well, when I was first ordained, I'm not sure if I had the same understanding of these things as I now have. By the time I was ordained, I had been in the seminary for twelve years, and we were pretty well brain-washed. I remember that I never really liked the idea of being a presider, and I never really liked the New Mass. I didn't understand all of the problems with it at that time, but I knew that there was something wrong. I knew that this New Mass was not what the Church had always done, and that, if you looked at pictures of Protestant services, there was really very little difference. So I was very troubled by it, but, at the time, I just thought that I was doing what I was supposed to do.

One of the things that they used to brain-wash us was the idea that the New Mass was like the Mass celebrated by the Apostles in the very earliest days of the Church. I didn't really believe that, but they really drummed these ideas into us over the years. The 1970's, of course, were a revolutionary period in the Church and in society, so we were trained that way, and we weren't really prepared to resist the brain-washing, since we were not given any strong spiritual life. There was really no emphasis in the seminary on prayer or meditation. Even attendance at Mass was, for the most part, optional!

Isn't the term "brain-washing" a bit of an exaggeration?

FR. H.: No. Brain-washing was very much a reality. We were always taught to go along with the system, even though it was very corrupt. We were always trained with the idea that Vatican II was the great hope of the Church and that everything before Vatican II had been bad. Many of our professors were ordained in the 1940's and 1950's, and they really had a lot of resentment toward their traditional training and toward the traditional Mass. That resentment and bitterness were drummed into us, almost constantly.

Is it possible to be a man of God, a sacrificing priest, when saying the New Mass, even in its most conservative form?

FR. H.: I don't think it is possible to do that with the New Mass at all, even if it is said in a very reverent way. I think that's the mistake that some people have, who want to find a priest to say the New Mass in a more conservative way. But I don't think it is possible to offer sacrifice when the New Mass itself de-emphasizes that aspect. Even if it is said in the Latin form, there are still some errors in it. The *General Instruction on the Roman Missal* does not emphasize the idea of the sacrifice of the Mass, rather, it puts the emphasis on the priest as the gatherer of the assembly.

Is there a particular feature of the New Mass which makes you say that it's not possible to be a sacrificing priest when saying it?

FR. H.: For instance, the Offertory prayers of the New Mass have nothing to do with the Offertory prayers of the traditional Mass. Even the Roman Canon, which is better, I guess, than the other "Eucharistic Prayers," as they call them, is still flawed in many ways, and it de-emphasizes the idea of sacrifice by the prayers which are changed. I think that some people have a mistaken idea that the New Mass is just an English translation of the traditional Mass, which is, of course, simply not true.

Is there a built-in conflict for the priest who tries to say the New Mass according to the traditional ideas of the priesthood?

FR. H.: Oh, yes! At least I can say that, in my case, there certainly was such a conflict. I don't see how it would be avoidable when a priest begins to understand what the traditional priesthood is. I don't see how he can continue to perform the ceremonies of the New Mass and live with his conscience. If he begins to find out what the priesthood is all about, and he realizes that he's not really living up to that when he celebrates Mass every day, I think that there would necessarily be a personal conflict.

How do priests who experience this conflict manage to go along with the system?

FR. H.: You would hope that such a conflict would cause these priests to refuse to go along with the system, but in some cases they purposely try to conquer their conflicted feelings, or to repress them. Or they just don't want to face reality! Some of my former colleagues have found a way to justify the new system and to go along with it. They know that there is a problem, but they don't think it is serious enough to do something radical about it. I remember, one time, telling a priest friend of mine that I had been saying the traditional Mass. He was not against the traditional Mass, but he asked me if I had permission. I said, "No, I hope I don't need permission!" He became very upset with me, because he thought that I was being disobedient.

What finally brought you to the celebration of the traditional Mass?

FR. H.: After I became a priest, I realized how very little I really knew! We didn't learn very much in the seminary–nothing of philosophy and very little of theology, at least not of traditional theology! So, I started reading on my own, because I knew that I had to learn something! I also began talking with other priests who were older and had more of a sense of what the Church was supposed to be. I began reading about Church history, about the Mass, and about theology. Then, I began to realize that there was something very seriously wrong and that it all flowed from the New Mass.

What happened as a result of this reading program?

FR. H.: When you're a priest who has been formed with the ideals of the 1970's, you do what you're told! You have liturgical committees, you have lectors, and you have ministers and all these other people who are telling you the things you are supposed to be doing. Half of the time, I found myself in conflict with the people who were in those positions, because they were doing things that even went beyond the way the New Mass was presented in the Missal. So, I began to realize that there was something really seriously wrong, but it took me a while, because we had been brain-washed and conditioned to believe that this was the way the Church was supposed to be. But, gradually, after about the mid-eighties, I began to realize that that position was wrong, and I began to do more and more research and study about the traditional Mass in particular.

How did you learn to say the old Mass?

FR. H.: Actually, I learned it from watching a video! Although I had some recollections of it from when I was an altar boy, I didn't remember that much. I watched that video, and then a parishioner gave me some books to read about the traditional Mass. After that, I came into contact with the Society of St. Pius X in Chicago.

Were you still a parish priest when you began to celebrate the traditional Mass?

FR. H.: Yes. I was celebrating it for small groups of people on Sundays and on Holy Days.

How did you manage to do that?

FR. H.: At that time, I wasn't completely aware of the situation. I was hoping to get permission to say the Indult Mass, but I was told that I couldn't, because that option was only intended for older priests! I eventually came to the realization I was either going to have to conform to the new system or get out.

There are people, both priests and layfolk, who think that the best thing to do is to "Stay in and fight," but I don't believe that, frankly. The ones who are really in control of the dioceses might allow a few things that are somewhat traditional, but the entire orientation is still toward the same revolutionary brain-washing that I experienced in the 1970's. So for me, although, I have to admit, it did take a while, the big difficulty was not how I would begin saying the traditional Mass, but how I could stop saying the New Mass! Saying the two Masses side by side, I was like Dr. Jekyll and Mr. Hyde. Finally, after a lot of thinking and praying, I decided to leave the Archdiocese. It took me over a year from that time until I finally left.

How did you leave the Archdiocese?

FR. H.: Well, when I had looked around for other alternatives which would allow me to stay within a normal framework, and I found that there simply weren't any, I went to stay in Post Falls, Idaho, for a while one summer. When the summer was over, I just didn't go back to the Archdiocese. I wrote a letter to Cardinal Bernadin, in which I told him all the reasons why I couldn't continue being a priest in the Archdiocese. He wanted me to come and visit him, but I declined the invitation. We wrote letters back and forth for a while, and he did threaten to suspend me, but he never followed through with it. I don't ever recall any mention of excommunication. I don't think they really believe in penalties and excommunication any more. They may use them in some cases with traditional people, but I don't know how much it really means, even to them. It was as if I had just quit my job. I was told, in fact, that I could come back any time I wanted.

You mentioned that, while saying both Masses, you were like Dr. Jekyll and Mr. Hyde. Could you develop that comparison a bit?

FR. H.: When the priest is exclusively saying the New Mass, there's just no sense of having to be a man of prayer or a man of sacrifice. I can say, from the experience of many of the priests that I lived or associated with, that there is a certain idea that the priesthood is a job. The morale among the priests was very low because of this idea, and I would think that it must be even worse now with all these scandals going on. There is no need to sacrifice, to give things up, in the new priesthood, and that worldly lifestyle, that consumerist lifestyle, could really be a problem for the priests.

I know that some of them are very sincere and want to do the right thing, but it's very easy, when saying the New Mass, to get into a worldly spirit and to become very much a "man of the world," and, from that, everything else follows. When you're saying the New Mass, it's hard to have a strong interior life. I suppose that there are priests who seem to be succeeding at that while saying the New Mass, but I still think that they're really fooling themselves. The New Mass is so superficial, so empty, that it really doesn't have a whole lot to offer to sustain the interior life of the priest.

Because of that, the priest's attitude towards things gradually changes. I'll never forget one priest I was associated with, who had been ordained in the 1930's (he's still living, actually). He had, of course, been trained with the old Mass, and he had said it until he was a priest for about thirty-five years. But I could tell that he had become more accepting of the new way of doing things. He would say, "Oh well, we were not taught that way, but that's the way it has to be now—everything changes!"

But younger priests, who don't really have any background in the traditional way of doing things, are not even sure what they've lost. I think that there is a great possibility for them to become worldly, not to pray much, and really to become social-workers.

Things change drastically when the priest begins saying the old Mass exclusively. For me, it certainly wasn't a change that happened over night. Obviously, the fact that a priest is saying the traditional Mass doesn't necessarily prevent him from being worldly, because you know that happened in the 1940's and 1950's when priests were only saying the traditional Mass! But I think that the traditional Mass helped me to understand better what the priesthood is all about, and it helped me to realize that the priest is really ordained to offer sacrifice. It strengthened my interior life in general. In my case, there was also more of a desire to say Mass. With the New Mass, it was really a struggle, especially for the last couple of years that I was in the Archdiocese, because I didn't want to do it any more. I did it only because I had to, but I didn't really want to.

Do you see any link between the Revolutionary training in the seminaries in the 1970's and the current scandals among the clergy?

Fr. H.: I think that there is a connection between these ideas and the scandals, although I haven't really thought about it profoundly. The Church of Vatican II has really become very feminized–it's an effeminate church. The

New Mass is a very feminine type of thing, because it tends to be sort of subjective, in the sense that they now put a lot of emphasis on the priest's personality: Does he smile? Is he folksy and friendly with the people? Does he say, "Good morning"? They are concerned about a lot of subjective things that are extraneous to the real priestly ideal.

They still say that they want priests, but they don't necessarily want priests to be strong and to be leaders. The priest is supposed to be somebody who is "one of the boys." Everything sort of pulls together in this question. The fact that the priest is no longer really a leader makes it very easy for him to lead a not-very-exemplary life! Since the Church has "opened up to the world" (and the New Mass is really at the center of that idea), a lot of abuses have resulted, including these scandals.

If you had to advise a priest who was concerned about his priestly life and thinking of saying the traditional Mass, what would you tell him?

FR. H.: Especially to such a priest who is searching, I would say, for the sake of his priesthood, that he should try to learn to say the traditional Mass and say it as often as he can. Frankly, knowing what I know about the corruption in a lot of the dioceses (which seems to be worse and worse all the time), I don't see how a really good priest, who wants to do what the Church tells him and who has a good idea of what the priesthood really is, could stay in the diocese. I would encourage him to start saying the traditional Mass, because I think it's going to help his priesthood. When I was at that point, I really believe that, if I had not done something quickly, my vocation would have been in jeopardy. The more often he can say the traditional Mass, the better it is for him, and the better it is for his priesthood. The problem is that, as far as I know, there are very few bishops who'd allow him to do that exclusively.

How can the priest who has never studied Latin hope to learn the traditional Mass?

FR. H.: It's not as though he is going to have to speak Latin all the time! A lot of priests, for example, speak Spanish, and if they know Spanish, they can certainly learn enough Latin to say the Mass. But I suppose he'd have to have the motivation to want to learn it. This is true for theology as well. It all depends on his level of motivation and his knowledge. You see, he's got to understand how deeply the Church is in crisis. If he doesn't believe that, then I guess these questions are not much of an issue.

So, these obstacles are not impossibly high as long as the priest has the motivation to try and overcome them?

FR. H.: Right, but he also needs greater knowledge. In the case of so many priests, who go to a lot of meetings, their lives become kind of bureaucratic. The fact is that there are fewer priests now, and, although it's true that they have a lot of lay-people doing what used to be priestly work, the priests are still very busy. I think that a lot of them don't have the time–or don't take the time–to read and to find out what's really going on in the Church. But I think that, if a priest is really interested, he can do it.

FR. EUGENE HEIDT

EDITED TRANSCRIPT

What year were you ordained, Father?

FR. HEIDT: In 1959. I started the minor seminary in 1947, as a freshman in high school. I went eight years and took my degree in philosophy at Mount Angel. Then, the last four years, 1955-59, I went up to Seattle with the Salesian Fathers, and they were still good. They hadn't been steeped in the new theology yet, so I got out of there just in time!

What did they teach you about the priesthood in the seminary? What did they teach you that the priest is?

FR. H.: I can tell you that they gave us a traditional understanding and teaching of what the priesthood is, and they spent a lot of time on the sacraments, particularly Holy Orders. They gave you St. Thomas's definition of the priesthood. At this moment, I'm not able to recall it word for word, but I know what the priesthood is. I know what's expected of us. And I know that, as long as we do what Christ and the Church want done, the Holy Ghost will supply all of the graces that we need to do whatever we have to do.

They taught you the priest is the other Christ, a sacrificing priest?

FR. H.: Yes, yes. And there was that very important thing in the Rite of Ordination where the bishop orders you to pray for the living and the dead. Those professors never missed a beat. It was all truly traditional teaching.

How did you react to the liturgical changes in the 1960's?

FR. H.: I was still a young priest when the New Mass first came out. One day, the pastor came in and told me that we were going to have to turn our altars around and say Mass in English, facing the people. I asked who had said that we had to do *that*, and he said, "Rome says so." Well, we believed everything that the authorities told us in those days, and so I went along with it. I never did like it.

Right after the New Mass came out, priests were innovating, one after another, and you couldn't find two parishes where the Mass was the same. They just kept on innovating after that. I never changed the Mass one bit from the way it came out in the Missal of Pope Paul VI. *I didn't like it, but I thought I had to do it.*

When did you first think of beginning
to pick up the traditional Mass again?

FR. H.: When the Indult Mass became available. The Archbishop got two young priests to write up the rules (because each bishop was allowed to make the rules for the Indult to allow the Latin Mass in his own diocese, you know). One was a Dominican, I believe, out of Chicago, and another was a wild, bold fellow here in the diocese who was always looking for novelty. And so they came out with this long list of rules. They said you couldn't have the traditional Latin Mass for First Communions, for weddings, for funerals, for Holy Days of Obligation, or for Sundays. They practically ruled it out altogether. Shortly after this was done, the young Dominican took off, and he went to work with the AIDS group, or some kind of outfit, as a layman, up in North Portland. Then, a couple of years after that, the other priest took off, too.

So you could only say the traditional Mass
at five o'clock in the morning on Wednesdays, something like that?

FR. H.: Well, it took me a couple of years even to get permission to say the Mass on First Saturdays.

Was it difficult to make the transition back to the traditional Mass?
How well did you remember the ceremonies?

FR. H.: I took the Missal, and I just sat down and kept on reviewing it for three hours in my head, you know, and then I went over and said Mass. It's kind of like riding a bicycle–you never forget. No, it was no problem getting back to the traditional Mass.

So, then you were saying both Masses for a while?
What effect did that have on your priestly life?

FR. H.: I knew that the New Mass I was offering was a **valid** Mass. (I didn't have any qualms about that. I didn't hate it; I just didn't like it.) But then, after reading more about the New Mass, about all the skullduggery they went through in stripping the Mass of its true meaning, even though I knew that *I* wasn't doing that, it kept involving me more and more. And I knew that the day was coming when I would just have to stop saying the New Mass.

I was talking with Fr. Marchosky [see p.73ff] around that time, and he was thinking about setting up some kind of a school, a kind of pre-seminary training course, I suppose, some place on the west coast. (He had been a seminary professor for years until his bishop turned him out.) He had gone to Rome, I believe, or Paris. He put me onto a priest who had written a number of theses on the New Mass, you know, all the objectionable doctrine and the change of attitude towards the sacrifice of the Mass. That's what got me interested. And then I started reading the things that Michael Davies had put out. He put out a pretty good book on the New Mass, *Pope Paul's New Mass*.

But I thought it was kind of a lost cause by then. Until I found out about this meeting, in 1986, of the nine cardinals who were called in by Pope John Paul II. Cardinal Stickler said that the Pope had asked the nine cardinals (and he had been one of the nine) whether the traditional Mass had ever been forbidden. So they said, "We understand that the Mass has never been abrogated or forbidden."

So obedience is not really an objection against saying the traditional Mass, when you consider that it's not forbidden by the Church?

FR. H.: Correct. There is no question of disobedience involved here, no way.

How did your convictions about the old Mass sit with the Chancery?

FR. H.: Things just got worse. A couple of years before, I had written a letter about what they called the "Stewardship Council." That was a program that they used to raise money for the operation of the Archdiocese. I told the people in the parish that we couldn't contribute to that. I black-balled the "Stewardship Council"!

Why did you black-ball it?

FR. H.: Because of the immoral causes that they were promoting. I named some of them in the letter I wrote. But I have to go back a little bit to explain some of this. It all came to a head with this question of the money for the "Stewardship Council"–that's what really got Archbishop Levada going. I remember coming home from meeting with him on one of those occasions. I said, "You know, that man isn't Catholic. The Archbishop is not Catholic!" I was telling the whole parish this. No wonder he got so angry with me, in the end of it all!

When Archbishop Levada had first come to the Archdiocese, I was the first one to have an appointment with him after he was installed. I went in there for an hour and a half, and I poured out my heart to him, because I was told he was a good, traditional, orthodox bishop, and that he was going to straighten this Archdiocese out. So I really churned my heart out to him, and he just sat there. He was like an episcopal vacuum cleaner, sucking all this stuff up and listening to it. I told him about the homosexuality in the Church, and I said, "I can name six or seven homosexual priests in the diocese. They call themselves the 'altar society.'" He said, "You've come in here with a bunch of rumors, and I'm not going to listen to that." I said, "Well, one day, somebody is going to have to pay!" But he wouldn't listen.

Every time I went to see him, I'd go in and argue with him. I think there is only one pastoral letter that he wrote, supposedly on the Mass and the Eucharist. I read the thing and I took it to his office, and I said, "Did you write this? Is this supposed to be a complete treatise on the Eucharist and the Mass? How did you manage to get through this whole thing without once mentioning Transubstantiation?" "Well, that's such a long and difficult term anyway," he said, " and we don't use that term anymore."

I said, "I don't think that's the correct estimate of that word. When I was in the first grade and our good little Benedictine Sister was preparing us for First Holy Communion, I can remember her putting that up on the board. She put 'trans,' and then she put a line. Then she put 'substantiation,' and then she went through and explained what each of those things meant. She was able to put it in terms we could understand, so that we knew that the Bread and the Wine are substantially different from what they were before the Consecration." He just repeated "That's such a confusing term!" So, I said, "Let's go on to the next item."

The "next item" was his having gone to Our Lady of Atonement Parish— that's what they called a "Catholic-Lutheran joint parish," where they have a priest on one end of the altar and a Lutheran minister on the other, and they go back and forth. I asked, "What did you do over there?" and he answered, "We concelebrated liturgy." "What does *that* mean?" I asked, "Did you and the Lutheran minister say Mass together? What *did* you do?" He just wouldn't discuss it any more.

And then, one night during all this "Stewardship" business, the Archbishop really got angry. He called me up, it was after hours, 5:05 p.m.! He was supposed to be on his way home, but he stopped and called me. He was *so* livid, he could hardly talk on the phone. He said, "You be in my office at ten o'clock tomorrow morning before the diocesan consulters and the other bishops of the diocese. Plead your case there!" I said, "Well, all right, I will be glad to come in and do that, but I haven't got any time to document all this." He said, "That's okay, just come on in and tell us what's on your mind."

So, I was in there probably an hour altogether, and those priests were lined up in a big horseshoe, you know, and I was at the table on the end by myself. I had my tape recorder, which I set up beside me, and, as I was trying to plug it in, I heard a voice up at the other end: "Hey, you can't use a recorder in here!" I turned around, and it was the archbishop. I asked, "Why not?" He said, "We don't record this kind of meeting." And I said, "Oh, all right, but I'll plug it in while I'm talking and unplug it while you're talking, how's that?" Then I set up a chair beside me, and one of the bishops, who used to be a very good friend of mine, asked what the chair was for. They were waiting for an attorney to come in, I suppose. I said "Well, that's for my Guardian Angel." And these priests looked at me like I was kind of crazy, you know.

At the end of my little speech, the Archbishop said, "Okay, I agree with you on everything except for the question of homosexuality in the Seminary. We took care of that a couple of weeks ago. Of course, you wouldn't know about *that* meeting, but it's already been taken care of." But he sided with me on the rest of the other complaints that I had.

Afterwards, he got on my case, and he finally told me to take a sabbatical. He said, "You can take your sabbatical if you want, and you are free to write up a proposal of what you want to do." I agreed, and I took a month to get my plan together and brought it back to him.

I told him that I wanted to spend five months or so studying the Council of Trent, Vatican I, Vatican II, and all of the papal encyclicals from the last two hundred years. But he said, "No, No. That's non-productive. You will go to the University and take their 'Credo' course" (which was an updating in theology). But I said "No, No." I said, like the boys said when it was time to go to Vietnam: "Hell no, I won't go! No thanks." So he said, "Then I'll send you to a monastery for your sabbatical, and I will draw up a course of studies for you. You will have a private mentor." I said, "No, I do not need a guru." Finally, he told me to go ahead and do what I wanted.

I said then that I wanted to spend the last couple of weeks of my sabbatical in Fatima, to talk all this stuff over with our Blessed Lady, and then I would come back. And he agreed. Well, I never got to Fatima, but in the meantime this place came up for sale, and I knew I had been had by that time. When I went back to see him, after the sabbatical was over, he told me that, because I had said the Latin Mass in "excommunicated" chapels, mainly Portland and Veneta [Oregon], he could no longer use my services. So I said, "Okay. You do what you have to do. ***But you're going to have to tie me up in chains to stop me from offering the Latin Mass.***" He threatened to suspend me if I didn't stop.

A month or so went by, and I got a letter from him telling me to get an attorney so that we could have a hearing in Portland. I thought it over, and I decided that, no matter who I got, the result would be the same. In conscience, no *Novus Ordo* priest could defend me, and, if I got one of the Society of St. Pius X priests, they wouldn't listen to him. So I wrote back to him and asked him to appoint an attorney for me. I sent this priest the whole case, and he read it and sent it back to me. He said to go back to the Archbishop and tell him that I was sorry and then submit and obey the Archbishop. And then, at the end of the letter, he said, "Besides, the traditional Latin Mass is a thing of the past, and within ten years it will be nothing more than a footnote in the history of the Church." And so I got nowhere with that. The next thing I knew, the Archbishop sent me a letter of suspension. I never did have a hearing.

I moved up here in 1988, the very weekend that Archbishop Lefebvre ordained the four Bishops. Then, I asked Fr. Laisney if I could help him out in the chapels in Portland and Veneta [Oregon], and he said, "Welcome aboard!" And I have been doing it ever since.

Has there been any change in your relations with the Archdiocese since the suspension?

FR. H.: Archbishop George was here for nine months before he went to Chicago as Cardinal, and I went in to see him twice: when he was first here, and then about two weeks before he left for Chicago. He said, "You're the only one in the Archdiocese that has a canonical penalty on his head, and I want to get rid of that before I leave." And I said, "You *know* that suspension over there in your drawer is invalid. There is nothing to it. Take it out, tear it up, throw it in the waste basket, and be done with it." But he said, "Oh, I can't do that, but I'll offer you the position of being Archdiocesan Chaplain for the Indult Mass. Then, whenever a pastor wants you to come in and say the Latin Mass for him on Sunday, you can do it." I said, "That sounds like a wonderful idea, but it's the job of the pastors to do that themselves!" I reminded him of the meeting of the Cardinals in 1986, and I told him that, if he would announce that and let the pastors do their own work, then he wouldn't need me for this. "It's a waste of my time and yours," I said. He suggested that the Archdiocese could buy the chapels in Portland and Veneta, but I said they weren't for sale.

Finally, he saw he was getting nowhere: "Well, I guess I'll have to leave you for the next Archbishop. He will call you and take care of the situation for you." I said, "Okay, now he's to call *me?*" He said yes, and I made him repeat it three times. I said I wasn't going to run after him. And I see now that the reason **he's** supposed to call me is that I'm considered a renegade. He's the father of the diocese, and it's up to him to call in his bad priests. I said I'd wait for the call, but I don't think he'll ever call me in. He's been up there two and a half years, and he hasn't called me yet!

So, you're a renegade because you won't give up the traditional idea of the priesthood and the Mass. How would you describe the new idea of the priest? What do they think the priest is, in those theological updating courses, for instance?

FR. H.: I don't know, because I never went.

You never went to a seminar?

FR. H.: No. I stopped that right in the beginning. They used to have three-day seminars, once a year. I went to the first one, and I stayed the first morning. At mid-morning, we met with the Archbishop, and we could ask him any kind of questions that we wanted. Well, the Archbishop started out with one of the directives that came from Rome, and he said that the Masses of priests who use anything other than unleavened bread and sacramental wine are to be questioned. But the Archbishop himself was pooh-poohing the idea. So these priests got the idea that they could go ahead and use pita bread, cookie dough, whatever. You could go down to Safeway and get a jug of wine or even grape juice! It didn't seem to make too much difference to him.

I poked the priest sitting to one side of me and said, "Hey, did you hear what he just said?" He said yes. I poked the one on the other side (he was a classmate of mine), and I said, "Did you hear what he just said?" He said yes. I said, "Well, in my book that's unacceptable!" and I got up and walked out the door and went home. And that's the last one I attended. I don't know **what** they say anymore about the priesthood, the sacraments, or whatever. I just don't pay any attention to them.

What about the priests who were your classmates, who went with the New Mass and have not come back?

FR. H.: They still believe that they are priests who offer the sacrifice of the Mass. They're a little bit older than I am, but there's two of them in particular. One of them comes up to visit me all the time, and he supports what I'm doing here one hundred percent. The other little guy said, "Damn you! You're always analyzing, always analyzing! You did that at school. *And if you would just quit doing that and do exactly what the Archbishop says you should do, you'd be okay.*" I said, "No way, I can't do it anymore." In their hearts, they have some semblance of what the Salesians taught them in theology, *but they don't have to live it anymore.* They just became worldly, that's what happened.

Is that the result of the New Mass?

FR. H.: I think so, yes.

How does the New Mass encourage priests to be worldly?

FR. H.: Oh, because it deifies man, first of all. Then, once man is deified, he becomes his own moral master. And then, after he becomes his own moral master, he can make his own rules. What kind of people are we? We're sinners! And so it's all going to go back to our passions, and to satisfy our passions we have to be worldly.

Do you think it's fair to say that the current scandals among the clergy are the result of the New Mass and the new idea of the priesthood?

FR. H.: Yes. I think it's fair to say that. That's part of the cause, at least. I suppose that the young priests today are being taught nothing about sacrifice in regard to the Mass. These priests are hood-winked into the idea that this glorious meal, hallowed meal, sacred meal, whatever they call it, has nothing to do with the sacrifice of Calvary. They take down the crucifixes in the church or make them into "glorifixes" (you know, with the extended hands and the glorified robes) and take away the idea that we are sinners, and that we need the forgiveness of God. Confession, I think for most of them, is more of a counseling service, because there's no such thing as sin.

So the priest is the counselor and the community leader?

FR. H.: In confession, he's a counselor, and in the pulpit and at the altar, he's a presider. He sees that things are operating according to *his* vision of what *this* celebration ought to be. How can these priests get up there and preach Sunday after Sunday? They don't have the Truth. What do they speak of, emotions, passions, politics?

Archbishop Lefebvre once said that, when the liturgical changes were coming in through the 1960's, he went along all the way up to the changes of 1967. He took out the genuflections, the signs of the cross, everything. But he said that he started adding these ceremonies back into the Mass on his own authority, because he could tell that his faith in the Real Presence was diminishing. Did you ever experience anything like that? Do you think the changes in the ceremonies had any effect on your faith?

FR. H.: Yes, those omissions make you more liberal. The New Mass, in itself, makes you forget the fact that we are sinners. *Once we forget that we are sinners, it's much easier to commit more sins.* The new priests' attitude towards the Divine Office is similar–if you miss the Divine Office because you had a hard day on the golf course or something, that's perfectly okay. You just kind of forget the important things. Meditation starts to go by the board. It all slides.

With the old Mass, did you find that the opposite was true?

FR. H.: Oh, yes. With the old Mass, you cannot do that. How a priest could be in mortal sin and offer the traditional Latin Mass is just inconceivable!

Too frightening a prospect?

FR. H.: That's right. You know *Who* you're representing then. You know how frightening that is, and so it keeps you focused on the practice of virtue. The traditional Mass keeps a priest on the right track: "I've got to do my meditation, my spiritual reading. I've got to be faithful to my Office." When a priest says the traditional Mass, all those things start coming back together. *It makes him behave like a priest is supposed to behave.*

One priest remarked that, when he was offering the New Mass, toward the end especially, his Mass became almost a chore for him. But when he started to say the old Mass, his Mass became the highlight of his day, the thing he looked forward to each day. Would you agree with that?

FR. H.: Oh, yes! Since I dropped the New Mass, I haven't missed saying Mass once unless I was sick in the hospital. When I was saying the New Mass, I'd go on vacation, and I didn't bother to take the Mass equipment along. But since I've been back to the old Mass, I'd have to be practically dead before I would miss it.

It's interesting what you say about being "on vacation."
Do you think it's fair to say that the New Mass
makes one look at the priesthood as a job?

FR. H.: Yes. As a *job*. Everybody is slapping everybody else on the back, and the priest is no exception to that. We have to be very careful that people are not patting us on the back because we're worldly and because we're "understanding" enough to allow them to practice artificial contraception and behave like the pagans do. *No, a traditional priest, I think, must come across to people as being someone hard-headed as far as Christ, His principles, and His teachings are concerned.*

Archbishop Lefebvre also said, when asked why he would not use the
New Mass in the seminary, that he thought that it was impossible to
form a sacrificing priest in a seminary which used the New Mass.
Do you think that's a fair statement? Would you qualify it at all?

FR. H.: No, I don't think I'd qualify that one bit. Because, if you don't have the idea of sacrament and sacrifice in the Mass, there is no way to teach it, and there's no way to form a real priest.

I think that there are still some young priests who know what the
priesthood really is, and they kept their mouths shut through the
seminary until they reached ordination. They believe that they're
other Christs, but they are beating their heads against the wall,
because the Mass that they're being asked to say goes against
everything they believe about the priesthood. How would you advise
such a priest, who wants to be a good priest but sees no way out?

FR. H.: He should go and find a place where he can offer the traditional Mass.

These places abound, surely, but what about his objection
that he doesn't know Latin or true theology?

FR. H.: He can *learn* it!

Is this possible for someone who has been all the way through the seminary already? Is it possible to teach an old dog new tricks?

FR. H.: Oh, sure! They can get enough of the theology behind the Mass, okay? And they can learn enough of Church Latin just to say the Mass. Even if a young priest did not know any Latin, and he just took enough Church Latin to say the Mass, he would still have the intention to do what Christ wanted done and what the Church wants done!

So he can do it if he really wants?

FR. H.: Yes. It's do-able!

What would you say to priests who are struggling with the idea of obedience? They would like to come back to the traditional Mass, but they're afraid they might lose their pension, or something? How would you advise them?

FR. H.: Well, most of the older ones have the attitude that they're over the hill, and it's not worth fighting anymore, so they're just coasting their way out. And it's true that they *are* afraid of losing their pension. Archbishop Levada told me there wouldn't be any pension for me. *But I don't care what the hell they do with their money.* I guess they need it to pay off their pedophilia cases!

The matter of support may be a big obstacle for such priests. But have you ever heard of a traditional priest whose needs are not taken care of by the faithful, who are so desperate for real priests?

FR. H.: No, I have never seen one starve to death yet! Yes, the faithful will take care of them.

Fr. Harry Marchosky

Edited Transcript

When were you ordained, Father?

Fr. Marchosky: In 1952. I just had my fiftieth anniversary Jubilee Mass this year!

Congratulations! You were trained in the seminary of Quebec, I believe?

Fr. M.: Yes sir! When I went there, I didn't know any French at all. They taught me French. The Superior there saw me at the end of the first year reading a book of John of St. Thomas. He was amazed that I understood it, and he said, "Don't think of going to the Dominicans–think of staying here and becoming a professor." I got a licentiate in philosophy after three years, and, by that time, I was convinced that I wanted to be a priest in that archdiocese. It was amazing that I was a foreigner, and I was made a priest in the archdiocese–not only a priest, but a professor of the seminary!

We had the best theology formation in the world! First, I was made a Professor of Philosophy there, and then I taught Dogma for years and years. *I just taught what I had been taught*, the best philosophy possible–Aristotle and St. Thomas Aquinas. Dogma was the same; it was all St. Thomas.

What did they teach you about the priesthood?

Fr. M.: They taught the best possible doctrine about the priesthood, the real, Catholic doctrine about the sacrificial priesthood. The priest was the other Christ. I believed in everything they said, and they were right! I had no trouble at all, as long as they stayed with that.

How did things change after Vatican II?

Fr. M.: I was teaching there from 1952 to 1971. After Vatican II, they started going with what they're teaching them in the seminaries now.

What do they teach about the priesthood now?

Fr. M.: I don't really fully understand what they think the priest is. He's a man who's like Christ, but you can't understand what they're talking about.

He's no longer the other Christ or the sacrificing priest. He's just the president of the assembly.

Do you think that the new idea of the priesthood flows from the New Mass, or the other way round?

FR. M.: The New Mass comes out of the new ideas of the priesthood that they were already pushing in the 1950's. They were already reading things that influenced them to get rid of the old teachings about the priesthood. These people were not taught the same way I was, and they were all reading different books about these new ideas. They weren't satisfied with the old doctrine any more. I was completely satisfied with the old dogma, completely satisfied, because it was true!

How did you keep from being drawn away from the true doctrine?

FR. M.: I didn't read all those new books–I read the "Book of Christ," the doctrine in the Bible. (I read the Bible every year.) These new books made it seem like we're smarter now, you know, smarter than the old people who believed the revealed doctrine. I believed what the Bible said!

How did they try to convince you about this new doctrine of the priesthood?

FR. M.: That didn't happen directly. *It all started with the new editions of the seminary textbooks.* I didn't believe in any of the new editions. I just kept on teaching what I had been taught. I taught there for nineteen years, and, after the nineteenth year, I couldn't take it any longer. So I came to the United States.

What was happening after nineteen years that made you unable to take it any longer?

FR. M.: They didn't want to teach St. Thomas any more. I had been trained in St. Thomas, so there was nothing left for me to do there. They didn't follow St. Thomas in the Second Vatican Council, you know, but all the Councils before that had followed the works of St. Thomas.

They didn't want St. Thomas, because, as Cardinal Ratzinger said, he didn't "grip" them any more?

FR. M.: Well, nothing else "gripped" me! *The new teachings just were not in line with Tradition.*

Did they try to re-educate you?

FR. M.: They wanted me to go to Rome and study Scripture, because I knew some languages. I did not want to do that. I just wanted to stay there and study and teach theology. And I won!

What happened when the first big changes were made in the Mass-when they started to use the vernacular, to get rid of the maniple, and so on?

FR. M.: I never put the maniple aside. It's wonderful–it's the sign of the cross, the "maniple of tears and sorrow." I would say Mass facing the people once in a while, but I never liked it, because it was completely different from what I had studied.

How did you react when the New Mass came out in 1969?

FR. M.: I did not like the changes at all, because I was in love with the old Mass. The theology of the New Mass was terrible. It was absolutely deficient; it was too radical. ***It was no longer clearly a sacrifice, even though they said it was.*** I read what Cardinals Ottaviani and Bacci said in the *Brief Critical Study of the New Mass,* and I agreed with their opinion. They said that "It departs in a striking way, both as a whole and in detail, from the theology of the Council of Trent." Yes, I read that book several times.

When you had said the New Mass a few times, what effect did it have on your priesthood?

FR. M.: None at all. I didn't like it, and I couldn't keep saying it. I believed in the real priesthood, and all the real priests were still saying the old Mass. I never had the temptation to give it up, ever. Even when I went to my class reunion, I did not concelebrate with them. They wanted me to say Mass with them, but I refused. There were fifty-six priests ordained in my class, and I was the only one wearing black!

Has the New Mass turned them from priests into presidents?

FR. M.: Yes. I tried to speak to them in the language we were all taught, but they just don't believe it any more.

Do you think that the New Mass is the reason why several of your good friends left the priesthood?

FR. M.: Oh, yes! One of them even married a Protestant woman in a Protestant church! I never spoke to him again when I went back to Quebec.

When you refused to go along with the changes, what effect did this have on your standing with the Archdiocese of Quebec?

FR. M.: They did not like it, but they supported me. They never suspended or excommunicated me, and I've always said the old Mass with permission of my Archbishop. They've just accepted that I will say only the old Mass.

What finally made you decide to come to the States?

FR. M.: After I left the seminary, I thought I could do more good for souls–that I could more easily spread my belief in the Gospel–in the States than I could in Quebec.

That's surprising, because Quebec is a Catholic province!

FR. M.: They used to be completely Catholic, but not any more! For instance, women wear pants there now–all the women wear pants!

What did you do when you came to the United States?

FR. M.: First, I was in Providence, Rhode Island. I didn't teach there; I would only say Mass. Then, I tried out a monastery for two years, but they were completely determined that saying the New Mass was the only right thing to do. When I saw that I couldn't stay there, I went to California, where I had some brothers. I stayed in California, and I decided to set up on my own and say only the old Mass. It was a very difficult decision, but I've always had the support of my Archbishop.

How did you first come into contact with the traditional movement?

FR. M.: I knew Archbishop Lefebvre a bit from his visits to Canada. In 1974, which was the seven hundredth anniversary of St. Thomas, I went to Ecône, and I gave a talk which was very favorable to Tradition. They all liked it very much, and the Archbishop said to the seminarians, "Don't you think that Father Marchosky should be teaching here?" I replied that I would like to, but that I had to take care of my elderly mother. She was supposed to live only six more months at that time, but she lived ten years!

What would you advise a priest to do who is struggling with his priesthood in the context of the New Mass?

FR. M.: He has to stick to the old Mass, or learn how to say it. No other solution is possible. *The old Mass is going to out-live everything!*

What about the priest who doesn't know any Latin?

FR. M.: He just has to learn it! Languages are easy to learn. It takes some work, but it doesn't take *that* much.

How would you reply to someone who objects that the New Mass in Latin, with the Roman Canon, said with vestments and incense, is just as good as the old Mass?

FR. M.: The New Mass is much better that way, but it's still not as good as the traditional Mass because Jesus Christ is not at the center of the New Mass, as He is of the old.

What about those who object that they can't say the old Mass because of the obedience they owe to their bishops?

FR. M.: They have a very different idea of obedience from ours! There's true obedience, and then there's false obedience. They should not be hindered by "obedience" which is not *true* obedience!

How would you answer the objection of the priest who is afraid of losing his support if he refuses to say the New Mass?

FR. M.: That's one of the best objections there is, but he's just got to make the sacrifice! It is possible–it takes a lot of courage, but it's possible. I made that sacrifice. I've remained faithful, and I don't have any money, but I don't care. *I'm perfectly happy without the money, because I know I'll go to Heaven if I stay faithful!* When I couldn't make it on my own any more because of my poor health, I came here to Veneta, and I've been treated better here than in any other place I've ever been.

To contact Fr. Marchosky:

Rev. Fr. Harry Marchosky
25269 East Bolton Road
Veneta, OR 97487
Phone: (541) 935-1873

Fr. Vidko Podržaj

Edited Transcript

When were you ordained, Father?

Fr. Podržaj: In 1994–I've been a priest for eight years. I'm forty-three years old, born in Slovenia in 1959, but I was not reared in a Catholic family. My parents were Catholics, but they didn't go to church.

How did you come to the practice of the Faith, having been raised in a non-practicing family?

Fr. P.: Well, it's a long story. My mother wrote an article in a Slovene newspaper, and a woman read the article, which impressed her very much. She was so excited that she wrote to the newspaper to ask for our address, and then she came to visit us. When I was living by myself she visited me and proposed to me that I should be baptized. I agreed with her proposal.

So how did you find a priest who would give you proper instructions?

Fr. P.: I was in a city where there was a parish priest, of a very big parish with many thousands of people, and I went to see him. The lady had told me to go to him, because he was very good. I received instructions, and I was baptized secretly in 1978, because the Communists were still in power, and my mother didn't want me to be baptized. My father wouldn't agree to my baptism either, but he did not oppose it.

You went into the seminary rather late, then, comparatively speaking?

Fr. P.: Well, I entered the seminary twice, in fact–for the first time in 1980, when I stayed for two years. After those two years, I couldn't believe that things could be so bad in the seminary! But I thought that I was just in the wrong seminary, so I tried to look for some religious order where the real Catholic Faith would be practiced and taught. I wasn't able to find such an order, because the situation was the same everywhere I looked. Finally, I just left the seminary and tried to find some job.

What drove you away from the seminary?

Fr. P.: I saw the difference between the Catholicism of the past and the Catholic practices of the present time, but I didn't know exactly what was wrong. I also read many books about the "Catholic High Mass," and I realized that this was very different from the current Mass. When I first entered the seminary, I didn't know that there had ever been any other Mass besides the New! I thought that the New Mass was the only Mass that had existed in the past. Then, in the seminary, they told us that the Mass was slightly different–much more complicated!–in the past. I was very interested in this old Mass, but they were glad that it had changed.

What did you do when you left the seminary?

FR. P.: I taught in an elementary school for some years, and then I decided to go back to the seminary. I entered for the second time in 1990.

How did you make it through the seminary this time?

FR. P.: The first time I had entered, I couldn't stay there, because it was just too much for me. But, by the second time I entered, I had grown a little bit older and was much more experienced, and so I was a little bit stronger–I could get through. But I must say that I was not accepted very well. Many, many seminarians–most of my colleagues–didn't want me to become a priest. I just kept trying very hard, and I said to myself, "God's Will may be done!" It was a miracle, but I made it through!

What kind of parish were you sent to when you were ordained?

FR. P.: First, I was a chaplain for two years, and then I was made pastor of a small parish. Oh, it was not very large–I had about three hundred and forty parishioners, something like that, coming from ten little villages. There were so few people because, in the past, the Communists didn't want them to go to church.

What first drew you to try and learn the old Mass?

FR. P.: As I mentioned, I had read about it before, and then one day, a gentleman met me in the street, and he gave me a bulletin written by a layman who was working in America, Canada, and Germany, translating many newspapers and bulletins about the current state of the Church. He issues a little bulletin for a few hundred people in Slovenia every month. I started to read his bulletin every month, and I learned more about this crisis in the Church and about the traditional Mass. Then, I was given some books by Fr. Paul Trinchard, who lives in New Orleans and says only the traditional Mass. After reading these books, I wrote to him, and he invited me to Phoenix, Arizona, for some conferences on the traditional Mass sponsored by Fr. Francis Le Blanc. I went to Phoenix with a seminarian who is also interested in Tradition. There, they taught us how to say the traditional Mass. I realized then that the traditional Mass is the only Mass I should be saying, and that it is not the same as the New Mass at all.

What did you do when you went back home?

FR. P.: First, I re-installed the Communion rails in my church. Then, I said the New Mass only on the "Tridentine altar," which was still there, behind the *Novus Ordo* table. Then, I told my parishioners to receive Holy Communion only on the tongue, and I told them that I wanted them to receive Holy Communion kneeling. After that sermon, a few older people told me that they were not able to kneel, because they were not able to get up afterwards, but all the others began receiving Holy Communion on the tongue while kneeling. I also wrote the Offertory prayers from the traditional Mass on a little card, and I would say those prayers and the traditional formula of Consecration in Latin during the New Mass! And, when I came upon something that seemed Protestant in the New Missal, I would just change it.

Did your Archbishop find out about these changes?

FR. P.: I expected every day to hear some "echoes" from the Archdiocese, but I didn't hear a word, until a neighboring parish priest told me, "They know what you are doing in your parish, and they are very angry with you in the Archdiocese!"

How did they find out?

FR. P.: When I came back from Phoenix, the seminarian who had accompanied me must have told someone in the seminary, because I didn't tell anybody. When I came back and went to visit my neighboring parish priest, his first sentence after we said "Hello," was, "Did you learn how to say the Latin Mass? If you say the traditional Mass in your parish, the Archbishop will suspend you!" I was very surprised.

What was your next move?

FR. P.: Fr. Le Blanc had encouraged me to speak to Bishop Bernard Fellay, so I went to Switzerland to see him for one or two days. Then, I spoke to Fr. Franz Schmidberger. He came and said the traditional Mass in my parish church twice, and he gave a conference (which was very well received) to a small group of faithful who are interested in Tradition. After that, I said the traditional Mass in my parish church about seven or eight times before I left to come to the United States.

How has the Archbishop reacted to your absence of almost a year from the Archdiocese?

Fr. P.: I was suspended, excommunicated, and threatened with expulsion from the ranks of the clergy if I don't return!

That's very severe! How did your fellow priests react?

Fr. P.: One monsignor from my deanery wrote me a letter at Easter, asking me to "Return, return back to the Catholic Church!" He sent me also a greeting card with a picture of his parish church. So, I wrote him back, and I said, "Well, I realize that you have a very nice parish church, but right in the middle of your church is a Protestant table. When you're saying your Mass, you're turning your back to our Lord in the tabernacle! So, I ask *you* to 'Return, return back to the real Mass'!" I didn't receive any reply to that letter!

Having been trained in a new seminary, how would you describe the idea of the priesthood which you were given?

Fr. P.: Well, things are a little different in Slovenia than they are here. My country was completely Catholic before Vatican II–there were only a few thousand Protestants then–so the situation is, perhaps, not so grave as in other countries. Our situation was a bit special, because we had forty-five years of Communist rule, during which the government was fighting against the Church. We have not been trained very well in the Faith, and sometimes we are very, very Liberal. In the seminary, we were trained in a sort of conservative way–sometimes it was even a little bit traditional. When I was in the seminary, the situation was not so grave as it is in the United States. But my reading about the past practices of the Church made me see the difference between being trained in the manner of the past and being trained in the modern situation. Now, they want the laymen to do whatever it is possible for them to do at Mass, to take over the place of the priest.

How is your vision of the priesthood different from the one which prevails now?

Fr. P.: Well, the priest is acting in the Person of Christ, and the modern idea does not agree with this. This idea is completely lost, and the priest has become a coordinator in the "*Novus Ordo* Sunday Show." But the bishops are very satisfied because of the great "participation" of the laypeople in this "Sunday Show."

For the priest, what is the difference between saying the old Mass as Another Christ and saying the New Mass as a co-ordinator?

FR. P.: I can only say that, saying the traditional Mass, one can feel like a priest who is offering the sacrifice of the Mass. In this "Sunday Show," it is not possible to notice that. I had to fight for my priestly position in my parish, because I felt that they were treating me like a religious worker, not like a priest. I really had to stand up and let them know what the real role of the priest is: that he is mediator between God and men and offers the Holy sacrifice for the living and the dead.

How did the people take it, when you started to stand up?

FR. P.: The older people and the Catholics who were still really Catholic in their lives agreed with me, and they supported me. But, of course, there were some who didn't like the direction I was taking, and they resisted, but I was insistent.

What are your plans for the near future?

FR. P.: I will go to Germany for a while, as Fr. Schmidberger suggested, and then, as soon as possible, I will return to Slovenia and start a traditional mission in the capital. There are people there who are very sympathetic to Tradition, and I hope to help them by saying only the traditional Mass and giving them only the traditional teachings.

To contact Fr. Podržaj:

Rev. Fr. Vidko Podržaj
Grabrovec 43
S1-8330 Metlika
SLOVENIA

Fr. Clement
Procopio, O.F.M.

How long have you been a priest, Father?

Fr. Procopio: I was ordained on June 8, 1944, two days after D-Day. I went to the minor seminary when I was going on fourteen. It was what they called the seminary high school in Lowell, Massachusetts. That same building was used for theology. The philosophy house was in Catskills, New York, and the novitiate was in Troy, New York.

Did you enter the Capuchin order or the O.F.M.?*

Fr. P.: The O.F.M.

You went straight into the O.F.M. at fourteen?

Fr. P.: After four years of seminary high school at Lowell, Massachusetts, we made our novitiate and that is when we received the habit. In those years we had great training and blind obedience and a lot of strict rules. In fact, just to point out one little thing: if anyone was caught going into someone else's room just to say hello, he was expelled. One time I made a mistake. A door was open…he just called me in to say something and a superior saw me; we had a hard time getting out of it, but it was just a minute or so–they were pretty strict on that!

What did they teach you in the seminary?

Fr. P.: In the minor seminary we had biology, history, algebra–the regular high school courses, besides, of course, apologetics. That was a very good class.

---

* The distinction posed in this question begs an explanation. "O.F.M." is an acronym for "Order of Friars Minor" of the Franciscans. In general, Franciscans are members of several Catholic religious orders following the Rule of St. Francis. There are three organizations of Franciscan friars: the Friars Minor (formerly called Observants), one of the largest orders in the Church; the Friars Minor Capuchin, less in numbers and known simply as "Capuchins"; and the Friars Minor Conventual. The Friars Minor, of which Fr. Procopio is a member, were made independent by Pope Leo X in 1517. Fr. Carl Pulvermacher, also interviewed in this book, is identified as "O.F.M. Cap.," meaning that he is a Friars Minor Capuchin.

Greek and Latin?

FR. P.: Latin, yes, of course Latin; Greek, we learned something but it was not a complete course. And I think one year we had Hebrew. Then, English, oratory and Italian. One thing I regret is I didn't come out speaking Italian like I should have, because then I volunteered to go to Central America, and then I picked up some Spanish.

What did they teach you about the priesthood?

FR. P.: We always had a very high regard for the priesthood. It was something to look up to. We knew that the course was long, and we were willing to go through what we had to go through to reach it. But we had that very high regard.

Did they teach you that the priest was another Christ?

FR. P.: Yes, *"alter Christus."* We knew that. You see, the respect was always there. Toward the end of the theology course our province was ordered by Rome to open up a mission outside the United States. And this foreign mission that they opened was in Honduras, Central America. They needed volunteers. Well, I still had a year to go in the theology course, but I volunteered because I always wanted to be a missionary anyway; so this was my chance. But they needed priests so bad to open the mission, that we didn't finish the last six months of the course. They examined us; it was an oral examination and I didn't know Spanish yet, so everything was kind of rushed.

You were ordained early for the missions?

FR. P.: We had been ordained a year ahead of time anyway, my class—we were what they call *simplex* priests who just say Mass. So we were already ordained; it was just a question of finishing the course. But, actually, when I was in Honduras I looked back, and said I don't know what I missed in the course, because you didn't need anything else. In October of 1944 the first three volunteers went down and opened the mission San Esteban in Olancho, Honduras, and then in January of 1945, my group and one from the year before went as the second group. The first group just went to open that area—there were no permanent assignments of any kind. So when we went down, they assigned us to places in Olancho, Honduras. There had been only one priest in the main city, Fr. Sancho from Spain. He was the only priest in the whole province, so we spread out into three or four other places in Olancho.

Can you tell us about the courses in the major seminary?

FR. P.: In our philosophy class Fr. Philip, who was our teacher, had a great way of teaching; he gave lectures, and we took notes. All the three years of philosophy we were all together in every class; there was a rotation. So, logic and then metaphysics, and back to cosmology, psychology. In those philosophy years, we had English, classes in oratory and things like that. We also had to practice preaching; that was during theology. We studied Duns Scotus, the Franciscan scholastic, but we also followed St. Thomas Aquinas. We also had the Roman scholastics, like Suarez.

What was your reaction to the changes of the 1960's?

FR. P.: When the changes came–this is another thing–we were accustomed to obey, so when the changes came, we didn't give it a second thought. For myself, I didn't like any change. I remember when they were trying to tell us, "Now you face the people," I didn't like that. I went in to say Mass and I didn't see the liturgical books there anymore. I was completely disgusted.

I built a church in a little town, Moyuta, in Guatemala. I had just finished building it–they gave us marble for the main altar and the steps, the sanctuary–donated to us from a marble factory in Guatemala City. Just as we finished, the changes came and we had to get a table and put it in front of the people. They couldn't use the old altar any more.

Did they tell you why, or did they just order it?

FR. P.: No, that is what I'm saying: we didn't even ask why, we just did it. I didn't like it and I remember thinking, "Now what are they doing?" We just thought, "Well, this is the way they want it now." That's how we looked at things. We were used to doing what we were told.

...When they were telling you to do what was right.

FR. P.: Well, before the changes, they *were* right. I thought that it was still the same way. At least, that was *my* attitude.

So what went wrong?

FR. P.: I got disgusted, in a way, seeing the way things were going. I was always complaining that something must be wrong. I was with the new way for a while, but I didn't know about the existence of the Society of Saint Pius X then or anybody else that opposed the changes. I had no idea. I would come up from Central America and wonder what was going on. I came up in 1965, just about the time the Second Vatican Council was going on. Little did I know that something big was going on in the Church, but I sensed something was wrong.

What were the biggest indications that something was wrong?

FR. P.: First, by what was being done to the beautiful prayers of the sacrifice of the Mass. They were eliminating too many things, and I knew something was not right. Of course, in the beginning, when the changes first came, the Mass hadn't become a circus yet, like later on. We figured that changes were being introduced with all due respect for the Mass. They were still trying to preserve respect for the Mass. When they first made them, the Mass was still in Latin anyway; then there were changes in English. At first I thought, "Well, that's a nice thing; we'll understand it." But, it wasn't that at all. I didn't realize that until later when I started to read books like Msgr. Kelly's *An American Bishop at Vatican II*, then *The Rhine Flows into the Tiber* [Fr. Ralph Wiltgen], and Dietrich von Hildebrand's *The Devastated Vineyard*.

I was starting to read these kinds of books. I was interested in any book that defended the old way. That's when I started concluding that there *was* something wrong.

What didn't you like about the new way?

FR. P.: The new way was a show. You had to be an actor. You were facing the people. That's the worst thing you could be doing, because when you're facing the people you think you have to entertain. That's the way a lot of the priests behaved. To tell the truth, as far as our Franciscan priests went, they didn't entertain; they just said the New Mass as devoutly as they could.

Then we saw other things. One time in Waltham, Massachusetts, a visiting bishop concelebrated a Mass at which he gave six sermons. Every time he had a chance he gave a sermon! In the first place, the idea of always facing the people to say Mass is a distraction. It distracts you from sacrificing. I always announced I was celebrating "the sacrifice of the Mass." I used those words, but I didn't know that the reformers were trying to get rid of "sacrifice" at that time. Though I was trying to emphasize it, I knew I was getting away from it little by little. I couldn't stand it any more.

So you had to swim upstream to stay Catholic?

FR. P.: Yes, to stay Catholic I had to swim upstream. And I was realizing little by little that I was in another world, a world that wasn't mine.

Thank you very much for

   a)   This is only par₁

   b)   The book you wante

   c)   The enclosed is fur

   (d))   The enclosed now com

   e)   Could you please send

   (f))   All is paid for, nothi₁

   g)

CARMEL BOOKS
P.O. Box 40
WELLINGTON TA21 8WG
phone/fax 01823 664751
Traditional Catholic Books

What did they want the priest to become?

FR. P.: The priest was not to be really concerned so much about doctrinal matters. The idea was that you had to have love and all that stuff. *That* is what he had to worry about now. That made me angry because that was taking away from, "Seek ye first the kingdom of God...." Now, the people are allowed to think that this is just handed to you. The idea of seeking God first has sort of disappeared. It became, "Seek ye first the things of this world, all the concerns of this world," and it made me feel that anything spiritual was out of place. You're not supposed to worry about adoration any more; you've got to get with the people here and now in this life. It was hard for me because I was supposed to give this new emphasis in my preaching. Though I remained orthodox, I preached these things. But I was getting the feeling I was in the wrong place.

Is the priesthood of this new way a sacrificing priesthood?

FR. P.: Sacrificing?! I found out that liberal priests—I use the word "liberal"—criticize everything priests used to do before. But they don't miss a trick, either. They get what they want and do what they want. Even the vow of poverty we followed—forget it. They take vacations, have boats; they have a lot of things, everything they want.

Even in the Franciscans?

FR. P.: No, diocesan. I was out in the missions for years so I wasn't with the Franciscans much. I'm talking about after I returned up here and was working in different dioceses.

What year did you come back to the United States?

FR. P.: In 1965. From 1945-65 I was down in the missions. In 1965 I came up here, and I was working in California in the diocese of Los Angeles which was then under Cardinal Manning. Cardinal MacIntyre had just gone out when I came up. I told Cardinal Manning that the Second Vatican Council had been about what the bishops and the laity should do. "Now," I said, "we should have a council about what the *priests* should do." I told him I missed the Gregorian chant. He said he did, too. But he didn't do anything about it. Then I got kind of discouraged.

Why were you discouraged?

FR. P.: The way things were going on in the parish. I sent a grievance to the chancellor about the rectory. I only had a little room with the window open to the church hall. If you went out of that room, you were on the sidewalk. I said I couldn't do much in this kind of a situation. The chancellor listened to me and I was sent to Orange County near Disneyland.

I enjoyed the parish in which I lived, but I took care of the hospital, and I visited all the retirement homes they had around there. The hospital itself was five stories high. One of the other buildings in back had a three-story mental health unit. It got me interested in the mental health field, so I went to nearby Chapman College there and took some counseling courses to learn what I had to know. I also went every night to the mental health unit.

You went back to Central America at some point?

FR. P.: In 1985 I went back to Guatemala. I was there for eight more years. So I was twenty-eight years in all in Guatemala. The first three years I was in Honduras, but the rest of the time I was actually in Guatemala.

Why did you go back in 1985?

FR. P.: After I had gotten my college degree in counseling, I ended up in Arizona where I was put in charge of Catholic Social Services in Flagstaff. I headed that for about eleven years. I was very active. I was enjoying my work as chaplain to the St. Vincent de Paul Society and Knights of Columbus.

The reason I did social service was because I was too disgusted with what was going on in the Church and I didn't want to be in any parish for that reason. But at social services the bishop gave me permission to be in my own place. I gave the bishop a good reason: "If I stay in a parish, then everybody will think that I'm serving that parish, and then I won't be able to serve the others. This way I can fit everybody in." That was all right with him.

All this time, I was feeling the urge to return to the missions. We had a new provincial by then. If I wanted to return to the missions, however, I had to return to my order.

Did you think you were more of a priest in the missions than you were in the social service office?

FR. P.: Oh, yes. I felt like a priest in the missions. The reason I periodically returned to the United States was to recuperate from mission life for a bit, then go back down and start over again. But the last time I went, I was in my seventies. I couldn't ride a horse or a mule those long distances any more. My last mule ride was returning from a place we visited only once a year. I just about fainted coming home. That was it; I couldn't go on any more. During Holy Week, I asked for a priest to help because I couldn't do all the services any more. So I returned to the States.

When did you first say the traditional Mass again?

FR. P.: I was saying it privately when I was living in my trailer at Flagstaff, when I came to Arizona after California. Of course, in the missions I couldn't. I didn't have a chance to say that Mass everyday in the missions, but in the States I could.

Since coming back this last time and retiring, I began reading books. I read *The Eternal Sacrifice* by Michael Davies. It didn't take too much by now to convince me that I should begin celebrating the Latin Mass again. I'm still reading; I've got all this material. I began saying Mass privately in homes so nobody bothered me.

How difficult was it to say the old Mass after so many years?

FR. P.: It wasn't very difficult for me because I *was* saying it privately. I didn't lose contact with the old Mass too much–only three or four years. However, I haven't *sung* the Mass for forty years, so I don't know what that will be like someday! I was on the fence for quite a while, but I finally said, "This is it." I was helping out at a parish at the time, but when in 1999 I made up my mind that the old Mass was the Mass I needed to celebrate, I began saying it privately at home.

This is when I was introduced to a situation in Clarkdale, Arizona, a mission of the Phoenix diocese. The priest was eighty-nine and couldn't say Mass anymore though he still lived lived in the rectory. For a while the diocese sent a priest to say a Saturday afternoon Mass but then they closed the church. People there knew I was celebrating the Latin Mass privately, and I thought to myself that maybe I could help them. I thought it might be Providence. The fact struck me that this was the only Catholic church in Clarkdale and the people didn't have the Mass at all. I thought they might stop going to Mass altogether. But my bishop of Phoenix refused me use of this mission church for the Latin Mass. Next door to the closed mission, however, was an empty Episcopal church which the **Episcopal bishop** was willing to let me use! What a crazy situation. I ended up renting the town hall and began celebrating a weekly Latin Mass there. Then I was introduced to people in Prescott, Arizona, and began celebrating the traditional Mass for them, too.

When did you rent the hall in Clarkdale?

FR. P.: About a year ago. I had been going on for two or three years saying just the old Mass. A pastor from a nearby church–a young priest–was sympathetic. He liked the old Mass. I was even teaching him. But he was afraid to make the move. He's sitting on the fence, I think.

Why are so many priests like that afraid?

FR. P.: They're afraid of what their bishop will do, afraid of breaking away from everything. It's hard for them. On my part, I'm not dependent on anybody, so whatever they do, they can't hurt me. I just keep on going.

One time a diocesan priest contacted me, "I want you to say the Latin Mass in this church." I replied, "You're the pastor. If I say the Mass in your church, you're going to get in trouble." He said, "Well, I'll ask the bishop to see if everything is all right with him. I'll just ask him and see what he says." Now, this priest was a favorite of the bishop, too, and he had no expectation that the bishop would have such a strong reaction. When he found out, it was as though the pastor had committed a crime!–"What is Fr. Procopio doing, saying that other Mass?" He was dead-set against it. The bishop called me right away on the phone and said that I couldn't say that Mass publicly, only privately without anybody around. I didn't argue with the bishop on the phone; I just listened.

Then the letter from the bishop came, with one copy to my provincial, declaring me schismatic, saying that he'd take away my faculties. I couldn't figure out why he hated the Latin Mass because he was ordained to say that Mass. I found out that his mother went to the old Mass and wouldn't go to the new one. His own mother! But after he became bishop, he must have forgotten all that. It's the chancery that changed him. All those people there got to him; that's what it was. He wrote and told me that he was the liturgist of the diocese. He wrote that he asked everybody if they wanted the old Mass and nobody wanted it. All I can say is that it must be a lie because I know hundreds of people who want it. He made it look like he had followed all the protocol, that he had gone through all the right departments, but he must have been lying. I know he was.

So you were suspended and your faculties were revoked. Were you thrown out of the Franciscan order?

FR. P.: No, but that almost happened. My provincial didn't know what was going on. He confronted me with how I disobeyed the bishop, how the Franciscan constitution states this and that, and that I needed to submit to all the penalties for having disobeyed the bishop. What he forgot was that the constitution also leaves latitude for conscience; it allows us to act so as not to violate our conscience. Anyway, I didn't argue. I wrote a nice letter to the provincial because, first of all, he is a very good man, and I always highly regarded him. I told him, "Wait, according to my conscience, I'm going back to the way the Catholic Church was before Vatican II, doing things according to St. Thomas Aquinas and all the old ways. I'm saying only the Latin Mass and I'm helping the Society of Saint Pius X. Now, if you can give me permission to help the Society of Saint Pius X, that's fine; if you can't, kick me out of the Order." He wrote back a letter showing he still didn't know what was going on. "Well," he wrote, "You can help the Society of Saint Pius X, but make sure you obey the bishop [of Phoenix]." I responded, "I don't have to worry about the bishop [of Phoenix] because I won't have to deal personally with him anymore. The Society will deal with the bishop of Phoenix, not me. I'm helping in one of the Society's missions. I have to celebrate the old Latin Mass there because that's the only Mass the priests of the Society celebrate. That's why I have to say it." He didn't bother me again. He almost declared me a *persona non grata*, but lately he's treating me very nicely as if nothing happened. But he still doesn't really get what's going on.

What made you feel justified in disobeying the bishop?

FR. P.: The fact that the Mass isn't meant to be said privately–Christ instituted it for everybody. So, if I'm going to say that Mass, I should be saying it for people, too, not just myself. Especially when people don't have a Mass. I especially base myself on the Bull *Quo Primum* of Pope St. Pius V which came out of the Council of Trent. I also base myself on the idea that it is the true Mass, and in my conscience I can't say the New Mass.

Do you mean "true" in the sense of "valid"? You don't think it's valid?

FR. P.: Well, some of them are not. They may be valid, but they may even be sacrilegious and sinful. I had a whole big article on that written by a priest who was anonymous, and he concluded that the New Mass was sacrilegious. I sent it to Cardinal Ratzinger. "Since you're the head of the Congregation for the Doctrine of the Faith," I told him in a nice way, "can you tell me if it is a sin to say the *Novus Ordo* Mass? Is it a sin for anyone attending it?" I'd like to have an answer from them.

How long ago did you write?

FR. P.: It was about six or seven months ago. *He* didn't answer me. But he must have forwarded a copy to Msgr. Perl [Camille Perl, Secretary of the Pontifical Commission, *Ecclesia Dei–Ed.*] who **did** reply to me saying he would need a volume to answer my letter. All I want to know is yes or no. He needs a volume!

What are your thoughts about the Indult Mass?

FR. P.: The Indult Mass lays down conditions. It's like the Mafia: "If you accept all the conditions, we have an offer you can't refuse." That's the way I see it; I don't care what anyone says. They don't really give you anything. The Indult always has something on you–"Accept the *Novus Ordo* Mass and then you can say the Indult Mass." Well, I don't need that kind of condition. I'm going to say it without any conditions.

How would you advise a priest who wants to say the old Mass but is struggling to work up the courage?

FR. P.: First of all, my situation is different. Since I was retired and was in social service, they can't take away any salary. But even if they could, that wouldn't have stopped me because the people would support me. The people will more than support you. The traditional Catholics are very generous. Don't be afraid as far as financial support goes. But, as far as the bishops go, the most they can do is take away your faculties in the diocese. I think the best thing to do is become a helper of the Society of Saint Pius X.

What about a young priest who doesn't know Latin and has no training in the ceremonies? How could he start saying the old Mass?

FR. P.: Go visit the seminary of the Society of Saint Pius X first [St. Thomas Aquinas Seminary, Winona, Minnesota–*Ed.*]. Learn a little Latin and the things the seminary says you need to know. That's the way I see it. I would never send anyone to any seminary unless it was traditional.

Do you think that the New Mass is the Mass of a new religion?

FR. P.: It's a whole different Mass. It's a protestantized, Lutheran-Calvinistic Mass. That's what it is. It's a whole new religion. Beginning with Vatican II, we have to admit that the Roman rite has vanished. "*Novus Ordo*" means the "new order" of the Mass, and that's a whole new thing. I'm suspicious of anything "new" in the Church. I preach that. There's nothing "new" in our religion. It develops and is explained, but there's no "new" doctrine. You mention something new, and you wonder what it is. "New evangelization?"–that's ecumenism, for instance.

Is the New Mass the Mass of ecumenism?

FR. P.: Yes, it's coming to that now. The Buddhist monks came to Fatima and the message of Fatima has to be dumbed down. Catholic churchmen want everyone to come and worship their own way. That's ecumenism; that's a heresy. The New Mass is all about that.

And then the new idea of the laity gathering around the priest and "celebrating Mass" with him: they're not priests. People get that confused–the ministerial priesthood with the priesthood of the faithful. They get that all confused. They don't know what's going on, and they make no distinction at all about a priest–to some the priest is just a layman, a minister, a presider, whatever else you want to call it–he's not even a "priest." That's a whole new religion. Modernism is a whole new religion.

That came out of Vatican II...while you were in the jungle....

FR. P.: Yes, well, I didn't know what was going on until I came north. I didn't want to stay in a parish. That's why I wanted to study and try to be a counselor or something.

They wouldn't let you be a priest, so why not be a counselor?

FR. P.: All the time I was a counselor, I enjoyed my work, but down deep I didn't feel like I was a real priest.

What effect has saying only the old Mass for the last two years had on your priesthood?

FR. P.: It makes me feel that I'm back on track now, so to speak. My mind was settled as soon as I had gone back to the old Mass. Before, there was a lot of confusion.

It's a little bit of a protection to be isolated.

FR. P.: Yes, that's right; I feel better under the circumstances.

You couldn't celebrate both Masses?

FR. P.: My gut feeling is that it's got to go back to the way it always was because that is the right way. And that is all there is to it.

To contact Fr. Procopio

Rev. Fr. Clement Procopio, O.F.M.
306 S. 18th Street
Cottonwood, AZ 86326

PRIEST
where is thy Mass?

MASS
where is thy Priest?

THE PHOTOGRAPHS

Fr. Christopher Danel

FR. FRANCIS LE BLANC

Fr. Paul Greuter

FR. BRIAN HAWKER

FR. EUGENE HEIDT

FR. HARRY MARCHOSKY

Fr. Vidko Podržaj

FR. CLEMENT PROCOPIO, O.F.M.

FR. CARL PULVERMACHER, O.F.M. CAP.

FR. RONALD RINGROSE

MSGR. RAYMOND RUSCITTO

FR. GRAHAM WALTERS

FR. PAUL WICKENS

FR. WILLIAM YOUNG

FR. STEPHEN ZIGRANG

Fr. Carl
Pulvermacher, O.F.M. Cap.

What year were you ordained, Father?

Fr. Pulvermacher: I was ordained on September 3, 1952. I was given a thoroughly sound formation in the Capuchins. Our professors were mostly older Capuchin priests and some had been teaching for fifteen or twenty-five years. But, for Scripture, we had one young priest who had studied in Rome, and he had quite a few new ideas. He would talk about the crossing of the Red Sea and the manna in the desert as events that were perfectly normal, anything but supernatural! We always thought, of course, that the crossing of the Red Sea was a marvelous work of God and that the manna in the desert was a marvelous miracle of God. We were scandalized.

What did your good Capuchin professors teach you about the priesthood?

Fr. P.: The Capuchin vocation was for my own betterment, my sanctification, my salvation. And I understood that the priesthood was to help other people save their souls through missionary work, confessions, retreats, and what-not. These were the things that a priest was supposed to do. A Capuchin was one who would go out among the crowd and teach people how to save their souls.

Where were you sent after the seminary?

Fr. P.: After I was ordained, I worked in the Indian missions of Montana for seventeen years. I spent twelve years with the Northern Cheyenne Indian tribe and five years among the Crow. In 1953, with the Cheyenne, things were normal. We had a school and mission stations. We taught the children the catechism, and we instructed the older people on the weekends with our sermons. Celebrating the Tridentine Mass and giving instructions were normal things that a priest had to do daily. Then I was sent to the Crow Indian tribe to take over for the Jesuits, who had been at the missions from the beginning in the 1870's and 1880's. I was the first of the Capuchins to go there. The first couple of years among the Crows were okay, but then we got a new bishop. He wrote a letter every week that was to be read to the people in church. First it was one change, then another and another. We had to put a table in front of the altar and open the Communion rails. I made a table and put it out there, but I didn't make many other changes. I left the statues and the Blessed Sacrament in their places, and I didn't touch the old altar. My superiors were unhappy with me because the parish was not changing fast enough. They complained that I did not have committees and activities for the parish. It was one thing after another. The Indians didn't want the changes, and they tried their best to avoid them. I just tried to keep on going the way we were. The superiors then demanded, "You must change; otherwise you'll either be fired or you'll have to resign." So I resigned, and I was sent to the monastery in Marathon, Wisconsin, our former Capuchin major seminary, for the next two years, where my work was mostly manual.

After Vatican II, did the new vision of the priesthood influence the Capuchins?

FR. P.: At the monastery in Marathon, Wisconsin, the priests had their regular work, going out to parishes and making contact with the people. There were a few straggling seminarians there who were not studying any more. When all the changes came about, everything was turned upside down. All the brothers, previously considered "dumb workers," were sent to school to progress in their education. Meanwhile, the priests stayed home, read books, washed dishes, mopped floors, and did the work that the brothers used to do. The seminarians went out to work among the people. The priests were confused. They didn't know what they were supposed to do. I couldn't understand it.

Again they said, "Well, you must change." I said "Change! Why do I have to change? And why do I have to stop celebrating the Tridentine Mass?" They responded, "The New Mass is the only one that is allowed now. You're not allowed to say the old one." Nevertheless, I said the Tridentine Mass as often as I could. So the real priestly work was not done by the priests, and couldn't be done by the seminarians. I helped out, mostly on weekends, teaching catechism. It was a tough job, but I did it. And then during the week I would stay at home at the monastery. It was a big monastery. We formerly had over one hundred students, with about ten or fifteen professors, and several brothers. The monastery had everything; it was self-contained–a beautiful place. I loved it, and I enjoyed working there. There was a lot of work, but none of it was priestly. I had to go out on weekends to fill in for any priest that was sick, or as chaplain in a hospital somewhere.

After two years there, I volunteered to go to Australia, because they needed English-speaking priests. I was there with the Italian Capuchins for three and a half years (from 1972-1976): two years in Sydney, a year and a half in Adelaide, and six weeks in Brisbane. Then I was sent to Perth in Western Australia to replace a priest who had gone to a seminar somewhere.

Did you ever go to such a seminar?

FR. P.: I never went to a seminar because they didn't want me to go! I would have caused a disturbance, so they never asked me to go! They thought they couldn't make me a New Priest. They wanted to change the priests' way of thinking. They had radical priests teaching that the use of the birth control pill was a normal thing. It was just tricking nature, and there's nothing wrong with tricking nature! All my three brothers went to the seminars. They were brain-washed. My older brother came back from one seminar completely turned around in reaction against what they were teaching. He syllogized that, if the Pope was teaching these things, then he was a heretic. Therefore the Pope was out of the Church. Therefore, there had not been a Pope since Pius XII, the last good Pope.

I also had two other brothers who were Capuchin priests. The older one, Fr. Pius, died recently. Since he would not disobey his superiors, he went along with the changes and said the New Mass. He was pastor in Castle, Wisconsin, and the people liked him because he was conservative. His celebration of the New Mass was so reverent that people would come to his parish from other parishes around. This made the other parish priests angry and jealous, and they finally got him out. The seminars didn't seem to have much of an effect on him, though.

My younger brother said that, if we had to go back to saying the old Mass, he would give up and not say any Mass at all! Can you imagine? The seminars worked on him. Now he's retired, living in Milwaukee, playing tennis, *etc.* He says that he is just going to have a good time and forget about the priesthood for a year. This new priesthood means being a social worker who runs many activities.

How would you describe the differences between your activity on the Indian missions and the activities of today's priesthood?

FR. P.: The activities now are mostly quick get-togethers like spaghetti dinners and other things which do not pertain to the spiritual growth of a parish. In the old days, there were real spiritual activities. A priest had to instruct altar boys, the engaged and married couples, and school children.

What is your assessment of the New Mass?

FR. P.: I think that the New Mass does not have any grace-giving qualities, and the priests who say it do not receive any more graces than they would if they simply prayed. The normal graces of the true Mass do not flow from the New Mass. You can see that from the fact that so many nuns and priests have abandoned their vocations. As sins of nature take their course, the priests, nuns, and people stop practicing the Faith, unless you have somebody charismatic who can really bring them back. But charismatics always promote a sentimental practice of the Faith. The Church has many wonderful preachers. They should be bringing in converts by the thousands! But it is not so. If Billy Graham can fill stadiums, how much more could the holy and faithful priest, who has an abundance of graces given to him, do so. I think the New Mass is a Protestant service, and that anybody who says it or goes to it will gradually become a Protestant. That is what is happening to our Catholic people: they are becoming Protestant because they are going to the New Mass. And our priests are becoming Protestant priests. All the New Mass does is makes Protestants out of Catholic people.

What are the chief things in the New Mass which make people into Protestants?

FR. P.: Firstly, the Offertory. It is not really an Offertory; it is only offering to God "the work of human hands" instead of an "immaculate host." The new Offertory makes no real sacrifice. They are going back to the old Testament of sacrifices of fruit and animals. It's a Jewish blessing prayer. I thought that the new Offertory immediately nullified the Mass. Also, the words of Consecration were changed several times. The first change they made was from "for many" to "for all men." The women didn't like that, so they changed it to "for all men and women." Then, some of the bishops didn't like it, so it was changed again to "for all." Maybe it was just an "ad-lib." They would shape the Mass any way they wanted. It was terrible! Every place you went, the Mass was different. I feel that the *Novus Ordo* Offertory and Consecration, even if they are said in Latin, even when you don't "ad-lib," still displease God, because the sacrificial aspect of the Mass was removed. It might be valid, but it's bad, just as a "Black Mass" is valid, yet it is bad because it is said in honor of the devil. They are dealing with the real Body and Blood of Jesus Christ. That's why it is displeasing to God, even if it's valid!

What was your reaction the first time you celebrated the New Mass?

FR. P.: The New Mass was easy! There was nothing to it. All I had to do was read the English. I didn't like it. For a long time, I would still say the form

of Consecration in Latin, and I would genuflect before and after the eleva-
tion, because I did not think that the new forms were sufficient. The New
Mass was incomplete. It was not our Catholic Mass–it was more or less a program in which everybody had to get involved. Even the children had to be in
on it. I remember a children's Mass in Adelaide, Australia, where they would
come up with their baseball bats, cricket bats, basketballs, and soccer balls,
and offer them up at the altar. I would simply skip over the kiss of peace (the
handshake of friendship), so that I would not be a part of it.

What effect did saying the New Mass have on your priestly life?

FR. P.: The New Mass made me angry because of all the monkey business. I thank God that I did not lose my faith. I was sorry that all this stuff was
happening, and I didn't want to help the New Mass along in any way.

How did you come back to the traditional Mass?

FR. P.: When I was yet in Sidney in 1976, I met up with a lot of traditional Catholics. They spoke to me, gave me literature to read, and asked me
to celebrate the Tridentine Mass for them. That's what prompted me to study
more about holding on to Tradition.

When you said the Tridentine Mass
in the parish church, what was the reaction?

FR. P.: They liked it. They wanted me to stay with the old Mass. But,
when I was in Adelaide, I could not find a church that would allow me to celebrate the Tridentine Mass, so I would make arrangements with parishioners.
They would set up an altar in a home, and I would celebrate the old Mass
there. When I was about to leave Australia, I made a firm resolution never to
say the New Mass again. I stayed until January 1, 1976, because I had made a
contract with the priests to stay and help with the parishes. After that, I flew
to Rome. There, I saw Pope Paul VI celebrating Candlemas on February 2,
1976, in St. Peter's Basilica. Then, after visiting Ecône, then Ars, Lourdes,
and a few other holy shrines, I came to Wisconsin.

Why did you stop in Switzerland on your way home?

FR. P.: I had met Archbishop Lefebvre in Sydney before I left, when he
had come to Australia for the Eucharistic Congress in Melbourne. He didn't
try to convert me or anything like that, and we got along well. When I got
back to Wisconsin to visit my mother, she was attending a traditional Mass
in De Pere, Wisconsin. One day, I went with her and met Fr. Bolduc. He
convinced me to go with him to Texas for a few months. Free from any obli-

gations, I accepted the offer and spent some time in Texas. So began my fifteen years at Dickinson and my work with Angelus Press, and the "Ask Me" column.

How did you get away from your Provincial?

FR. P.: I told the Father Provincial that I was not coming back to the Province until the Province comes back to the Catholic Church. He said, "Well, if that's how you feel about it, don't look to us for any help or medical insurance. You'll have to take care of that yourself." He didn't excommunicate me or tell me that I was thrown out of the order. He finally said, "Okay, that's all right. Go ahead."

Was it a hard transition to return to the traditional Mass?

FR. P.: No. I had been saying the old Mass the whole time. I never had any trouble getting used to saying it again–in fact, I enjoyed saying it. I felt a lot more at peace because I didn't have to worry about the validity of the Masses I was celebrating. I felt that I had been displeasing God by saying that New Mass, so I was very happy to get away from it permanently.

Archbishop Lefebvre once said that he could not use the New Mass in his seminary because he thought it was impossible to form a sacrificing priest with it. What is your opinion?

FR. P.: That is very true, because the idea of sacrifice is missing from the New Mass. I think that a priest has to have some idea of sacrifice. If he doesn't, he's not going to last very long as a priest. That is the reason why we have no vocations–children are growing up without the idea of sacrifice. The parents are giving in to them all the time. When I was growing up, we always made sacrifices during Advent and Lent. We offered to our Lord the sacrifices we were making.

Do you think there is a connection between this lack of sacrifice in the New Mass and the current scandals among the clergy?

FR. P.: Sure. This New Mass gives no graces. The priests have no help from God. They get as much grace out of the New Mass as Protestant ministers get out of their Protestant services. These priests do not have the sanctity which is required in the priesthood. It can also happen to priests who are saying even the traditional Mass! Why sacrifice yourself, if you are not a sacrificing priest? This business of pedophiles and homosexual priests becomes a normal thing. That's how corruption is brought into the Church, by ordaining gay priests.

Many *Novus Ordo* priests are trying to live good priestly lives in a system which is working against them. What advice would you give such priests?

FR. P.: I've met many priests in various parts of the world who told me that they were completely confused. They should give up the New Mass. They should go to a traditional bishop who has his head on straight and ask to be conditionally ordained, because there are a lot of traditional-minded people who will not go to the Mass of a priest ordained in the *Novus Ordo* since they think his ordination is invalid, and thus he is not a true priest.

Can a priest who has been formed in a modern seminary make the transition to saying the traditional Mass?

FR. P.: If he wants to do it, he has to go to a traditional seminary to get some training first. Otherwise, he will have nothing but trouble no matter where he goes.

How will such a priest find the necessary support?

FR. P.: I think, if he prays his Office, says his rosary, and celebrates Mass devoutly, he will never have to worry about his livelihood because the good Catholic people will support him. Catholics are so grateful for a good priest that they are even more generous than necessary.

To contact Fr. Pulvermacher:

Rev. Fr. Carl Pulvermacher, O.F.M. Cap.
4580 Southwest 65th Avenue
Davie, FL 33314-4315
Phone: (954) 792-3162

FR. RONALD RINGROSE

EDITED TRANSCRIPT

So, Father Ringrose, you were ordained in what year?

FR. RINGROSE: Which time? [*Laughter*]

**Your ordination in the normal context,
before you knew there was such a thing as Tradition.**

FR. R.: Well, okay, my original ordination was in 1979.

So you said the New Mass for how many years then?

FR. R.: For two and a half years.

**From your formation and your experience as a diocesan priest,
how would you describe the Conciliar concept of the priesthood?**

FR. R.: You have to understand I started in the seminary before Vatican II, and I was in the seminary during Vatican II. I left temporarily right after Vatican II, in fact a few years later. So, the concept I was given was more traditional. I was aware of what they were putting forth after Vatican II, but that wouldn't be my concept of the priesthood. My concept of the priesthood is the priest has the character of Holy Orders and primarily offers sacrifice and administers the sacraments in order to glorify God and save souls by exercising the priesthood, as the Church has always done. The new concept is that the priest is the presider over the community, the facilitator, the enabler, and he is almost anything but a ***priest***.

**Did they try to sell this concept to you in your
last years in the seminary, before you were ordained?**

FR. R.: No, you see, even after I took the eight years off, the seminary I went to (St. Mary's, up at Roland Park) was more or less traditional, certainly by *Novus Ordo* standards, and the theology that we got there was pretty sound. I mean there were a few wacky professors here and there, but they were more than offset by sound professors, particularly in moral theology, but also in dogma. So, it was not like places like Mount St. Mary's Seminary in Emmitsburg, where it was radical all the way through. Even though they were using the *Novus Ordo* at St. Mary's, many of the traditional positions were still in place.

What about your bishop?

FR. R.: I was from a very liberal diocese, and of course the diocese favored the Mount St. Mary's model of things. And of course all the talk in the diocese would have been that the priest is the builder of community, the enabler and all these things, a presider, you know. There was very little talk about the fact of the priesthood as traditionally understood: the priest is one who offers sacrifice, one who is there to save souls. Anything spiritual like that was ridiculed and discouraged.

So, as far as you can see, which model of the priesthood is portrayed in the New Mass as it actually stands in the typical edition, abstracting from all the abuses?

FR. R.: In the New Mass, you have to answer that, clearly, the priest is a presider, not an offerer of sacrifice. In Pope Paul's Missal, the Missal of 1969, it is very clear that he is a presider. But that's not a unique insight that I have. I think that is very clear from the text. You see the thing about the *Novus Ordo*, the danger of it for many, is its ambiguity. What happened, from my recollection, is that the the old-time Catholics who were raised the old way, the pre-Vatican II way, such as myself and people older than I, would accept the *Novus Ordo*, interpreting the ambiguities in a traditional manner. And the text, being ambiguous, permits you to do that. So we were steeped in the old catechism, and we were going to look at it from the old-catechism point of view. Now, if you take the younger ones, who are in school and being raised on the new catechism, where they are not being taught that the Mass is a sacrifice, but simply a happy meal or whatever, a holy picnic, a liturgical picnic, they are going to be looking at the ambiguities from a Protestant point of view. And that is the "beauty" of it. ("The beauty," I say in quotation marks.) It shows the diabolical hoof print that is on it, that it is able to be interpreted in either way. So that when people object from the traditional side that this Mass is not good because it's Protestant, it says nothing about sacrifice, says nothing about the Real Presence and so forth, they would say, "Oh, we're not denying any of these things."

Is it a strain for the priest who sees the priesthood in the traditional light to say a Mass which is this ambiguous? Is it natural to interpret it in a traditional light, or is it a strain?

FR. R.: There is a certain strain, but the strain can be diminished in a way. I'll only say for the brief time that I offered the New Mass (and I wish I'd never offered it), I offered it with a Catholic mindset, simply because I've always had a Catholic mindset. I would have interpreted it pretty much in a traditional way, in its ambiguity, and the manner in which I offered the New Mass was, externally speaking, as close to the old Mass as I could make it, while still following the Missal of 1969. In retrospect, I would say it was a strain, but at the time I wouldn't say it seemed such a strain. The real strain was, and maybe I am jumping ahead to other questions, the real strain was what people were doing around me and how they were counteracting what I was trying to do. I was successively in two parishes as a diocesan priest. The second one, where I was for maybe a little over a year, was a very radical place that was out of control, and a more traditional-minded pastor was put in. But he didn't clean up a lot of the liturgical things, because I think he just thought he had to take things step by step. But to me, you know, to be trying to offer Mass in as traditional a manner as possible and then having some gal strutting across the sanctuary in a miniskirt with a ciborium, you know, obviously there is some conflict here. So the strain would have not been within myself, but the strain would have been the contrast between what I was trying to do and what they were trying to do. I was trying to stem the Revolution, and they were trying to further the Revolution.

So you would say that the New Mass, even in its typical edition, helps the Revolution by its ambiguity?

FR. R.: Oh yes, sure, that is what it is calculated to do.

And so that, for one who says the New Mass in a traditional manner, because of the others around who are saying it in a radically liberal manner, there will be a great strain in trying to interpret the New Mass as it stands in a traditional way?

FR. R.: Oh yes, certainly as things played out in the diocese where I was and in the parish where I was, *the odds were stacked in favor of a revolutionary interpretation*, rather than a traditional one.

What affect does the old Mass have on the life of the priest? That is, how is the priesthood lived differently with the two Masses?

FR. R.: In my own experience?

In your own experience, sure.

FR. R.: You see, I tried to live the priesthood as traditionally as possible, even while in the *Novus Ordo*. But there certainly is a conflict, and I think there is *a certain amount of self-deception*, rationalization, trying to make a sow's ear seem like a silk purse, and trying to be kind of a *Wanderer*-type Catholic, or *Wanderer*-type priest. There certainly was a conflict in that, and I can see now, in retrospect, a real dichotomy between what I was trying to live as a priest and the Mass I was offering. I can see that very clearly now. I could somewhat see it then, but I don't think I *wanted* to see it, so I tended to try to *avoid* seeing it.

What would you say was the root of this ambiguity, this dichotomy?

FR. R.: Well, I think it is the **horizontalism** of the New Mass. The focus is clearly on man. It portrays the relationship of man and man "horizontally," more than that of man to God "vertically." A traditionally-minded priest offering the New Mass is trying to live his spiritual life on the model of man to God vertically (or rather God to man vertically), but he is offering a Mass that tries to mute that vertical aspect and tends to emphasize the horizontal, which is only secondary. I think that is the root of the conflict. Of course, once the priest begins to offer the traditional Mass exclusively, that conflict is removed, and I would say that this is a great enhancement to the spiritual life of the priest because this unnatural contradiction is taken away. In other words, now the Mass that the priest is offering expresses better the kind of spiritual life he is trying to lead as a priest. Saying the New Mass and trying to be a traditional priest is kind of like trying to put a square peg in a round hole, and, you know, when the same priest begins saying the traditional Mass it's like putting a square peg in a square hole.

If you had to point to one feature of the New Mass in which this horizontal aspect is most clearly seen, what would you say that was?

FR. R.: I don't think it is possible to point to one thing. It's true of the New Mass as a whole. First of all by the very fact that, if you take the Constitution on the Sacred Liturgy from Vatican II, there is, for example, the statement that there are all these different roles in the Liturgy, and that one may not transgress on the roles of the others. And, of course, the whole point is to insinuate that everybody has some kind of external activity to perform, and to imply that, in the traditional Mass, the people aren't doing anything while the priest is doing everything.

The physical orientation of the priest, the altar, and the people in the New Mass also emphasizes the horizontal aspect. In the traditional Mass, the priest is facing the altar, the people are behind him. (I don't like to say that the priest has his back to the people, because they use that as a club, but the real orientation is that the priest is facing the altar, the altar is facing east, and the people are behind the priest.) And what's the priest doing? The priest is offering sacrifice to Almighty God as a priest, and the people, *through his priesthood* are offering *their* sacrifice, being behind the priest. So they are all headed in the same direction, leading up to God. The people are down there; the priest is up here on the altar; God is up there. So it is all in progression up to God; God comes down to the people through the priest; and the people's prayers and sacrifices go up to God through the priest. That is all very clear in the old Mass. In the New Mass you've got them all standing on the same level, you have the priest on one side of the table; you have the people on the other side of the table; and they are dialoguing back and forth. In addition to that you have all these sub-ministers doing their thing, distracting really from whatever of any value is happening on that table. Just the physical arrangement itself is striking: physically, mystically, symbolically, ritually, in every aspect.

How did you come to the end of this self-deception?

FR. R.: What a question, what an interesting question! I think we have to go back to where the self-deception began: I absolutely did not believe that the Church could ever change the Mass. And on that day, the first day of Advent in 1964, when they first started introducing a little vernacular, turning the altar around and so forth, I really knew it was coming, but I just never thought it would ever really come. The absolute disbelief that it could happen threw me into a great deal of confusion, and the only thing I could say was, "Well, you know, it is the Church of God; it is infallible as the Church of God, and somehow or another, there is a problem with me that I can't see how this is all traditional and not contradictory, and so forth. Therefore, even though I don't understand what is going on, and I can't process this, I will accept it because the Church knows better than I do." So I kind of muddled along with that until I came here, in 1982.

What was the key of that self-deception's coming to an end?

FR. R.: Well, see, I never *really* embraced the New Mass, and I certainly never, under any circumstances, in any form, embraced the new theology. In fact, before I was ordained, when I was teaching in the public school, I used to attend Mass every day, a *Novus Ordo* Mass (the only thing I knew was available at the time). And I would sit in the back and read my old missal and just sort of block out what was going on. What led to my coming back was first of all, I think, being made aware of the fact that there were many priests offering the old Mass. For instance, I became aware of Archbishop Lefebvre in 1976 when the big brouhaha occurred over the suspension. I'd never heard of him until then. I would say at that time–deep down inside, I wanted to join up with him–but I said, "No, he's disobedient, and I have to obey the Church.

So I can't go that way, although I am very much inclined to." So, I let that go and got ordained, but I could see that *there was no way of doing any kind of restoration of the true Faith in the* Novus Ordo, *under the* Novus Ordo *mainstream set-up*.

Any little advance I would make in the direction of Tradition would be undone by five other people. And, of course, the whole diocesan bureaucracy was against me, and, when push came to shove, there was no battle I could win for Tradition, because all of the cards were stacked the other way. That's thing number one. Thing number two which brought an end to the self-deception was that, by Providence, there was a gentleman who lived very close to the parish I was in. I always heard confessions on Saturday afternoons, and he used to come to me for confession. He would not come to the parish church for Mass, but he would come to me for confession. Anyway, one Saturday he slipped me a note saying that there was a church that offers the traditional Mass down in Virginia that needed a priest. (This was during Lent.) I just took the note and kind of sat on it for a while. I would say that my immediate inclination was to find out more. But I sat on it because of the obedience question. At some point, just seeing more and more of the handwriting on the wall, I began to see that I could do a lot more good as a priest there in Virginia than I could where I was. I began to read traditionalist writers to see how they were justifying doing these things. These people wanted to be Catholics, they obviously wanted to save their souls. Somehow, they didn't see a problem with obedience, so what was I missing, was I missing something? So I began to find myself more and more in agreement with the traditionalist writers, and I came to see where they were coming from. The only obstacles that remained, ultimately, were the questions of the validity of confessions and the validity of the marriages witnessed outside the normal diocesan structure. That question of supplied jurisdiction was solved for me. So then I simply became convinced that, not only was it good for me to return to Tradition and say the traditional Mass, but that I was obliged to.

So, what finally provided the impetus for you to make the change?

FR. R.: It was a combination of things, and, of course, the gentleman who passed me that note was certainly the catalyst. He really blasted me out of neutral, put me in gear. I owe a great deal to this fellow.

How did you learn to celebrate the old Mass?

FR. R.: I grew up attending the old Mass. I served it in the minor seminary. I served it until it changed, every day, sometimes several times a day. So I knew exactly what the priest was doing, and while I was attending the *Novus*

Ordo Mass before I returned to the seminary, I was reading the old Mass in the missal.

You were reading it in Latin? With the rubrics and everything?

FR. R.: In Latin, with the rubrics, the little tabs on the page and everything. Using the same missal I still use when I travel.

So the transition was very, very easy?

FR. R.: No one had to teach me to say the Mass. I think I basically went through a book of rubrics or something, just to kind of brush up. And, of course, I knew Latin very well, so the Latin itself was no obstacle. I was, by the way, reciting the Roman Breviary in Latin since 1961, although once I was obliged to say the Office, then I said the *Novus Ordo* Office. The *Novus Ordo* Office is very distasteful and just as much butchered up and botched as the New Mass: I mean, "A Reading from Dag Haamarskjöld"?

Did you begin to say the old Mass in your parish, or did you begin when you came to St. Athanasius Church?

FR. R.: No, I didn't say the old Mass in the parish. Once I had made up my mind that this was the way I had to go, I thought that, in justice, I had to go to my bishop, and I did. I began talking with him basically in the vein that there were a lot of revolutionary things going on in the Church that I could not in conscience continue to go along with. I started with Communion in the hand, because that's very obvious. Before I started out though, I said to the Archbishop (this was Archbishop William Donald Borders), "I will not accept that there is anything wrong with me or that I need to see a shrink or anything else." I said "*These are clearly objective abuses, and the problem is not with me. The problem is with these abuses*. So, respectfully, I am simply stating that I will not accept the idea that I have a problem." And then I laid this out, and I laid out the problems with the New Mass. The way I put it, I knew he would say no; I knew he had to say no, but I had at least to put it this way, and I had to say "I want your approval, first of all, not to distribute Communion in the hand, and I want your permission to say only the old Mass." And, of course, he was one of these apparently compassionate liberals, you know. He was listening with great pain, as I was talking about all of this. So then finally he let me spin out what I wanted to say, and then he said, "Well, I can see you're in a lot of pain. You're under terrible stress, terrible, terrible stress, and you really need to see a counselor to deal with this stress, and you also need to see a competent theologian." [*Laughter*] You know what "competent theologian" means?

"Competent" means certified by the diocese?

FR. R.: There you go! First of all I said "Well, I'm not accepting that I need to see a counselor. The problem is not with me. It would do no good at all to see one of these theologians." Then the Archbishop said, "Just go back to your parish and think about this a little more." So, I went back, and I spoke to my pastor, with whom I got along very well. I think he liked working with me a great deal, too, because deep down inside he was traditionally-minded and was happy not to have a radical for an assistant. Besides that, I was quite a work-horse in those days, and it was a big parish, a busy parish. He'd had other assistants come and go to the alcohol-treatement homes and that sort of thing. So I told him of my discussion with the Archbishop, where I was planning to go and what I was planning to do (which I had not yet told the Archbishop). He regretted my decision, but he said, "Well, if this is what you think you have to do, this is what you have to do." I told him that I wanted him to have the time to be able to make arrangements to replace me, to have somebody assigned to take my place. I wrote a letter to the Archbishop telling him where I was going, what I was doing and my reasons for doing it. I finally made the move on the Friday before Pentecost, after having received the original note about St. Athanasius in March.

Could you describe the first time you said the old Mass?

FR. R.: It went through without a hitch, you know. Like I'd been doing it for years. Yes, it was like I was flying! I'd been weighed down by this whole struggle.

Were there any sanctions from the Archdiocese?

FR. R.: I came down here, and I heard nothing from the archdiocese until October, when I got a letter from the Archbishop saying, "Well, you've been gone for a while now, and I really thought you were going to take my advice. I'm sorry about this, but you really need to come in and talk to me about your future with this Archdiocese." So I went up to see the Archbishop and, more or less, laid out the same things. The Archbishop, who was very kind to me, insofar as he could have been, said, "Well, it seems that you have pretty much decided what you are going to do, and the only thing I can say to you is that, although I'm not going to suspend you, I'm withdrawing from you the faculty to preach and to say Mass publicly. So if you want to continue saying Mass privately, you're perfectly free to do that." Now, when he told me I could say Mass privately, he knew which Mass I was saying, obviously. There's a new Archbishop there now, Cardinal Keeler, whom I have met, so he knows that

I'm here, and he knows what I am doing, and he has chosen basically to leave things as they are.

So no suspension, no excommunication?

FR. R.: No suspension, no excommunication. I'm still a priest incardinated in the Archdiocese of Baltimore and, far as I know, in good standing.

Do you have your faculties now?

FR. R.: I do have all my faculties, actually! See, he removed them at first, but I stayed on the mailing list because I wanted to pray for the priests as they died, so I could offer five Masses for each deceased priest, which was the custom. So, they kept me on the mailing list, and when the new *Code of Canon Law* came out, they had to reissue faculties. So, you see, they just reissued faculties to everybody on the mailing list, and my faculties were renewed, and they've never been revoked. I can hear confessions, according to the new *Code of Canon Law*, anywhere in the world!

What about your family?

FR. R.: They thought I was making a mistake at first, but they supported me. Eventually, I like to think they came around.

Archbishop Lefebvre once said that one could not form a sacrificing priest in a seminary using the New Mass. Based on your experiences in a 1970's American seminary, how would you react to that assertion? Would you qualify it at all?

FR. R.: I don't think the *Novus Ordo* Mass can be used to form a sacrificing priest. I think the Archbishop was exactly right. In the minor seminary, we were not only given all these courses in Greek and Latin, and so on, that I told you about, but we were getting good solid, traditional, Sulpician spirituality, and there was, of course, the old Mass only. But I'll tell you this: when once you begin attending the New Mass or begin offering the New Mass, whatever the case may be, even though there is nothing openly heretical in it, *the ambiguity of it and the Protestant flavor of it begins to have an influence on the way you look at things*. To borrow an example that Bishop Williamson once used, it's kind of like you're being "marinated in liberalism." And, you know, even though we are trying not to be liberal, we are in a liberal environment, and we are all influenced by this liberalism. So, in one sense we are all picking up the flavor of liberalism. I think if you apply that same kind of a notion to the *Novus Ordo* Mass, we are being marinated in a certain ecclesiastical liberalism, Protestantism, whatever you want to call it. And I myself, even though I never held any positions that were in any way against the Faith, I certainly was willing to cast a blind eye, even if a somewhat disapproving eye, at humanism, religious liberty, things like that. In other words, I would not approve of the concepts, but I would kind of look the other way, and sweep them under the rug. The only way to overcome that is to be rid of the New Mass and to say only the old Mass, or attend only the old Mass, and I think it even took me a couple of years. I think that there's a certain liberal flavor that was given to me, despite my best efforts to remain Catholic, simply by saying or attending the New Mass. The only way to get rid of that liberal flavor is to separate yourself from the New Mass.

For me to say that Archbishop Lefebvre was right? I mean, you have to laugh! But there's no question the Archbishop was on target with that statement, that you cannot form good, traditional, sacrificing priests with this liberal marinade, with the New Mass. I mean, look, you put a steak in this or that marinade; it's still a steak, but it's going to have a different flavor to it.

If you had any words of encouragement or advice for some priest who was vacillating and thinking about what to do about this question of the New Mass versus the old Mass, someone who is sitting on the fence, what would you say to such a priest?

_**FR. R.:**_ It depends on what is holding him back. If it is the obedience question, he needs to get a true notion of obedience. I think, as simple as it is, the little flyer put out by the [St. Thomas Aquinas] Seminary ("Where Is Catholic Obedience Today: Not Where You Might Think"), says it all very clearly. He needs to have a true notion of obedience, that's thing number one. If his problem is that he's afraid that he will be destitute and poor because there will be no diocese taking care of him, he has to know that the traditional people value their priests far more than the _Novus Ordo_ people ever will. They're grateful to have a priest, and I don't know any traditional priest who has in any way ever been lacking for any of his material needs. So that shouldn't be an obstacle. Myself, I never really worried much about the material stuff. I figured if I was doing the right thing, and this arrangement didn't pan out, I could always say my Mass and sell shoes for a living. It would be much better for me to offer Mass privately in my home and sell shoes to support myself, than to be a _Novus Ordo_ priest in the diocese in a big parish.

If he's worried about what his fellow priests will think, or worried about losing friends or whatever, well, we have to have courage, you know! We have to be a good example to our fellow priests. We have to put Christ first and let all the other chips fall where they may. I mean, you know, _**we are in a war**_, and we have to be willing to be thought of as odd, strange, whatever, however people want to think of us. The first time such a priest says the old Mass, after saying the New Mass, it will be like a big weight lifted off his shoulders in the sense that he will know that he **can** be a priest as God wants him to be a priest. He **can** be a priest as he himself will feel happy being a priest. He will no longer be kicking against the goad, trying to swim upstream.

How would you defend yourself against charges of rigorism for holding to these views?

FR. R.: I would say, "Jesus Christ yesterday, today, and forever." *There are certain truths that can't change and don't change, and we are only kidding ourselves if we think they can.* It is not rigorism to follow the truth! Rigorism is slavish and unreasonable. I just can't see how being steadfast in the truth is rigorist.

It is a question of intolerance.
How would you explain the intolerance of the truth?

FR. R.: See, there are some things that are tolerable and there are other things that are intolerable. Error is intolerable because it is a manifestation of evil in regard to the intellect. Yes, you have to be intolerant of evil, and intellectual error is evil.

Is the New Mass erroneous? Is it evil?

FR. R.: Well, there you've got the crux of the problem. See, insofar as it is a Mass, of course, it can't be evil. But, insofar as any Mass is schismatic, it is evil. The sacrifice of Jesus Christ is of infinite value and is infinitely acceptable to the Father. But the circumstances of the Mass can be evil, and certainly if it is a Mass said by a schismatic, it is evil under that aspect. *The New Mass is evil under the aspect that it is Protestant, ambiguous, not a clear expression of Catholic doctrine.* No Mass is *per se* evil, but it is evil *secundum quid* (under a certain aspect).

One last point. The priest sitting on the fence might say, "You can't teach an old dog new tricks! I'd better just keep on as I'm doing!"

FR. R.: Well, if he's an older priest, and he has already said the old Mass, it is just a matter of relearning it, and I think he would slip back into it fairly easily. If he has never said the old Mass, he is probably not so old that he couldn't adapt to something. But I think, if he were inclined to come to Tradition, he would already be wanting to say the old Mass. It's just he doesn't have the courage, or something is holding him back from doing it. So I think he should be willing to learn new tricks.

How about for the priest who never learned Latin?

FR. R.: The only way out of that that I can see, and I'm just offering a personal opinion, is that he has to learn Latin, and probably, if he's never learned Latin, he needs to learn theology, too. The best thing to happen in a scenario like that is that this priest would stop saying Mass altogether and maybe spend several years in the seminary, learning Latin and maybe getting some kind of a crash course in philosophy and theology. At some point, once he has been brought up to speed, then he can say Mass.

That's not an easy thing to say...

FR. R.: That's not.

But none of these obstacles is insurmountable?

FR. R.: No, nothing, by the very fact that he's a priest, he will have the grace of Holy Orders to help him.

To contact Fr. Ringrose:

Rev. Fr. Ronald Ringrose
Post Office Box 1627
Vienna, VA 22183-1627
Phone: (703) 759-4555

Rev. Msgr. Raymond Ruscitto

When were you ordained, Monsignor?

MSGR. RUSCITTO: I was ordained on May 30, 1953. I entered the Minor Seminary of the Pontifical College Josephinum on September 11, 1941; then the Second World War broke out in December of that year. The Josephinum took boys from all over the United States and gave them a scholarship-type education for twelve years.

Was your formation fairly orthodox?

MSGR. R.: It was very good. We had four years of high school and two years of college. Then, in the Major Seminary, we did philosophy for two years and theology for four.

What did they teach you that the priest is?

MSGR. R.: Priests are "Men taken from among men, who are ordained for the things of God in the service of men." It's from Scripture, there's no question about it. It was only subsequently that they started talking about a part-time priesthood, based on new ideas that took different directions. The priesthood was no longer to be a totally dedicated life–you could *retire*! We never had ideas of retiring when we entered the priesthood. It was "for keeps," and you died with your boots on. The new priesthood was a *career*. We, on the contrary, were given the old-fashioned ideas that you did your job wherever the bishop sent you, and you didn't get into politics. At least the ideal was set before us that our bishop was going to be our overlord and that we were going to serve as he directed us.

As a sacrificing priest, an *alter Christus*?

MSGR. R.: Yes. But years after my ordination, the local bishop decided that there were going to be "teams" in the ministry. There would be priests who lived in one parish house but who would go out to serve the various parishes and then come back to a sort of "home base." It was sort of experimental. We did not know what was going on. I just kept my nose to the grindstone. I kept things as conservative as possible, wherever I was, and I didn't care too much about what was going on elsewhere.

Were these new career priests, "team ministers," to be sacrificing priests, or were they to be more like social workers and enablers?

MSGR. R.: Well, I'm sure the idea was that they were to be sacrificing priests and "other Christs," but we called them the "Young Turks," because they were ready to experiment according to the new "liberation" that was coming out of the Council. There was a division of mentalities between the young priests and the old priests. The young priests were having their meetings, and they were making their plans for the new liturgies and all that crazy stuff that first came out, guitars and dancing. The idea was, "We are liberated, and now we are going to show you how it is done!" And everything became humanized.

What was the result of their "humanizing" the priesthood?

MSGR. R.: They wanted to have parties and contests and sports–all the stuff that brought them "closer to the youth" or to the people. They dressed in their "civvies," as they called them. They went out and played softball, and so on.

Did you see any of the older priests going along with these practices?

MSGR. R.: Some wanted to be "gung ho"; they wanted to be in with the new trend, so to speak. But most of them, for example the older Irish priests, did not want it. They did not completely conform with the American image, but even some of them were ready to jump in and lead the way. *They didn't want to lose the control that they had, and they sort of sacrificed their authentic priestly efforts in order to go along.*

What was your reaction to the New Mass in 1969?

MSGR. R.: Well, you've got to keep a certain perspective. The New Mass was given to us by degrees; it wasn't a sudden change. First, the traditional Mass was said in Latin with some English, and then Mass facing the people came in. People were stunned and ill at ease, in my parish at least. They said "Well, this is what we are supposed to do, so we'll do it. We don't understand it; we don't really like it, but we'll see what comes of it!" So they followed along, and I did the direction. You know, we had meetings; we had demonstrations; and we had expectations. We had guidelines, and the bishop was pushing, by degrees, the different aspects of the changes, like turning the altar around. I was one of the last ones to do that. It was commanded by the bishop–what was I supposed to do? So I did it as conservatively as I could.

Why were you so reluctant to accept the changes?

MSGR. R.: I'll tell you, if you really want to get the history on this. It started when I was in my second assignment. By 1958, I had got in contact with some people who were members of the John Birch Society, and they gave me some literature to read. I never joined that group, but I read the materials, and one of the things that opened my eyes was a book by a retired admiral who told the real story of Pearl Harbor. I learned for the first time that the United States intelligence forces had broken the Japanese code and that they knew the attack was coming. We were never told this in the news media! I was totally stunned, trying to figure out how this ignorance could be supported.

So, I began to study, and I got into areas that I didn't know existed. I had no axe to grind, and I came to some conclusions slowly but surely, turning over every pebble. *It was long and hard, confusing, and very painful as a matter of fact, but persistence has brought the reward of understanding.* I learned about espionage, sabotage, the Council on Foreign Relations, the Roundtable. All of these were foreign terms, and I had no idea what they meant. I had no one really to guide me, and I had to sort of fish for myself. It meant a lot of reading on political topics. I began to see connections that were invisible to a superficial glance, but discernible if you searched for them.

So, I searched, and I read and read. That was before the Second Vatican Council was announced. When the preliminary materials on the Council came out, they were produced by the Paulist Press. This was slick material, Madison Avenue stuff. I said, "This is not Catholic, because we usually just have cheap pulp-paper stuff, and this doesn't fit the pattern." When Pope John XXIII was elected, the world took to him like filings to a magnet, you know. I said, "This is not Catholic! They hate the pope, and yet the world is just running to him, and we don't even know that much about him yet."

So, I was suspicious on those two counts: the announcement of the Council in that fashion, and all the promises being made and all the upbeat predictions about undoing what had been detracting from our Catholic Faith and practices, and what-not. With all of the information I was learning about in the political field, I was suspicious to begin with, and I began to try to understand what was coming out of the Council, in one general overview, because I was very busy in the parish. *I saw that they were moving from very clear ideas to more ambiguous ideas, and I just kept saying, "This is not Catholic!"*

Could you give an example of this ambiguity?

MSGR. R.: Well, take the priesthood, for example. I remember a cartoon where a housekeeper was answering the door and saying to the people who were looking for the parish priest, "He's not here. He's out on some crusade or other." I said, "That's the story now, they're not in the rectories anymore. They're out doing things with kids or working for social causes." We were losing our perspective, our orientation. Instead of being in the confessional, instead of preaching sermons based on doctrine, they were giving political speeches. *That was the trend. It was a move away from a God-centeredness to a human-centeredness.* I said, "We are abandoning the divine aspect for the human agenda, the social gospel." They were quite open about it: "Yeah, that's what we are doing. We're getting out there, meeting with the people. We're going to address some causes now, because we've been too stand-offish and aloof."

Did this new trend conflict with the traditional Mass which you were still saying?

MSGR. R.: I was suspicious about the whole thing, you know, watching it and getting bad vibrations about it all. But I said, "I've got to obey, and I'll go along as far as I can, while keeping things as conservative as I can." This was my attitude until the bishop forbade me to say the traditional Latin Mass altogether.

By that time, I was only celebrating the old Mass on the first Sunday of each month at eight o'clock in the morning, and all the Italians would come to that Mass and respond to it in Latin. But he forbade even that, and so I said "Why? The Pope has never forbidden it!" Then the bishop gave me the Apostolic Constitution of Paul VI, and I read through it again. "Well," I said, "He's promoting the new liturgy, but he hasn't taken away the old." The bishop read it, and he was confused! He said "If I'm wrong, I'll retract my letter forbidding the Latin Mass, but first of all, we'll check with the Apostolic Delegation in Washington, D.C." The reply he received was not satisfactory: it was just news clippings and other irrelevant materials.

Then the bishop said, "You must write to Archbishop Benelli and ask if the old Mass is forbidden." Well, we never got a reply, so he just hardened his position. I saw that I could not hold the line if the bishop was not going to back me up, and so, in 1976, I decided that I would take early retirement. That's how I got out of the obligation to keep saying the New Mass.

What happened then?

MSGR. R.: I had some marriage cases to sort through, so I wound them up and gave my financial report. I turned everything over very smoothly to the next priest, who took over on June 1, 1976. I moved out, and he moved in. I was not allowed to say Mass. When the bishop told me this, I said to him, "Well, Bishop, you've done more than all the Masons put together by forbidding me to say Mass. They couldn't do it, but you've done it for them." (I didn't put it quite that bluntly, but that was the idea.) "Why are you forbidding me to say the Mass, when I've done nothing wrong?" I asked. But he wouldn't listen. This was a case of tyranny! I said, "He's got the authority to do what he wants to do, and I'll just have to take the consequences, but I'm not going to create any more problems than necessary." So, I retired quietly and never said Mass once for the whole following year.

What prompted you to start saying Mass again, despite the prohibition of the bishop?

MSGR. R.: Well, Fr. Eberhardt was saying the traditional Mass twice a month here for some people whom he had known before. (As a matter of fact, he was saying the Mass right across the street from my house.) These people saw me sitting here doing nothing, and one Sunday they came over to me and asked why I wouldn't say the other two Masses, on the Sundays Fr. Eberhardt was not here. "Well," I thought, "Nobody is going to take care of these spiritual outcasts, and I'm here doing nothing. I've spent my year on probation; I didn't create any problems." So, I said "Yes, I think I can go ahead and say the Mass for you." And that's how I began to celebrate Mass again, in response to the needs of the faithful whom no one was taking care of.

Let's go back a little bit and talk about the New Mass itself. What were the problems that you had with this Mass?

MSGR. R.: When the New Mass came out, I was the director of CCD for the diocese, and I was put on the committee to review the proposed general catechism. We got preliminary papers, and I read through it all and said, "This isn't Catholic!" The definition of the Mass in the Missal of 1969 was "The gathering of the people under the presidency of the minister." I said, "That could be a novena! I mean, it's so vague! This is supposed to be the definition of the Mass?" I couldn't accept this vagueness, this disorientation, and I was very uncomfortable because all that new stuff was so disruptive. It was not promoting that spirituality that we were supposed to develop in the parishioners. ***These things represented a disorganization, a disorientation of our very human faculties, let alone our spirituality.***

Another thing that I noticed was the Masonic set-up of the New Mass. The altar is turned around and placed in front of the "president's chair" (or the grand master's chair). You've got your wardens (one's going to take care of the announcements, and the other will read the Gospel or the Epistle, or whatever they do), the master of ceremonies, and so on. Anybody who has studied the background of these things could see their relation to Freemasonry, but the others who didn't know about Masonry couldn't recognize the change which was taking place.

They also took the tabernacle out—not only did they set it aside, but they even put it in a different room. They put Christ out of the sanctuary! So, the whole *milieu* of operations, at that time, told me that they were subverting our Church, our ministry, our sacrifice. Then, they began changing the words in the formula of Consecration ("*pro multis*," which means "for many") to "for all men." First "for all men," then "for all men and women," and then "for all"! It was ambiguous because Christ **did** die for all, but the *Catechism of the Council of Trent* explained very clearly why our Lord said "for many," and not "for all."

What really opened my eyes was the New Theology that everybody is saved. "For all" means that even those who are not Catholic, even those who don't know about Christianity, are saved. I said, "That's contrary to what we've been taught!" I was astounded. They not only put a Protestant twist on things, but the capital letters in which they used to print the words of Consecration were gone. *The text was now in a narrative form, retelling a story, and not in the old form, where the formula of consecration was clearly a sacramental form.*

Then came the ecumenical movement, joining the other religions in prayer, which is absolutely forbidden by the First Commandment, you know. This is doctrine that we were taught, and the leaders were doing the exact opposite. I said, "This cannot be accepted," so in conscience, I couldn't follow.

In what other ways is the New Theology expressed in the *Novus Ordo* Mass besides the idea of universal salvation?

MSGR. R.: Well, the Eucharistic ministers don't have to have consecrated hands, and women in slacks can come up to the tabernacle and bring Communion to those in the hospital. All of that is a sort of madness. *It's as if the priests are being put out of business.*

What did you think about the new Offertory prayers?

MSGR. R.: That was one of the big points, because you know what these are—these are Jewish table prayers! I knew that from the beginning, because I had read up on it. They were trouncing the essence of Mass, in that they were not putting in Offertory prayers (which emphasize the sacrificial nature of the Mass), but prayers for the "preparation of the gifts," which will become "our spiritual food and spiritual drink." This is so ambiguous that Protestants can use these prayers now! In fact, I've heard of Baptists and Lutherans using the same "missalette" the Catholics are using. They don't accept the Mass, the sacrificial Mass, but these prayers seem to present no difficulty for them. Bishop Manning told us that there was a Catholic priest who "concelebrated Mass" with an Episcopalian woman "priest." I thought, "My goodness, how could they go this far?" but they went even further than that.

In what way?

MSGR. R.: One of my own more serious episodes happened when I was told that I had to officiate at a mixed marriage between a Jehovah's Witness girl and a Catholic boy. Since she wouldn't come to the parish church for the wedding, I was told to go to the Jehovah's Witness church and officiate with the Jehovah's Witness minister. I resisted, but arrangements had been made, and the bishop ordered me to do it. I was ready to go ahead, but it was like a sword through my soul. Fortunately, the congregation refused to let me in! So I didn't have to officiate, but the bishop just dispensed them from the canonical form of marriage and allowed the Jehovah's Witness minister to officiate at that wedding all by himself! It's against the Divine Law! I decided that, if they ever told me to do that again, I could not comply, but, by then, I was on my way to retirement.

Why is it so important that the Offertory has been replaced by a "preparation of gifts" and that the consecratory formula has been changed into a "narrative of institution"?

MSGR. R.: Because the reality of the sacrifice was very clear before, but now it's ambiguous. The same pattern was obvious in all the changes—we have gone from clarity to ambiguity. I saw that this was not supportive of our Faith, so I could not go along with the program. It's not just the Mass, but everything has gone this way now.

Given all of this ambiguity, the down-playing of the idea of sacrifice, and the changes in the Offertory prayers and the formula of the Consecration, is it easy for the priest's proper intention to slip away, and thus for the New Mass to be invalidly celebrated?

MSGR. R.: Absolutely. *The whole context of the New Theology, as expressed in the New Mass, is towards a man-centeredness and away from a God-centeredness.* That's why, today, there are Catholic priests who no longer believe in the Divine Presence in the consecrated species. They think it's just a memorial, like a Protestant service, and not a sacrifice. They pass the Host around as if It's just common bread, and whatever falls on the floor is thrown away.

There was one parish bulletin that said, "Please be careful with the Hosts, because we have to sweep them up after Mass." One lady said, "When I had my daughter's wedding in your church, they gave us these little white hosts, and I pasted one in the marriage book." What a desecration! I was told about one parish here where the priest allowed his First-Communion class to receive the Host by intinction. One of the boys didn't like the taste of It, so he spit It out! I protested, but the bishop just said that the priest ought to give better instruction and preparation. So, I saw that there was just no concern about such sacrileges.

Once, when I was already retired, a priest who was serving at one of the parishes as a guest in the diocese wrote me a letter to try and address some of these abuses anonymously. He said that the Franciscan priests in that parish were making their own hosts with sugar and other things. "I don't know what to do," he said. "If I report this to the bishop, I might be thrown out or sent away." So I wrote a letter to the bishop and explained what was going on, and about three months later he issued a bulletin to the priests saying, "Be careful to conform to the canonical requirements for the making of hosts." He didn't explain anything further. So, I saw that things were just going to go on as before, and nothing has changed. At least my conscience was clear. I raised the flag of warning, but I couldn't really do anything else about it.

How does all of this ambiguity harm the faith of the people?

MSGR. R.: Well, you see, ambiguity is more of an academic thing; it's at the level of the understanding of the principles involved. What really touches the people is the outcome of the ambiguity. They see these things through Catholic eyes, so they are scandalized; they are shocked. They don't understand why, but they see things that they cannot weave into their Catholic patterns of thinking. They're scandalized, not so much in theory as in the results of the ambiguities.

The people are disheartened, and some of them will leave the Church to go nowhere. Others will leave the Church to go to some more satisfying and spiritual religion, even to the Pentecostals, although they feel uncomfortable there. At least it is more spiritual there than in the jangle of confusion which dominates the new liturgies now.

What do these ambiguities do to the faith of the priests?

MSGR. R.: That is a question not only of psychology but of spirituality and *diabolism*, I would say. ***This astounding blindness is almost diabolical.*** They say that the corruption of the best is the worst, and when priests fall, they fall like a ton of bricks. They lose all sense of propriety, of spirituality. They may have been hanging on by their fingernails before, but they really drop all the way upside down when they fall. They think they're going up instead of down. It's the spiritual operation of error which Scripture talks about [II Thess. 2].

Archbishop Lefebvre once said that he went along with the changes in the Mass all the way up through 1967 (removing genuflections and signs of the cross), but that he put them back again, on his own authority, after trying the 1967 revision for some time, because he could see that his faith and his devotion at Mass were slipping. Does this correspond to your own experience?

MSGR. R.: Absolutely. There's a slow drip that begins to erode the substance of the Faith. We have to support the substance of the Faith with back-up helps of every kind. We are human, and we need these things to eliminate the dangers, because in our fallen condition we are "inclined to evil from our youth," and we have to pull away from evil. If we lose these supports, then we're down to rock-bottom basics, and if those begin to slip away, then there is an inversion that takes place.

What do you mean by "inversion"?

MSGR. R.: God created all things out of nothing. In that creation, there is a positive side that is *reality*, but there is a concomitant negative side that is *illusion*. We are constituted in our rational nature to receive external reality *intellectually* within ourselves. When we judge external realities correctly, we are operating according to reality. But when we judge them incorrectly, for whatever reason, we begin operating according to an illusion. We are in an inversion of reality. Only later do we find out that we were mistaken, and we have to change our false judgments to conform to reality, to truth. If we do this, if our choices are proper, the Truth will lead us to good results.

But we are in danger of falling prey to illusion when we don't conform our false judgments to the truth. We can create a false religion and think we are serving God. As our Lord said, "A day will come when they will put you to death, thinking they are doing a service to God." This was the problem with the bishops who pushed the changes through. Their ideas were not in conformity with reality. They were into politics; they were great administrators. They were doing all kinds of things, except the spiritual things they should have been concentrating on.

So, despite the fact that almost every bishop at Vatican II had a doctorate in Thomistic philosophy or theology, moderate realism was not really a part of them?

MSGR. R.: No. They were just studying to get a "sheepskin." They went through with whatever it took to get the diploma, but Thomism didn't get into their bones, so to speak.

And so, by entering into this illusion, this inversion, they set up for themselves a parallel "reality" which is not real?

MSGR. R.: I would say that it's more than a parallel reality–it's a "counter-reality."

But they must have taken some wrong turn to have ended up in this counter-reality. What was that wrong turn?

MSGR. R.: It comes from the real abuses which existed. These things were not at variance with the essence of the Faith, but there were abuses–personality conflicts, heavy-handedness, a sort of tyranny. Superiors would demand more than they had a right to demand. Things became very politicized. Behavior was, in a certain way, "out of synch" with the Gospel. They entered the counter-reality in reaction to abuses that were not part of the traditional way, as such, but which were subjectively identified by them with Tradition as such. So, when they threw out the bath-water, the baby went too! Then, they wanted to start all over again.

They had their opportunity with the Second Vatican Council. Bishop Donohoe told me that, when they were called to Rome, they didn't know what it was for. They went expecting to put their time in and come home. But, as we have now read in Fr. Wiltgen's book, *The Rhine Flows into the*

Tiber and Bishop Tracy's book, *An American Bishop at the Second Vatican Council,* the American bishops were subverted by those Liberals from northern Europe. And they were persuaded that they could more usefully put their energies into overthrowing the Roman Curia, which had behaved toward them in the past somewhat as a heavy-handed overseer. They fell in with this whole liberalization process, and, as Fr. Wiltgen said in his book, they threw the whole agenda for the Council in the waste-basket during the first session. They just threw it away! All that preparation for nothing!

So, then they had a new agenda which had been formed by the Northern European Liberals, and they were going to meetings, being lectured to. They had no notion of what they were doing or what they were going to do. So they fell in with the leadership that was already in place behind the scenes.

This was all engineered. It was just like the Communist program, how they take over meetings with just a handful of supporters. They know what they are doing, and they know how they're going to get it done! The same thing took place at the Council. You couldn't always identify who was doing it on purpose and who was the unhappy victim, but the agenda was being pushed through all the same.

It's like that movie *Rosemary's Baby,* the story about this child of the devil, whose mother loves it when she first hears it cry but is horrified by it as the child of the devil. **What the bishops brought into existence at Vatican II was demonic, but since it was their baby, they embraced it at all costs.** They have even persecuted us, as Catholic priests trying to hold the line, because we wouldn't accept that demonic baby! It's not even a *doctrinal* baby! It's a *pastoral* baby, but they made it seem as if it had authority from heaven itself. This is the subversion, the inversion that's taken place. It's accompanied by a blindness that certainly preceded Vatican II, and the politics of "Americanism" made it possible.

Are the new ideas about the priesthood a counter-reality to the real priesthood as well?

<u>**MSGR. R.:**</u> Yes, the whole idea is to get rid of Christ. The devil wants to take Christ's place, but Christ is very powerful, so he has to get rid of the Blessed Sacrament. And then he's got to get rid of the priesthood. To get rid of the priesthood, he's got to subvert the Catholic culture and to do all that he can to destroy the creation of God–nature.

The illusion is against the State as well–the whole social structure has to be turned upside down. They did that by brainwashing people all during the sixties and seventies. Take a look at what was happening at that time! We have largely forgotten about it now, but go back and get those magazines and see what was happening–the academic strikes in the universities, all the demonstrations ("Ban the bra!"), nudism, the confusion of civil disobedience, the "rock and roll." These things were battering the minds of people. It was quite a period of turmoil, and, in times of turmoil, the mind becomes more open to suggestion. People were confused.

All those who had power and authority were suddenly bereft of it, and they were looked down upon. An older priest came out to visit me, and he said, "You know, the Bishop is always going to the young priests now. He's ignoring us as if we are an embarrassment to him!" I said, "So, it's turned around; it's upside down! And I'm not surprised!"

By then, I could see the pattern; it was happening right in front of my eyes, but nobody else seemed to recognize it, even when I pointed it out. I said, "Can't you see what's going on right here? Look at it!" *But, no, they wouldn't look, because they wanted an easier life, because they had been worked hard, and the new ways were supposed to give them that easy life.*

I had seen the old priests, before the changes, when they were "put out to pasture." They got a room on the third floor of the rectory, and they were ignored. Is that supposed to be the outcome of a long life of service to the Church? So the priests would buy properties, and they'd try to make money. They'd prepare for their old age, because they didn't feel secure that the bishops would provide for them. Not all of the bishops, but enough of them, would just say, "Thanks, goodbye, and sorry–fend for yourselves!"

There were abuses which were almost fostered, and the young priests were longing to correct them. They wanted to do away with the tyranny, and to have an easier life by having lay people to "participate" and do some of their work for them. They ended up by sitting back and reading the newspaper while somebody else is reading the Gospel or the Epistle. Some of the laity just love to do that, so it was no problem! Those lay people want power. The idea of the struggle for power in the Church is very much a part of this crisis.

The whole agenda across the board was the fabrication of a New World Order without Christ, without Christianity. But there was room for a substitute Christianity which had the appearance, but not the substance, of the real thing. They had to destroy the Church, and they did that with Vatican II and its aftermath!

Would you say that the New Mass is the substitute Mass for the substitute Church?

MSGR. R.: It's really more of a substitute spirituality. Christ gave us the legacy of the Holy Ghost, "Who will teach you all truth," but this operation has now been subverted by a false spirit.

People refer to Vatican II as the "new Pentecost." Do you find any significance in this?

MSGR. R.: Well, it depends on which side of the fence you are sitting on! It's a new Pentecost for *them*, because now they're liberated from all this tyranny, all this dogmatism, all this triumphalism; now they're going to become "more authentically human." But those of us who saw the barnacles on the ship (which was still sailing) saw the ship being sunk. The ship went down, but there were no more barnacles!

So it wasn't a new Pentecost so much as a funeral pyre?

MSGR. R.: Absolutely. I'll go along with that! It was a false spirituality. I gave a talk one time on false mysticism, and what it really amounts to is occult mysticism. You've got to study the occult to recognize and understand it. I have learned some surprisingly spiritual principles from studying the occult and by turning the occult principles exactly around. It showed me facets of the truth which I did not even recognize until I saw them in this backward manner.

Could you give an example?

MSGR. R.: Like the spiritual principles of grace, in reverse. We have supernatural grace that comes from God. The devil mimics that grace–he inspires his followers with a certain like-mindedness. It doesn't have to be overtly coordinated, but by diabolical "inspirations," they all work together for a common purpose which they may not even see. This common purpose is orchestrated by the diabolical spirit which has entered into them by their leave.

Another principle is that of illusion, like when a building casts a shadow. The building is a substance; the shadow is the illusion of that building, but it's not a haphazard shadow. The shadow has to follow the lines of the building. God has made creation as it is, and the devil cannot escape the lines of that creation, even though he's working in the shadow of it. What you see as a shadow indicates the building itself. So you don't look at the building, but you see the shadow, and you have an idea of what the building is like by its shadow.

The grace of God reversed is the diabolical "black grace" that Satan uses to inspire his people. But he has to stay within the lines of God's creation, so he's bound by the structure, but he's free to turn it around, which he does by disobedience. Those who sin are disobedient, and they are automatically brought into the devil's camp. That's why we fight against sin–it's a reality that, "You cannot serve two masters"!

What would you say about the worthiness of the New Mass, even in its most conservative form?

MSGR. R.: If the Protestants can say it, there's something wrong. But we have to remember that the Mass is Christ's sacrifice. It's the continuation of Calvary. So, no matter how it's cast, as long as Christ is authentically the main Priest, and His intentions are still operating through the liturgy, we would still have the sacrifice. We can accept that there may be different forms of the liturgy–matter, form, and the proper intention are all that are required for validity. This makes it, in fact, pretty hard to invalidate the Mass, but if the intention is subverted or the matter vitiated, you've lost the essence of it.

I wouldn't get too hung up on the precision of the Latin Mass and all its elements. Take the priests who were in prison camps as an example–they got hold of some bread and a little bit of wine from a medicine bottle, and they said Mass. What did they say? They didn't go through the prayers at the foot of the altar! They said "This is My Body; This is My Blood," and they had the Consecration; they had the Mass. When you have the Consecration, no matter what its attendant aberrations are, you have the Mass.

The problem is not just the New Mass, though–it's the New Theology that goes along with the New Mass! If somebody says the New Mass with the right theology, with a good intention, and the matter and form are intact, it's a Mass, even if it's not what we're used to.

By the same token, is the validity of the traditional Latin Mass guaranteed? No! If the priest deliberately doesn't intend to say Mass but just goes through the ceremony, does the Church supply his intention? How do we answer some of these questions when we're dealing with invisible realities? It's difficult, it really is, and so we have to take the safer course. That's one thing, at least, that distinguishes us from the *Novus Ordo* clergy: We take the safer course. They say "Hey, you don't have to do all that extra stuff! We're already saved, we're redeemed, and we have to celebrate!" That's why you get the balloons, the Coca-Cola, the tortillas instead of hosts, and the picnic atmosphere in the New Mass. *And that's why I say that we are not bound in conscience to attend it!*

Having celebrated the New Mass alongside the old for several years, how would you describe the influence of each Mass on the life of the priest?

MSGR. R.: To say the New Mass, even as conservatively and reverently as possible, produces anxiety—at least it did for me. I told the people from the pulpit, "When I say this Mass, I intend to consecrate the host and the wine into the very Body and Blood, Soul, and Divinity of Christ. So there's no doubt as to my intention." But it was so uncomfortable; it was a sort of agony.

What is the root of that agony?

MSGR. R.: The traditional Latin Mass was so clearly a sacrifice. It was embraced by all the saints. It is oriented to communion with Christ. The New Mass sort of fades away from the heavenly Host and concentrates on "My brothers and sisters."

How does this effect the priest's vision of himself as Another Christ?

MSGR. R.: I think it would tend to indicate a sort of part-time service, not total dedication. "We have other agendas! We must make speeches in public forums, lead marches," etc. It comes from a social gospel that is not germane to the Gospel of Christ. The priest has taken on an aura that fits this world, which we are not supposed to be a part of. We live *in* the world, but we are not *of* it. Priests have gone after human respectability, accolades, promotion, power. It's a question of pride, and all of these things feed into pride. If you don't have a genuine spirituality, it's easy to fall.

What about the current pedophilia scandals among the clergy? What would you say is the root?

MSGR. R.: It's the aftermath of abandoning the old books on ascetical and mystical theology in the seminaries. They abandoned them for mimeographed sheets which combined liturgy and sociology. When I first found out they were doing this, I was stunned, but I knew something bad was going to come about as a result of the vacuum created by that change. That vacuum was bound to be filled with something, but I didn't know it was going to get this bad.

You can't live the priestly life without an authentic spiritual life! If you don't have any solid spirituality to begin with, how can you pass it on to the people whom you're serving? Then, Catholicism becomes bingo games and building projects and the social gospel. And we enter into an inversion of reality.

Priests are only human, and the words of Cicero come to mind: "Nothing human is foreign to me." A priest can become as merely human as anybody else without spiritual support! He can want marriage, family, the pleasures of the world; he can want sin; he can even want devil-worship. He can invert even that far! He needs that support which comes from the Holy Ghost in the context of Christ's Mystical Body. If he doesn't have it, he can fall, as we are all inclined to do as human beings. When I talk to my bishop, I am not talking to a bishop–I'm talking to a *man* who's a bishop. He's got authority; he's got power and responsibility, but he's still human. And if he's got a bad temper, for example, he's going to be a bad-tempered bishop!

The one thing that I sought in my retirement was to study how it could be possible for this crisis to happen in the Catholic Church. I wasn't concerned with finding out *who* did it, or *how* it's been done–what interested me was the theoretical question, the philosophical question: How was it possible for this to happen, in view of Christ's promise, "I will be with you always, even until the end of the world"?

The answer that stands out from all my studies is this: As long as we have human elements involved in the Church, we have the potential for subversion, even in our leaders. We've all studied the history of the Church. There have been morally bad Popes, but they kept the Faith, or at least they didn't fight against it! Now, we have Popes who subvert the Faith, and that is a conundrum! The reason they have subverted the Faith is that they have abandoned the supernatural to enter into the natural arena, and that's where they met the devil and made this turn-around.

Nevertheless, the Holy Ghost is still with the Church, and she's still holy–but the external, human side of the Church! It's like a rose window–from the outside of the church, it looks gray and ugly, but that's not so important because, on the inside of the church, it's bright with color. Maybe these Popes never did really enter into the spiritual structure of the Catholic life! They only see the outside, the human side, and that's all they deal with, while they pass by the beauty that's on the inside because they never saw it! And if we can't convey that beauty to our traditional people, they won't see it, either!

Is it easier for the priest to see the window from the inside when he says the traditional Mass?

MSGR. R.: The old Mass is no safer for the priest than the new if the proper theological mindset is not in place. We do have some good priests in the *Novus Ordo*, but they're on the borderline–they're more susceptible to subversion. But that doesn't mean that traditional priests are all secure and safe just because they say the old Mass! For instance, they can get into an excessive rigorism. We have to keep a prudent balance, and that's why we need the Holy Ghost, because we really can't achieve that balance by ourselves. Without that interior grace, being naturally balanced isn't enough, even at its best.

How can a priest who was ordained before the subversion of the Church find his way back to this prudent balance? Can he escape from the inversion?

MSGR. R.: The first question is this: Knowing the theology he was trained in, why doesn't he go back? Can he find out why he has not done so already? Is he lazy? Is he fearful? What is the reason, not the "good reason," but the *real* reason underneath it all, why he has not already gone back? *Let him address that, and if his convictions are strong enough, he will be able to overcome whatever other barrier may seem to stand in his way!* He can overcome it if he sees that it's his duty, and if he's got a conscience sensitive enough to push him in that direction.

What can the younger priest do? He's probably never had a proper theological formation, for instance.

MSGR. R.: He's got to take the time and study what he's not been given so far. He labors under ignorance. The only world he knows is a sort of passing show. He's got to get back into history, back into philosophy, back into theology. He's got to do his "homework" all over again, but from a healthy, valid approach this time.

If there were one or two books you could recommend for such a young priest to look at, what would they be?

MSGR. R.: Well, he would probably have to go to the books in English. There are a lot of good theology books in English from the pre-Vatican II days. Of course, it goes without saying that he should read Tanquerey's *Spiritual Life*, because he has to sharpen up his own spiritual life. That doesn't come just by wanting it–it has to come by living it, through the various stages of conversion, and that is a very personal program!

He will need a spiritual director. It has to be a one-on-one spiritual formation, I'm afraid. Such a director can guide him past his mistakes, undoing them, and bring him on to an authentic spiritual life. *He has to learn what valid spirituality is and why–he cannot just memorize the doctrine, but he must understand why it's necessary!* That's a philosophical understanding which will lead him to strong convictions. Then, God can kick in with His power, His enlightenment, His strength, and His zeal. Once he lights the fire, it will burn according to the logs he throws onto it–his studies, his efforts, and so on. But he has to have that fire to begin with, if he's going to get anywhere!

What about his objection that "You can't teach an old dog new tricks"?

MSGR. R.: The grace of God can overcome that, but it normally happens by means of a really traumatic experience. It's like with people who are used to their own way of doing things, but they want to change, only they really don't know how. They won't change until, for instance, death strikes close to them or their loved ones, because they'll see, for the first time, the shortness of life, the eternity after death, and how they have wasted what little time they have. They see that they'd better get going, or it's going to be too late! Or they can lose it altogether and say they don't care, or "It's too late!" That would be giving in to the temptations of the devil. They simply have to read what the Scripture says: "If a sinner leaves his sin and turns to virtue, I will forget his sins, says the Lord." But, by the same token, "If a man gives up his virtue and turns to sin and evil, I will forget his virtue."

It's the present moment that God looks at, not at the past, not at the future, but at what we're doing here and now. If you say, "I'm sorry," your conversion is good here and now. That's how God's love works. It's like you were holding a spring back by your disobedience, but when you let the spring go by conversion, it bounces right back, just that quickly! That's God's love! You can't measure the infinity of God's love by human standards. The turning of the soul to God is a case of hope and mercy working together. You can teach an old dog new tricks!

But, having said all that, the priest who gets serious about changing is not going to have everything served to him on a platter. He's got to go after it! It's like with studies–if you're not really interested in what you're learning, you'll forget it all, because it doesn't mean that much to you in the first place. But, when you really have to pay the price for something, you're going to keep it. So, let him search; let him work!

It's like I tell my people: "Look! I'm not going to save your soul! I don't save souls–I'll save one, maybe, my own. And you're only going to save one, maybe, your own! But you can't save anyone else's–not your husband's, not your wife's, not your children's, not your relatives', not your friends'. It's one-on-one; the salvation of your soul is on your head. Now, if you want the prize, you have to pay for it. Heaven is not free!" How often I tell our people that! It's not free! "Christ died for you, but you better do your own part now, too!" *So, if it's worth that much to the priest to re-learn what he needs to know, he'll be willing to pay the price.*

What about the "good reason" of obedience, which many priests will put forward as their excuse for staying with the current practices of the Church?

MSGR. R.: They have to understand the "mirror image" of reality, which the devil holds up to confuse us. Everything created contains within itself a potential for good use and a potential for evil use, at the same time. That's where the illusion is. This question of obedience is a good example. There is a true obedience and a false obedience, a true authority and a false authority. The Pope is supreme in his jurisdiction, but his authority is not absolute! He's under God, too, and he may not go against God, even though his authority is supreme on earth. If he tries to do so, his use of authority is invalid–he has no authority to go against God! And we have no obligation to obey in that case.

It's easier to see the point when we bring that principle down to a lower level. Let's say that a pastor oversteps his authority–I don't have to obey him, and, in fact, I may have to oppose him. This has all been brought out in our traditional theological training. But when we refuse to exercise false obedience, we have to be very sure about the principles, and we have to be very careful which side of the fence we end up on. *We can't just decide these questions subjectively–we've got to know the principles and know how to determine whether the superior is within his rights to command.* Otherwise, we're going to end up twisted around somebody's little finger.

What is the weight, in your opinion, of the objection of the priest who is afraid of losing his support if he should refuse this false obedience?

MSGR. R.: He may say, "I'm too old! I'm too sickly, you know!" Well, we have to give consideration to that. But what's in his heart? Does he accept the subversion, or does he reject it but feel forced to abide by his limitations? There are priests who are hung up like that and who say, "I'm too sick! I just cannot do any more." They just survive or get by. But, if they go along with this subversion which is called "the New Theology," or with this practice of making your own hosts out of doubtful matter, their other objections are not authentic.

Some priests have authentic objections but really feel bound by certain limitations. We have to remember that they are not bound to do what's impossible. If it's so difficult for them to break out that it's practically impossible, God will distinguish, so we shouldn't judge them. We'll do the best that we can and leave their judgment to God. But we can't let up on our own efforts.

What will happen to the priest who does decide to "launch out into the deep"? How will he live?

MSGR. R.: Oh, God will provide for him! If he's got intelligence and capacities, even though he may not be able to work with his hands, he would still be able to teach, counsel, serve with prudence and caution a traditional lay group, or if worse comes to worst, he could wash dishes. There are always options; God will provide!

Fr. Graham Walters

Edited Transcript

FR. WALTERS: I went into the seminary in 1955 and studied under the Vincentians in Houston at St. Mary's Seminary. I was ordained in 1963, just before the changes started coming. I was from the local diocese, and it was a co-diocese at that. It was the Diocese of Tulsa-Oklahoma City. We were sent to different seminaries because we didn't have our own seminary here. I was trained totally and fully in the traditional Mass. None of the changes were even foreseen when I was ordained. This all came to me as an utter and absolute shock. When I was in my first assignment in Tulsa, at St. Francis Xavier Church, the first of all these changes appeared in turning the altar around. Then we had what I called the "picnic table on wheels," and the pastor, who was a very dutiful Bostonian Irish Catholic, lived to regret all of this himself. But in those days, you know, we did what we were told to do. The bishop wanted this, and we thought this was what we were supposed to do, so we did it. For my own part, I certainly did it with a lot of grimacing. I was very upset.

So even when you were deacon, they were not preparing you for any of this?

FR. W.: Not at all. The seminary faculty was very old hat, so to speak. Maybe there were some more modern views put forward by the Scripture professor, but the only ominous signs that I ever noticed in the seminary were the occasional visits by clergy from the diocese. They were planting their little ideas and their little seeds. And, of course, many of my classmates were very gung-ho about this. But I was a convert, and this didn't sit well with me at all.

What was the definition of the priesthood which you were given in your formation in the seminary?

FR. W.: The priest is the mediator, the one here on earth in the person of Christ who offers on behalf of Christ (on behalf of the Church) the sacrifice of Calvary. He is the *alter Christus.* This was very explicit in the traditional Mass. Here is the visible celebrant, but the one who is actually celebrating is Jesus Christ. We are but the instruments that He makes use of to extend His Presence in time and place after He ascended into Heaven.

How were you coerced into adopting the changes?

FR. W.: There was a great lack of cooperation on my part, all the way. In fact, in about 1972, the local Archbishop of Oklahoma City, the very young John Raphael Quinn, who was to become the Archbishop of San Francisco and then resign to become a professor at Oxford, told me that something was simply going to *have* to be done with me because my theology wasn't current. Fortunately, I had the presence of mind to thank him! He had very large eyebrows, and I'll never forget his reaction. They just sort of raised up, and his eyes (he had a very intense glare, very beady eyes) looked right through me. I thought, ***"Well, this is not the Church I embraced as a convert, and so I'm not going along with this, which is, for me, a new religion."*** I didn't tell him that at the time, but that was the basis of my position and my thinking.

What was the red flag which suggested to you that this was a new religion?

FR. W.: Well, there were so many red flags! I mentioned to you earlier that I was brought up, not in any zealous way, in the "Christian Church," and then I went on my own to the Episcopal Church, which was the church of my maternal grandparents. I decided I would start going to the Episcopal Church because there was an attraction there, a beauty, a ritual. There was a formality; there was something that the others didn't have that I liked. But then, of course, I started reading more because of my curiosity, and I looked into encyclopedias and histories and what have you, and everywhere I came to see a red flag, except with the Catholic Church. This was the one Church that had the real continuity. Not just that it was there centuries before any of these others –there was no interruption at all in the history of this Church. And I thought, "Well, this is the one that I want to be a part of."

After my conversion, the red flag against the New Mass was this new brand of thinking, this indifferentism, this sloppiness and dumbing-down. Everything became more and more dumbed down from the moment the New Mass came in. Maybe the new liturgy, the New Order, is a charism for the dumbed-down!

I've had, particularly, one priest, only a year out of the seminary, come to visit me. He had studied in Rome for five years. He just came to talk to me and visit with me and to cry on my shoulder about the situation. One of the expressions he used was that everything has been dumbed down. He felt that it was quite a challenge to try to do anything with these people. Again, they have been so downgraded or dumbed down in every way. They come to church dressed in tee shirts, jeans, cut-offs and sandals, with thongs and caps (turned around backwards!) on their heads–you see every kind of thing imaginable. They don't know better, because they've not been taught anything better. And the priests, the clergy, have not taught them anything, because they themselves are dumbed down.

This was totally opposed to everything that I had ever hoped to embrace when I became a Catholic. *What had begun as my greatest love, my greatest joy, became my greatest disappointment.* The Catholic Church as an organization, as an institution, that is to say, the material and human part of what it had become with all of the changes, became the greatest disappointment of my life. Something had to be done in my life, personally, for me not to suffer the same fate as practically every one of my classmates, who left the priesthood after they were ordained in the late sixties. Some of them stayed no more than a year, some even less than that.

As bad as all these preliminary changes were, what happened in 1969 when the New Mass came out? Was this the straw that broke the camel's back?

FR. W.: No, it wasn't, it was just the deepening of a spiritual crisis that I was enduring in my own life. It just added fuel to the fire. I was becoming very much worse than lukewarm–I was indifferent, soured.

Actually 1969 was the year I became a pastor for the first time. And I was put way out in Southwestern Oklahoma, in a remote area. It was a nice parish, as far as the physical plant was concerned. But I was very much alone, and I was very much saddled with this new church. I was very recalcitrant in many ways with regard to what was happening, and the Archbishop, whom I previously mentioned, was very intent upon straightening me out.

I was constantly receiving calls from Helen, the Archbishop's secretary: "The Archbishop would like for you to come to lunch." Well, they had other things to be concerned about than lunch! There were pep talks, what have you. He would give me a brow-beating to try to correct me. So, I would have to get in the car, and I would have to drive ninety miles to have lunch and to be mentally beaten up and to be told my priesthood was going down the tubes. I was down there in the parish by myself. I was doing things with the lovely place (the people were very, very generous, helpful, and supportive). It was a modern-looking church, but I got beautiful things for it. I redid the Blessed Sacrament altar and hung some beautiful tapestries. I got a new tabernacle and a lovely sanctuary lamp to try to bring some focus on the Blessed Sacrament, but none of this sat well with His Excellency. He would come down there and never say a word to encourage me about anything, because I was not a part of this New Order.

Did they send you to seminars for re-education?

FR. W.: They tried to.

And you refused to go?

FR. W.: I would go, until they would become so irksome that I would leave.

And no consequences ever followed your leaving?

FR. W.: Well, I'm sure there were consequences, because I was transferred after only four years. Usually, a pastor would hold a parish for seven or eight years. The Archbishop told me he wanted to move me to a little place in the wheat-fields of Bison, Oklahoma, where there was no operational income, or what have you. That time, I prevailed and was not moved, but the following year there was no discussion about it. He made me a hospital chaplain (for both Baptist Medical Center and Deaconess Hospital in Oklahoma City) and gave me two missions which don't exist any more. So, I did that for five years before finally leaving the archdiocese.

Why don't we speak a little about that?
How did you become determined that you were
going to abandon the New Mass and its new religion?

FR. W.: Well, it goes back a way. Of course, I was prepared in the seminary to say the traditional Mass. And I said it after my ordination for almost a year before the changes started creeping in. At my first parish in Tulsa, we had three priests: six Masses every Sunday, one of which was a solemn high Mass! When I went along with the incremental changes, I found myself groping for something.

I had many people coming to my Mass, and that was probably one of the reasons they wanted to railroad me out, because there was hardly standing room when word got out that Fr. Walters was saying more of a traditional type of Mass. I had Benediction and other functions, you know, in the normal fashion, and the people came. Plus, I preached and tried to give them something substantial when I preached. And the church was full.

Finally, when I was in Altus in the early seventies, I found out what I was groping for. There was a small group of mostly elderly people, pillars of that parish, who were always ready to help out and give whatever was needed. I said to them, "You know, I'd like to say the Latin Mass." "Oh, Father, you would do that?" they replied. I said, "Yes, let's do it!" So we fixed up a little altar in a room next to the parish church. I got all of the necessary items, altar cards, candlesticks, and what have you, and I started saying the traditional Mass down there. I said "You just keep this quiet," but they were the only ones who came to daily Mass anyway.

Things changed drastically, though, when I was put in the hospital chaplaincy. This shows how my own spiritual life went down in a spiral. I was on call twenty-four hours a day, and none of the other priests offered to help me; none was willing to help me. I hardly ever got a vacation. I even carried a beeper (that's why I hate these cell phones hanging on every hip, because I hated those beepers even in the early seventies). I lived at the "Pastoral Center," which was five miles away from the hospitals. I've been to those hospitals twice in the same night: deaths, car accidents, and what have you. I've been into the morgue to see bodies torn asunder, and then gone back and tried to get some sleep. I did that work for five years, and I offered the New Mass in the most horrible chapel which had been set up for the retired priests. No one would even attend my Mass. I must tell you that I just quit saying Mass altogether.

You wouldn't concelebrate with the others?

FR. W.: No, I always detested concelebration. A bunch of nitwits. It's so lackadaisical, so sloppy! They're all standing up there like they're ready for a group photograph. It's so stupid! They don't even know what to do with their hands. It's the silliest conglomeration I ever saw in my life. No, I never concelebrated. And, of course, that just ostracized me even more.

Did saying the New Mass bring your priesthood to this point?

FR. W.: The New Mass almost caused me to lose my faith. It was no charism for me. Maybe it's a charism for some of them, I don't know because I don't know what kind of faith they have, but I don't think it's the true Catholic Faith. ***The New Mass was an obstacle to my Faith, and that is the reason I had to leave.*** I went out into the cold and the dark blindly, but I knew that I had to keep my faith. I had to ask God to lead me, and He led me and showed me the way. It was not easy, but He was with me every step of the way through everything that has been accomplished in the last twenty-two years. (I was seventeen years in the archdiocese.) Every step of the way in this apostolate, I have been blessed. I've had serenity, and peace, and a relationship with God that I did not have while saying the New Mass. I've had silence and time for God to speak to my heart. But when I was in that other situation, I didn't have a chance.

Then, the old Mass protects the priest's faith and helps him to live life as a true priest?

FR. W.: It certainly has been the case for me! I would have gone down the tubes just like all my classmates if I had stayed. A couple of years ago, I went out to see the current Archbishop, and I took him a picture of my ordination, which he had never seen, of course, since it was 1963. There were ten or twelve of us, some of them from different seminaries, and I pointed to this and that priest. He had never heard of them. I told him they were my classmates; they were ordained with me. And I'm the only one left in the priesthood! Two of them studied in Rome. One of them studied in Innsbruck. One of them studied in Louvain. Thank God I didn't go to Rome! I almost went to Rome. My pastor had offered to send me to Rome if I wanted to go, but I said, "I'm an only child, and my mother and father are not well. I don't believe I can go over there and stay four years." So I didn't, and maybe it's good that I didn't!

Those years were so frustrating. I even stopped going to retreats after I went to one at the Benedictine Monastery in Shawnee and walked out at two in the morning because my brother priests were drunk. Of course, the Archbishop called me in and asked, "Why did you leave the retreat?" I said, "You were over in your Bishop's Suite, but I was up in the dormitory, and I couldn't sleep because of all the carousing going on up there. I'm not going back!" And now they're having all these moral problems and what have you among the priests in the diocese. The chickens are all coming home to roost!

Would you say that the current scandals are the result of thirty years of the New Mass?

FR. W.: It's a formal breakdown. When I was in the seminary, there was never even a hint of anything like that. I've read recently this book, *Goodbye, Good Men*. I've been out of all of this since 1980, for twenty-two years, almost twenty-three years, almost a quarter of a century. I have been away from the New Order of things, thanks be to God! But when I read that book, it even shocked me. I knew the situation was bad. I knew a lot of things, but I had never experienced anything or seen anything like that. One of the priests who comes here for confession was ordained in the seventies, and he told me things that certainly verified what Michael Rose had written. He even said that the Prior of the monastery where he was as a deacon had made advances to him.

Their vision of the priesthood is totally different from yours. What do these new priests think they are? What do they think a priest is? What did they try to make you think a priest was when they were trying to update you?

FR. W.: It's an entirely humanistic approach now, you know. There's only a worldly God. And they've debunked and thrown the concept of sin out the window. No wonder they're acting the way they're acting!

Does this new vision of the priesthood come from the New Mass, does the New Mass come from this new vision of the priesthood?

FR. W.: In a way, I think the new religion was already there, and the New Mass just implements it.

Could you discuss some points in the New Mass which embody this new religion?

FR. W.: The notion of sacrifice is left out. "The love of God be with you!" The whole outlook has changed. They have dropped the preparation, the prayers at the foot of the altar. So the priest comes out and says "Good morning." The banality of it all! It's like a caricature of the Mass. And the sloppiness helps in forgetting totally the idea of sacrifice. The Offertory perished completely. I tried so hard to enhance it the best I could, but I didn't have anything to work with.

Is it possible to dress the New Mass up with Latin and incense in such a way as to make it less damaging to the priesthood?

FR. W.: If the true notion of the sacrifice of Calvary is lacking, then all of those enhancements are just window-dressing. The New Mass is absolutely a sow's ear, out of which, as the saying goes, you cannot make a silk purse!

What was the reaction of the archbishop when you left in 1980? Were you suspended?

FR. W.: I was never formally suspended. He wrote me a very rambling letter, which was obviously right off his tongue. It was totally distraught. He said that I was the last one he could ever, ever imagine that would do something like I did. But everything would be fine if I would come back. So that was as far as it ever went. I never had any problem with him. It was very awkward, very difficult for me to leave my two little parishes. But I knew I had to do something, because by staying, I would be just continuing up a blind alley. And it was very dangerous for me. I promised the bishop who ordained me reverence and obedience to him and to his successors. But I never foresaw such a mess!

It was like, when you buy something, you buy what you contract for. You have to be given what you purchased. Well, I bought into something that turned out to be totally different, at least in practice, from what I was ordained for.

You mentioned that the continuity of the Church was one of the main reasons you converted?

FR. W.: That's right. In a thousand years I would never have joined this new religion. I joined the Catholic Church; I didn't join their New Catholic Church or whatever it is. And I never would have. There was nothing about it, and there is nothing about it that could attract me. If it were not for this apostolate, I still couldn't be one of them. I don't know what I would be, but I could not be one of them. I don't have any choice; that's why I'm here.

Archbishop Lefebvre claimed that it is impossible to form a sacrificing priest using the New Mass in the seminary. Would you agree with that statement?

FR. W.: Yes, I would agree with it. As I say, there's just nothing in it for me. It offers nothing to the formation of the priest.

What do you see happening among priests who say the New Mass and who are trying to hold on to the real concept of the priesthood and trying to retain their faith (and help others to do so as well)?

FR. W.: For some of the young priests I know, it's interesting to see that there is a curiosity beginning to arise about the last three or four decades. They are beginning to wonder what is really going on in the Church. But most of the priests who are my age have done this new thing for thirty to forty years, and they believe, you know, that this is the only way. The new way is terribly hard for them to swallow in some cases, but they are committed to it.

Was it very difficult for you to recall the rubrics, the ceremonies of the Mass when you began celebrating it again?

FR. W.: No, it really wasn't, because I had always revered them and cherished them so much. There was only one part of it that was a little bit difficult for a while–you get a little rusty with the Latin pronunciation. At first, you know, that was a little bit difficult, but I always loved Latin, and so that was really the only obstacle that I had (and it wasn't all that much of an obstacle).

If there were any advice that you could give to a priest who is frustrated and questioning whether something must be done differently in his priestly life, what would that piece of advice be?

FR. W.: We have our Faith, and God is going to help us. He assured us that if we trust in Him, He will help us, and I think that He will—I'm sure that He will. We're His children, He loves us, and He will lead us through the storm. There *will* be a period of storm, but there will follow a period of calm. It's a very difficult thing, the situation right now with those that are supposed to be in authority. I have visited with the authorities; I talked with them about trying to resolve some of these things, but I don't believe there is any human resolution to it. I've dealt with the *Ecclesia Dei* Commission, and it's like going up against a brick wall. Visiting with the Local Ordinary, you might as well be from Mars, or Jupiter or some place. We are not two peas in a pod; we don't see things the same way at all. *Ecclesia Dei* is going to be a flop, and I think it's designed that way. There is no way for us traditional priests to function under a New Order bishop, and until the Church gives us bishops of our own, till we have our own jurisdiction, our own autonomy, it won't work. I have believed ever since I left the archdiocese that that is the only solution, and I continue to believe it. In time, I know God will work this out, because He's in charge, He's in control, and we aren't. In His time and in His way and in His plan, it will be done.

In the meantime, it's been taken care of. There are places like this chapel; there is the Society of St. Pius X. It's growing! Rome recognizes that, and Rome appreciates power (that's the *only* thing she recognizes as important right now: it's not faith, it's power and prestige). In a way, it's not surprising; it's just the human side of the Church. She is One, Holy, Catholic, Apostolic, and *human*. There is a human side to the Church, and we have to deal with it. But with God working at our side, I know it will work out. In my own little, minuscule microcosm here, that's the way it's always been. It's been uphill all the way, but it's UP, at least—always greater progress. Praise God, He did impossible things, it seemed like. We had the whole neighborhood against us, you know, when we were trying to build our church. We put it in God's hands, and He took care of it. Then, how to come up with the money for the church? He took care of it. I put a great deal of my own inheritance in it. God provided for it at the right time; He made it available. He's making it possible now that I can regain some of it so that I will have something, eventually, to live on in my old age. But I'm not worried about it because God is taking care of it all the way. If we had tried to do it all ourselves and control it ourselves, it couldn't have been done. He and the Blessed Mother did it. We put it in their hands, let them call the shots and decide the time frame, and they did it. I've never seen anything like it.

Have you ever seen a traditional priest go hungry or go without a place to say Mass?

FR. W.: No, no, never. And they are mushrooming up all over the place. So we are here to just steer the ship for the time being. The New Order is corrupt, and it will rot of its own accord; it will self-destruct.

Some priests will object, "You can't teach an old dog new tricks. It's impossible for me to learn the traditional Mass, the Latin, the theology and philosophy." How would you answer that?

FR. W.: Oh, you can learn anything! I was from a Protestant background, and when I came into the Catholic Church, I didn't know *what* was going on! I saw this large congregation bobbing up and down, kneeling here and standing there and following missals in Latin and what have you. I didn't know any Latin, but I got a missal and started listening. Then I started reading, and I started following the Mass in Latin. I was a teenager! I took Latin in High School, and I almost flunked, because I had never learned to study properly, but I put my nose to the grindstone, and I kept with it. I started learning and doing a lot better with it. Obviously, it was a challenge, but it's good to give the intellect a challenge!

You know, the main point was that I was in love with something in the Church that attracted me very, very much, and I was willing to make the effort. I didn't know what it was all about, but I learned, and I think if I could do that as a fourteen-year-old boy, someone older, someone who is already a priest, could do at least as well. We are supposed to be intelligent beings, so we can learn. If we are convinced of the authenticity, the integrity, and the truthfulness of something, then we have to go for it and embrace it with our very being.

To contact Fr. Walters:

Rev. Fr. Graham Walters
Post Office Box 12183
Oklahoma City, OK 73157-2183
Phone: (405) 752-0004

FR. PAUL WICKENS

FR. WICKENS: I was ordained in 1955. The Church was relatively healthy then, although she can always use internal improvement, or "reform," if you want to call it that. Unfortunately, what happened was a revolution, it wasn't a reform. So we threw out the baby with the bath-water, you might say.

Everything was going along smoothly, and, when Vatican II was convened in 1962, we were not suspicious. We had an orthodox bishop, as most of the bishops were, as far as we knew. So, then, little changes came in the Mass during the sixties, and we were told that they were good, that they were going to increase conversions, that it was going to be good for the youth, that it would increase vocations. But, of course, you and I know that just the opposite happened.

The goal of the people who promoted these things, *i.e.,* the modernists, was not really to make merely superficial changes. They actually wanted to make substantial changes. As Fr. Crane, in England, said, they couldn't attack doctrine directly, so they attacked the expression of the doctrine.

We would get notices from the Chancery office: the *Confiteor* would be in English, and the Prayers at the Foot of the Altar would be in English. But the traditional Mass was still intact. Then, of course, in 1969, the New Mass, the "Normative Mass" as it was called, came into existence. Personally, *I had funny feelings about it, but I didn't express them, because we were brought up to have trust in our superiors.*

What was the root of your "funny feelings"?

FR. W.: One root was that there was less reverence, and another was that doctrine was ambiguously expressed.

Can you give some examples?

FR. W.: Yes, no one ever denied that the Mass was a holy sacrifice, but it wasn't mentioned very much. The liberals, the Modernists, would ignore the primary effect of the sacraments and just talk about the secondary effects. For example, with Baptism: it's only an initiation for them. Well, it *is* that, but that aspect is further down the line. Primarily, the effect of Baptism is the removal of Original Sin, the conferral of Sanctifying Grace, and it makes one eligible to receive the other sacraments. It's the same for the Mass: they talk about the meal part of it and don't talk about the re-enactment of Calvary, the Holy Sacrifice.

Certainly, the Mass *is* a sacred banquet, like one of the most beautiful Eucharistic antiphons says: "*O sacrum convivium, in quo Christus sumitur, recolitur memoria Passionis ejus, mens impletur gratia, et futuræ gloriae nobis pignus datur.*" (O sacred banquet, in which Christ is consumed, the memory of His Passion is recalled, and a pledge of future glory is given to us.) But they leave out the fact that Christ is offered in sacrifice.

Also, the changes were a departure from our traditional piety: there were fewer genuflections, and there was more noise and external activity going on. It wasn't any longer a quiet, reverent act of worship.

And so, I had funny feelings about it, from the get-go. But I didn't verbalize them. I know that there a few priests who said, "No, this is wrong!" And, of course, if you go and read the famous *Ottaviani Intervention*, it said, even before the New Mass was issued officially, that it would lead to Protestantism, that it was a radical departure from the doctrine of the Council of Trent, *etc.*

I think it was the *sensus catholicus* which made me have the "funny" feelings. That's a certain way we think and act, a certain way our feelings are directed to God. This New Mass was a departure from that. But I did not refuse the *Novus Ordo*. I said it for a period of, well, let's see, almost fourteen years. And, as you know, we were softened up for this by the little changes that came before. If you objected to change or you wanted to be able to say the old Mass, well, "It's human nature to be slow to change," they retorted.

The Modernists who were in control of the chanceries and the liturgical committees would continually promote it, and, pretty soon, even though you might have had an aversion towards it at first, you'd begin to tolerate it, and then you'd embrace it. Of course, many people had an aversion to it and didn't tolerate it. They either left the Church or became lukewarm Catholics.

They didn't have the strength to fight?

FR. W.: Yes, you know, it's the frog in the water thing: he'll stay there until he cooks, as long as the temperature is only turned up little by little. Well, during the next decade, other things came in, like Communion in the hand and concelebration. And I knew these things were not approved by the Vatican at the time. A group of priests in our diocese, who were gung-ho for the changes, got together and had these little workshops. They were unofficial; they were not sponsored by the diocese, but they'd get together a workshop for three or four days and invite nuns and priests, and liberal priests would give lectures. (Almost every one of those priests left the priesthood, almost every one of them!) They were so enthusiastic about these things, and they'd marginalize you and make you feel as if you were not going along with the times. "You're not up-to-date. You're not modern!" That's how teenagers get caught up in drugs and things like that. And they used the same principle for adults. It's called "peer pressure."

I *did* draw the line at Communion in the hand. So, when that came in, I said, "I'm not going to do it! I'm going to follow the principle by which they got into power, which was to 'follow your conscience.'" I was curate in a relatively small parish at the time, and I announced that it was against my conscience to give Communion in the hand, but if anyone insisted on it, the pastor would take care of them after Mass. We never had a problem with it. Nobody ever insisted. ***People follow the leadership of their priest on the parish level.***

Even when we had a non-parish Mass, such as a wedding or a funeral, and visitors would put out their hands, I would simply place the Host towards their mouth, and they would comply. (There were probably one or two exceptions, like some feminist or a very militant nun might take me on and turn and walk out, but I never fought with anybody.)

But then we went on priests' retreats, and they started to concelebrate. During the concelebrations, they made a big thing out of the "Prayers of the Faithful." They'd go around, and people began to editorialize, as it were, politically. "That we get out of that terrible Vietnam War, let us pray to the Lord!" Then I would say, "That we stay in the war to defeat the Communists, let us pray to the Lord!!" It was ridiculous that they would editorialize like that. I was not yet a Traditionalist, but I felt we had to do something about this. We could not let the liberals win.

I had some lay people behind me, and so we decided to combat this Liberalism. I went to the diocesan newspaper and asked if I could put in some conservative columns, and they were seemingly gracious about it and said that I should send in some samples, which I did. Well, they never called me. They appeared to be "democratic" and to want to hear all sides of the question, but they really didn't. You know, Liberals believe in "diversity" in everything except when it comes to allowing orthodox views!

So, I began to object publicly. We started a newsletter called *New Jersey Catholic News,* with a small circulation, but it grew and grew. The idea was to point out the lies of the Modernists.

Why couldn't the diocesan paper tolerate your kind of "diversity"?

FR. W.: Because of morals. That's the bottom line, it's morals! The bottom line in business is money, and the bottom line with religious people is morality. They don't want anybody telling them that fornication is wrong or that pornography is wrong or that birth control is wrong (it's usually sins against the Sixth and Ninth Commandments). They don't want anyone to tell them they have to go to Mass. They don't want anybody to tell them they have to be unselfish. So, even if they want to be pure or unselfish, well, they don't want to be told to be. They just want life to be devoid of higher laws and higher authority. That's why they're opposed to things like heaven and hell.

And they're opposed to the old Mass on the same grounds?

FR. W.: Oh, very much so. They hate the old Mass. I'll give you an example of this, it just happened this last week. Some of the people who come here to Mass sometimes are not solid traditionalists. They just live nearby. They like the priest, or they like the St. Anthony statue, but they're not theologians. They're just good people. So, two of these people happened to go to a Saturday evening Mass at a parish in the next town. A new pastor was being installed that night, and he stood at a receiving line at the back of the Church, while these people congratulated him on his new post. "We don't come here very often, because we go to our *own* parish," they said. "Where *is* your parish?" (You know, the famous question.) "Oh, we go to St. Anthony's with Fr. Wickens." Well, the priest had a fit, actually. He held up the line for ten minutes, and ranted and raved that Fr. Wickens was against God, against the Pope. And he went on until he almost said that everything at St. Anthony's Church was invalid. They don't use the word "invalid" at all, except with us! They don't use the word "obedience," except with us. They don't even *believe* in those concepts.

I wrote him a note, and I said, "Let's get together," but he's not going to respond to the note. If these people had said to him, "Father, we go to a Lutheran church," he would have said, "Oh, God bless you, my child! You just follow your conscience, and go to the Lutheran Church!" Or, if they had said, "You know, Father, we own a topless bar," he would have said, "Well, that's perfectly all right." Everything is okay, except Tradition, because Tradition is a protest against their way of life, which is self-centered.

And, by the way, all these *Novus Ordo* parishes are dying. These people who reported to me said that there were only fifty people there that day. I remember this church; it was the mother church of the area, covering a huge area. They had fifty people at Mass where they used to get five hundred. I know that people are more mobile now, and all that, but, nevertheless, whole generations have been lost to the Faith.

As a case in point: I was reading a diocesan paper from a bishop in Texas who's supposed to be reasonably conservative. He seems like a pretty good guy, but, if you read his publication, he's talking about the loss of the faith among the Hispanics. The reason he gives for this loss of faith is that they haven't heard about Vatican II yet! It's just the opposite–Vatican II destroyed their faith! *After Vatican II, there were no vocations, there were no traditional Masses, there was no traditional teaching, so people slipped away from the Faith.*

But he says a lot of people have become Protestants because they haven't heard the good news of Vatican II! What good news? That if you are divorced and re-married you can still go to Communion?

Is the New Mass killing the parishes, or are the parishes killing what's left of the Mass?

FR. W.: Good question, let's see... The *Novus Ordo* Mass is killing the parishes. You see, the *Novus Ordo* Mass, besides being ambiguous, also changed the way people look at responsibility. We went to Mass, I would say, in the old days, because it was *our duty*. We went to keep holy the Lord's Day, to fulfill the Third Commandment and the Precept of the Church to attend Mass. I went to Mass because it pleased *God*, and not because it pleased *me*. What they did with the liturgical changes was to switch that around. "Go to Mass because we have guitar music and a lot of other shenanigans. Go so you will enjoy it!" So they go to Mass now because of their enjoyment, their pleasure, their satisfaction.

Consequently, when the thrill of it eventually dissipated, as must happen, then there was no sense of obligation left. "Oh, I'm not going to *that* Mass, because it's not entertaining, or because it's dull, or because there is no folk music." People used to say things like that to me: "Hey, that was a good Mass, Father!" Can you *imagine* Christians in the first century saying to St. Paul or St. Peter, "Hey, that was a good Mass, St. Paul! I'd rather go to your Mass than St. John's!" The New Mass took away the sense of duty, obligation, and worship from the Catholics' way of thinking. *And so the reason why these parishes are going down in attendance is because the majority of the people don't think they have to go to Mass unless they get some emotional satisfaction from it, and that's not enough to bring people to Mass.*

It's too subjective?

FR. W.: It's just like a guy going to work to raise his family. If he thinks the only reason he goes to work is to get some emotional satisfaction out of it, he'll end up not going to work at all. The Liberals did things that had an immediate, (seemingly good) effect on people's enthusiasm, like a guitar Mass or hootenanny Mass. It was "entertaining," it was enjoyable, and people were talking about it. But these things had a disastrous long-range effect.

To give you a parallel: if children come home from school and say, "Mommy, I'm hungry," a *good* mother would say, "Here's a glass of milk and a peanut-butter sandwich. That will hold you over till supper." Now, a *Liberal* mother would say, "Okay, I'm going to give you candy and ice cream," and the kids would say, "Oh, Mommy, you're wonderful! We love you more than the lady who just gives us milk and peanut-butter sandwiches!" But the sweets and the jelly beans and the twinkies and everything that the liberal mother gives them, will fill those kids up and make them happy, but it will deteriorate their health and their teeth.

So, that's the way it happened with these changes. There was a seemingly good immediate effect, there was a blip of enthusiasm on the radar screen, but then everything went down the tubes and stayed down. What they're doing in the parishes is getting almost ludicrous. They try tricky things to get people back: they put banners up, "Come on home!" or they change the confessional box so you can "rap" one-on-one, face to face.

The Pope even has these youth rallies! Here are these kids at World Youth Day who don't even know the Ten Commandments, they don't know the Apostles' Creed, they don't know the Precepts of the Church, but there's a lot of enthusiasm that doesn't have any long-range effects at all. *None of these changes in the Church had any long-range good effects, but they had long-range fatal effects and changed the way Catholics were thinking.*

The ones who engineered all this were Liberals, and they've made Catholics into Liberals. The etymological meaning of *liberalism* comes from the word *freedom*, and the Liberal wants to be free from any laws or restraints. In order to be "free" like that, they had to build a whole theology and philosophy of freedom. It's not just the Mass; it's not just one thing! Liberals crave freedom in doctrine, but especially in morals.

Your comment about a man not going to work unless it made him feel good seems to apply to the priests you spoke of, who left the priesthood after having led the focus groups during the changes in the Church. Is that why they left the priesthood?

FR. W.: Yes, I think so. They left the priesthood because, first of all, they didn't like the confinement of the priesthood. They didn't like celibacy any longer. See, we were told over and over at these workshops that, unless you're married, you're not really a full person. As a matter of fact, at these workshops, there were nuns and priests holding hands and dancing! ("There's nothing wrong with dancing....") was a common mantra.) See, the Liberals shot down the idea of Original Sin and the effects of Original Sin, which are the Seven Capital Sins. So, if you *want* to practice celibacy in imitation of our Lord Jesus Christ and the Apostles, well, you can't do those things such as dancing and dating and holding hands and showing physical affection, because human nature is prone to the Seven Capital Sins. Rather than keeping a check on these inclinations, that behavior would encourage them.

Is it fair to say that the New Mass keeps the priest from worrying so much about the Seven Capital Sins, for instance, whereas the old Mass makes him be more careful because he's more aware of what he is?

FR. W.: The New Mass eliminates the idea of sacrifice. "The fear of the Lord is the beginning of Wisdom." It's like with a building. If you don't have the foundation, that building is coming down. Our foundation is the fear of the Lord. You don't have religion without it. If you don't have fear of the Lord, you don't consider our Lord as the Supreme Being, the Judge of the living and the dead. Then you must have to admit that you really don't have true religion. You don't look *up* to God. Michael Davies said Modernists are atheists. They don't really believe in God! Oh, they might use the word "God," but it's only a word.

How did you come back to offering the traditional Mass?

FR. W.: Well, that will take some telling! The bishop didn't really like the fact that we were exercising "freedom of the press" with our newsletter, because we were critical of various diocesan policies, and the new catechisms, and the crazy liturgies and so forth. Then, it came to a boiling point when the State of New Jersey made it mandatory to have sex-ed in grades K through twelve. Along with a lot of other citizens, I objected to that, and we went down to the State Capital. We got down there, and who was lobbying for it, but the Catholic bishops! They were lobbying for classroom sex-ed! My bishop didn't like the fact that I ran into some of his lobbyists on the floor of the Senate. They were promoting sex-ed, and I was objecting to it. One of the bishop's lobbyists screamed at me on the floor of the State Senate, you know. The bishop was out to get me after that, but I didn't care.

I belonged to a little group of people who objected to sex-ed, and we called a press conference. I was the spokesman, and I said, "If this sex-ed goes through to the Catholic schools, we have to boycott the parishes!" Well, I had said the magic word, "boycott." The next day (this was in 1983), I got a letter of transfer. I was ordered to leave the place where I had been for twenty-eight years. I had all kinds of things going on, but I was supposed to be out in six days! So I said, "I can't be out in six days!" Then the bishop took off, and went to the Caribbean for a month of vacation.

(It was Ash Wednesday, by the way. Remember that the Liberals never lack for "creature comforts," and that's why they like to become pastors and bishops—because they get their hands on the Dough, Ray, Me! They live high, like kings, really. Oh, but they pretend to love the poor! But they don't! They don't live with the poor, like the Saints did. As a matter of fact, they probably make fun of them behind their backs.)

So, the bishop transferred me, but I couldn't get hold of him since he was out of the country. I decided to apply for an early retirement. So, when the bishop came back, he said, "Just leave the rectory, and we'll look into it." I called a Canon lawyer, and he said *not* to leave the rectory, because otherwise I would never get a hearing. The bishop threatened me with suspension if I was not out of the rectory in ten days. So, after ten days, I was officially out of the parish, but I stayed there in residence for a year. I forced him to evict me!

Was it during this time that you first said the traditional Mass again?

FR. W.: I had two rooms in the rectory. Since I could not use the church, I said the traditional Mass there in my room. *As soon as I celebrated the traditional Mass, light bulbs lit up over my head!* I saw that the New Mass was really the crux of all the problems in the Church. To get rid of the Mass of all times was the major victory of the Modernists. And I never went back to the New Mass after that.

After almost fourteen years, were you able to say the old Mass just like that, without any difficulties?

FR. W.: It all came back immediately, immediately! In the days following I started getting phone calls. As a matter of fact, one of the Society (SSPX) priests came to the rectory to see me. I wasn't able to see him, because the Pastor wasn't being very nice at the time to people who were looking for me. He just said, "I don't know where he is," and then slammed the door or hung up the phone. This SSPX priest came with a couple of seminarians, because he had read about my situation in the newspapers.

I got a call from some of the faithful I knew who were dissatisfied with the New Mass, and I began to say the traditional Mass at their chapel, which was about fifty miles away. I continued to live in the rectory, and I even had some converts under instruction there. I continued to do that until I was evicted, and then I rented a small building and offered Mass there for about three years. We had about fifty to seventy people coming, and then someone offered us a large American Legion building with more parking, which was better situated. We were able to add a second Mass, which immediately doubled and then tripled the attendance because of the convenience of the situation. We stayed there for quite a while, until we raised the money and built the current chapel on three and a half acres here.

What is the difference, for the priest, between offering the New Mass and offering the old Mass?

FR. W.: Other people have said it before, but the immediate impression with the old Mass is that it is God-centered; it is the worship of God. This is not just playing around; it's not just feelings or emotions. To quote St. Augustine, our hearts were ever restless, but now they're no longer restless because they are directed towards our Creator and our Savior. *I felt clean and purified, like I was doing what I had been ordained to do.* And this feeling was just an added prize–the real prize was in worshipping the Holy Trinity and gaining the graces that were there for the asking.

The traditional Mass expresses just about every major truth in the Catholic Faith. The *Novus Ordo* doesn't express them clearly at all. It's like a silly little performance that you're going through. Some people think it's only the Mass that we're interested in, but it's all Catholic doctrine and morals. When you get going in Tradition again, you have greater appreciation for the Scriptures than ever before. You have greater appreciation for the saints, the lives of the saints. And you start learning things that you didn't learn much about before, like about St. Pius X and his fight against Modernism.

What is a priest in the *Novus Ordo* context?

FR. W.: Well, I haven't been in the *Novus Ordo* for almost twenty years now, but I know in that, in twenty years, they've slid further down the slippery slope of Liberalism, and there's hardly any real priestly work done at all in the parishes now. In the parishes that I'm familiar with, the priests are not on duty–they're gone all day, almost every day. They don't instruct converts. They don't instruct for Confirmation or for First Communion. *The priesthood is kind of a feel-good thing now. It's almost like a weak form of Anglicanism.* Everybody is nice, and they're shaking hands, and it's so nice to go to Mass, but no one has any sense of obligation. There is a tremendous amount of inactivity in the dioceses. Don't get me wrong: we all have the inclination to be slothful, obviously. But they seem to think it's okay to give in to that inclination. We don't, because it would bother our conscience, and we'd have to go to confession.

But they stay busy running around to meetings, don't they?

FR. W.: Even that has diminished a lot. A lot of those changes that came in like a lion have gone out like a lamb. I remember when they changed the confessionals. Oh, they were going to make it possible to go to confession in person, face to face. There was a lot enthusiasm about it, and they spent thousands of dollars changing the confessionals into "reconciliation rooms." That was a waste, because hardly anybody goes to confession any more.

Another good example is the parish councils. I was there when parish councils came in. "Oh, this is the greatest thing in the Church–parish councils!" You'd have an election every other year, but that's all dead and gone. It's great on paper, but parish councils don't mean a thing.

The priests are keeping active in things that are unimportant. Human nature is that way–they want to feel they are accomplishing something. You can see this with the Liberals, the Hollywood types. They don't want to keep the Ten Commandments, but they want to look busy, so they'll save the whales or something like that, you know. All these things are substitutes for the Faith.

You see the same thing in the Church. All these little programs are just *substitutes* for the true Faith. But, in practice, there's a tremendous amount of sloth, materialism, and sensuality. Unfortunately the secular media are revealing much of this moral corruption.

Would you say that's a result of the New Mass?

FR. W.: Yes, it's connected with the New Mass, definitely, because there's no more fear of the Lord left in the New Mass. Now, we're males, we have red blood in our veins, and we know there's temptation out there. But the love of God and the fear of God keep us from falling into these things. But, if you remove the fear of the Lord and the love of God (or even if you spell it "l-u-v"), what's going to stop you from falling? Not only is there no fear of the Lord, there is no objective moral law at all. If you just "follow your conscience," and there's no Law that's based on the Divine Essence, which is unchangeable, everything's up for grabs! The average *Novus Ordo* priest doesn't think about that. In the seminary, they only get little workshops on the sacraments, not real moral theology.

Does this subjective morality come out in the confessional?

FR. W.: The priests don't even want to hear confessions. A priest friend of mine, who is still with the *Novus Ordo* and doing the best he can, went over to a local university to go to confession. So he went into the chapel. The priest who was the confessor for that day was in a back pew wearing a yellow cardigan and reading the newspaper. "Excuse me, Father, can I go to confession?" "What do you want to go to confession for?" "Well, I want to get absolution, you know." "All right, I guess you just want to hear that God still loves you. Okay, come on in." They don't even think about forgiveness of sins! Confession is just a reassurance that God loves us. It's not a cleansing, it's not purgative, it doesn't forgive your sins. It's so far gone!

How have your classmates fared with the changes in the Church?

FR. W.: I've been ordained for forty-five years. I went to a class reunion. My priest confreres don't see a problem. They just don't understand what we're fighting about. They don't understand that we are called the *Church Militant* for a reason! These are men all trained in the 1950's, like I was, ordained in 1955! They said things to me like, "Why don't you come back to the Church?" or "lighten up." They refuse to be concerned about the loss of grace and salvation.

Do they have the fear of the Lord?

FR. W.: No, they don't. That's it! If I could pinpoint any one thing about the destruction of the Church since Vatican II, I would say that getting rid of the fear of the Lord is the key. St. Theresa of Avila had a vision of hell, and she said that that was the thing that kept her on the straight and narrow.

Could you pinpoint some of the areas in the old Mass which help to establish the priest in the fear of the Lord and some of the areas in the New Mass that take away this fear?

FR. W.: The traditional Mass starts right off with the *Confiteor*, quote, "through my fault, through my fault, through my most grievous fault." The whole atmosphere of the traditional Mass is that Christ died for our sins and saved us. What is He saving us from? Hell! Our posture at the Mass expresses fear, reverential fear of the Lord.

There are eleven genuflections in the traditional Mass. There are three, I think, left in the *Novus Ordo*. The most significant genuflections are left out at the Consecration. In the traditional Mass, when the priest bows over the altar and says the words of Consecration, what does he do? He genuflects *immediately*; he recognizes the Divinity present on the altar. In the *Novus Ordo* they don't do that. They say the words, then they elevate, and *then* they genuflect.

One day, I was talking to a priest friend of mine, who was falling for the "Spirit of Vatican II." We were just sitting around having a cup of coffee, and I said, "Oh boy, I'm grateful to my Guardian Angel for such and such." He said, "You don't believe in angels, do you?" So, at that moment, I knew there was a chasm between us. Because, you see, they don't believe in angels, but why don't they believe in angels? It comes back to the fear of the Lord, because if there are good angels, there are bad angels. Where are the bad angels? They're in hell. And why are they in hell? Because they disobeyed God. So, in order to eliminate the fear of the Lord, you have to eliminate a lot of things that lead to that, including the angels! It's the domino effect. One doctrine after another topples.

Why do these Modernists challenge the creation story in Genesis? To them it is a "myth," because it involves the disobedience of Adam and Eve, because of which they lost Paradise! "Well, that's just a myth, you know! God doesn't hover over you. God doesn't worry about what you do. He just wants peace in the world and for people to be nice to one another." Modernists have no idea of the moral law! or obedience! or culpability!

But "the fear of the Lord is the beginning of Wisdom." Holy Scripture teaches that; it's nothing we invented. You must fear God, as we say in the Act of Contrition, "Because I dread the loss of heaven and the pains of hell." They've changed that around, too. Now, it's "Because I fear Your just punishments," and pretty soon they'll water that down, too. It's always the slippery slope to disbelief, one denial or ambiguity at a time.

Some would object that the New Mass can be acceptable when said in its official form, without abuses, but you disagree. Why?

FR. W.: You know, I did say the *Novus Ordo* Mass once since 1983! Here's how it happened. In 1985 or 1986, a group of traditional priests got together (organized by Fr. Le Blanc, from Arizona) for a one-day convention in Chicago. One of our resolutions was that we should go to Rome (we were a little naive then!) and put some pressure on the authorities. Our attitude was "If only the Pope knew what's going on, he'd do something about it."

I was the first one to go. Somebody contributed some money for the plane fare, and so I journeyed to Rome. Then, someone from the Society of St. Pius X house in Albano picked me up at the airport and was supposed to take me to stay there, right outside Rome. But it turned out that my second cousin, who was a German nun living in Rome, asked me to stay at her convent. I stayed there finally, because Albano is too far out from the city.

We made connections to a priest who was able to arrange attendance at the Pope's daily Mass. The Vatican monsignor directed me: "You come to the bronze door tomorrow morning, and bring your alb and stole." I asked why. "You're a *priest*, aren't you?" he said. When I got there, there were about ten visiting priests. We went up to a sacristy, put on our albs and stoles, and concelebrated with the Pope!

You did? What was it like?

FR. W.: I was not impressed by that Mass at all, which was a *Novus Ordo* Mass, of course. A Spanish nun read the Epistle. There was not a lot of nonsense, but it was still enough to show me the deficiencies of the New Mass, even at its best. I actually concelebrated Mass with the Vicar of Christ! Well, you'd think that would have had some kind of an impact on me, but I just felt a big emptiness. It just seemed so shallow. I thought, "It's a shame that the Pope is celebrating this Mass."

So, even when said in the most conservative form possible, even in that very conservative papal chapel, the New Mass was not acceptable?

FR. W.: No, because it was not God-centered. After it's over, you take off your alb and stole, and you come into a large living-room, and the Pope comes in and goes to each person, shakes his hand, and gives him a Rosary. He says a couple of words to each of them. The *Osservatore Romano* photographer was there, snapping pictures like crazy. They give you the chance to buy your photos if you want to. I was in four or five pictures, so I bought a number of them and brought them home and had them reproduced and dropped out of a plane all over the Archdiocese! What do you mean I don't acknowledge the Pope?

No, I do respect the Pope, but I feel sorry for him, not because of his old age, but because he doesn't enforce whatever rules he makes. Well, I know I wouldn't want to be in his shoes, because this is a time of crisis, a real crisis!

There isn't one diocese in the United States of America (and probably not one parish) that teaches integral Catholicism. All the statistics have proven that, because the churches are empty. We have only 40 seminarians in this diocese. The Jesuits have maybe that many, but they used to ordain about 200 or so every year!

How would you answer the objection that traditional priests are being disobedient by clinging to the old ways?

FR. W.: How are we being disobedient? Since Vatican II, the priests and bishops don't want to do combat with the modern world any more. It's like being in a stream: you can't float with the current, or you will be taken downstream. If you want to cross the stream, you have to actually fight against the current, and that's what a priest has to do. The current we had to fight against used to be just the World, the Flesh and the Devil, but now it's the Church itself, Modernism in the Church, which was summarily condemned by St. Pius X. That takes effort, it really takes effort!

Some traditional priests even quit and go back to the *Novus Ordo*. They get tired of being disliked. Archbishop Lefebvre said that the Modernists use "obedience" to the authorities to promote disobedience to God. This is the handy little cliché they use: "You've got to obey your bishop." What law is there? What Church law says that, if you say the old Mass, it's a mortal sin? I don't think there is one! So, if there is no sin at all, which is basically what they say now, how can we sin by saying the traditional Mass?

Now, when my bishop suspended me, I didn't advertise the fact, because people would have thought I had done something wrong. I went to the Canon lawyer of the diocese, and I said, "Isn't it true that a censure such as excommunication or suspension is an added penalty the Church puts onto an existing grave sin, in order to accentuate its gravity? What grave sin did I commit?" "You have not sinned," he said. I said, "Well, I must have a sin–mortal, venial, or something, to have an extra penalty put on top of it!" "No sin that I can see," he said. It's just a joke! They play with words. They label you, like they labeled Archbishop Lefebvre and the bishops he consecrated.

If Rome says, "You're excommunicated," or "You're suspended," the faithful, the innocent lambs out there say, "Well, he must have done something wrong!" How can you defend yourself against that? The more you try to defend yourself, the worse you look. Mark Twain said something like that: "Don't worry if you're losing an argument, just call your opponent names!"

When I was "dialoguing" with the local bishop, he'd never discuss orthodoxy, or sex-ed, or the Mass. He would just say, "You've got to obey your bishop!" But we don't have to obey our bishops in those cases! We are not obliged on pain of sin to obey our bishops. But they make us think that we are. There is a principle of jurisprudence; no human law binds in a case of grave reason or if a higher law prevails. Divine laws we must *always* observe. Human laws depend on the circumstances.

How would you advise the priest who wants to be true to Tradition but missed the traditional formation in his seminary studies?

FR. W.: Some of the younger priests think that they would have to know Latin to come to Tradition, and that scares them a little bit. ***If we meet a priest who is sympathetic towards Tradition, we have to try and get him to start saying the Mass***. He doesn't have to understand Latin. Just like an opera singer who sings beautiful Verdi arias doesn't have to be conversant in Italian, the priest doesn't have to know Latin perfectly. Latin is the easiest language to pronounce, and you don't have to speak in Latin, you just have to recite it.

How would you reassure the priest who is worried about his support if he stops saying the New Mass?

FR. W.: I never worried about money, because I knew God would provide. I didn't have any salary, or insurance, or anything like that when I was dismissed. But I wasn't *that* broke, because I came from a big family, and I knew I could always fall back on a sister or brother. Once in a while you get a priest from another country, from India or the Philippines, who seems to be overly concerned about his support. That's because they have no safety net. Somebody from America can always fall back on a brother, or a cousin, or someone.

I would say that *Novus Ordo* priests usually don't want to face the fact that they should come back to Tradition because their fear of losing two things: *money* and *reputation*. They are afraid of losing their reputations. When you say the old Mass, you can become a sort of pariah among your family; they just don't understand. You would also become unwelcome in other parishes, because you'd get labeled. People are afraid to get labeled. That's a normal reaction, but we can't let these fears keep us from doing our duty before God.

If they are afraid of losing their sustenance, well, they just have to trust in God. They have to believe what Christ said, that "The foxes have their holes, and the birds their nests, but the Son of Man has no place to lay His head." They really have to take that chance. Priests are kind of afraid to "launch out into the deep." They really are. But I don't know of a single case where a traditional priest didn't have a place to lay his head! It always seems that the traditional lay people come through, because they have great respect for priests.

The traditional people are just wonderful—the sacrifices they make! They bring their kids here. They travel an hour or two to get to the sacraments. They contribute generously.

We opened this church six years ago, and it took two years to build it. When we started, we didn't have that much money, but it's amazing, the generosity of the people! There's an old saying: "Dig a hole, and people will start contributing." They know that something positive is being done, and so they don't mind giving. We had a big mortgage, but it was paid off in three years.

Yes, the people are a great inspiration to us priests. If I decided to leave my parish, give up my work, and go fishing every day, I'd never save my soul, so I'm not going to do that! The people need their priests, and that helps the priest to see how important his priesthood is. If I retired, I'd still have my Mass and my Breviary, but the people don't have that—they need the priests; they need us. That's the way God made it, that the *alter Christus* is the mediator between God and man.

To contact Fr. Wickens:

Rev. Fr. Paul Wickens
1360 Pleasant Valley Way
West Orange, NJ 07052-1313
Phone: (973) 325-2233

FR. WILLIAM YOUNG

EDITED TRANSCRIPT
What year were you ordained, Father?

FR. YOUNG: I was ordained in 1976, but my road to the priesthood started back when I entered the Dominican Order in 1960, after I graduated from college.

But you didn't stay with the Dominicans?

FR. Y.: No. I got a scholarship to go back to Catholic University of America, and I was torn between becoming a Dominican and continuing my studies outside the order. I decided that I wanted a degree that would be recognized in secular areas, and the Dominicans, at that time, only offered degrees which were recognized within their own communities. So, I went back to Catholic University and got my graduate degree in philosophy.

In what kind of Philosophy?

FR. Y.: Don't forget that all of my studies before the seminary were in a pre-Vatican II context, before the Revolution. At that time, Catholic colleges were still really Catholic. My undergraduate work, at the University of San Francisco between 1956 and 1960, and my graduate work at Catholic University, were very sound. I was finished with the philosophy degree by about 1966, so all the courses were basically Scholastic–we had Franciscans and Dominicans for professors. If you looked at the course-catalogue, all the courses were Scholastic: St. Thomas Aquinas on Social Justice, St. Thomas Aquinas's Epistemology, St. Thomas Aquinas's Natural Theology, St. Bonaventure's thought on this or that.

I was formed completely in St. Thomas's thought, and, by the time I went to the seminary, I had already been given a fairly intensive formation in the traditional theology of the Church. That formation made me relatively immune to what was being taught in the seminary.

What was being taught in the seminary about the priesthood?

FR. Y.: Well, you know, you have to remember that we're talking about the years from 1972 to 1976–things were very confused! In a sense, I cannot recall there having been a systematic theological approach to the priesthood in our seminary studies, because there wasn't a systematic theological approach to anything! They were moving away from the model of the priest as the *alter Christus*–the priest who, when he administers the sacraments, acts *in Persona Christi*. They were moving away from the idea of the priest as the mediator between God and men towards a more "social justice" oriented model.

In fact, we had some people in the seminary at that time who had no belief in the supernatural at all. They saw the Church as a vehicle for promoting "social justice," and they saw themselves, wearing the collar, as having a certain authority and being able, perhaps, to get more done in the area of "social justice."

As far as the idea of the priesthood went, in terms of its theological dimension, there was just a lot of confusion. Before the Revolution, there had been a systematic program in the seminaries, in which one point of view was presented as a cohesive, coherent, logical whole. Whereas we would just get all these different view-points about every question. It was like a collage, you know. They didn't give us textbooks, just xeroxed materials about different view-points, some of them manifestly heretical.

Take abortion, for example. We would get different kinds of articles representing different points of view, but we never got a systematic moral theology in which abortion would have a specific place. You could never fit anything into an overall whole–it was very eclectic.

Of course, there was a pretty clear rejection of some of the traditional ideas of the priesthood. There was no emphasis on celibacy at all. Basically, it was seen as an arbitrary rule imposed by the Roman authorities that had little, if any, value at all. It was something one simply had to follow if he wanted to be a priest. In a similar vein, the rector actually apologized for having to ask us to promise to say the Divine Office! "I hate to do this, but you know, this is part of the formality."

The other thing that stands out in my mind was the rejection of what was seen as "clerical triumphalism." The wearing of the cassock was not explicitly forbidden, but one fellow got hauled up before "the committee" for having been spotted in a cassock on the grounds. The idea was that we were no longer to be in a separate "caste." Basically, we were expected to be "with the people," rather than separate from them. There was a breakdown, not theoretically but practically, of the distinction between the ordained priesthood and the "priesthood of the laity," which is theirs by reason of their baptism.

How did this non-systematic approach to studies present the theology of the Mass?

FR. Y.: Well, again, there wasn't any clear, well-structured theological view of the Mass either. The Masses we experienced were so bizarre–some of them *quite* bizarre–and so varied, that you wouldn't get any single impression of the meaning of the Mass from observing these kinds of celebrations. We had one priest who celebrated what we called the "Navajo Mass." He would come in wearing burlap vestments and use pottery vessels–it was very casual, very informal. And we had one priest who celebrated what we called the "Japanese Mass." He had a little table in front of him, and he would squat and put both hands on the table for the consecration. (Both of these priests ended up leaving.) Sometimes, the priests from the Vatican II Institute would come to say Mass, and they were really a mess! They would concelebrate in various kinds of albs that looked like rags, and they'd wear these grotesque multi-colored stoles, usually hanging all askew.

When we went on retreat once, the Jesuit retreat house provided yet another experience of the Mass. The retreat master came out in very casual lay clothes, actually just a Hawaiian t-shirt! He had no Missal–no book whatsoever–and he began to improvise. This was going on in a store-room setting; there were big windows, a big disco-type globe, and, of course, through those big windows, we could look out over the whole surrounding area. We thanked God for this beautiful scene; we thanked God for our community; and they improvised. At some point, they did something that was meant to resemble the consecration, although they didn't use the words of consecration, and then, after a certain point they went into the Our Father. Then, the Blessed Sacrament (?) was distributed like *hors d'oeuvres*–it was very much a cocktail-lounge atmosphere. I don't remember any last blessing–they just packed up and left the "altar."

What was the common thread which tied all of these bizarre liturgies together? What were they emphasizing?

FR. Y.: The emphasis was on the Mass as a meal, as you would expect. The notion of transubstantiation was never formally denied, although we did have one priest who insisted that the Fathers of the Church used "bread" and "Body" indifferently to speak of the host before and after the consecration, and he tried to suggest, without actually saying it, that the notion of an actual change in the host was, perhaps, a later development that was not emphasized at the beginning of the Church. That, of course, is false, but he didn't actually go that far. Very often, these people would stop short of formally contradicting the Church's doctrine, but they would make these innuendoes and implications that the doctrine was wrong.

Was transubstantiation ever mentioned, other than in the insinuations that it was not essential to the Faith?

FR. Y.: In my whole course of theology, I don't recall any discussion of transubstantiation from a philosophical or a theological stand-point. The emphasis on the sacrifice of the Mass was radically down-played. Rather, the emphasis was on the community coming together to tell their story. Remember, it's not the consecration now—it's the "institutional narrative." They come together, they tell their story, and they share the Meal of the Lord.

We were merely presented with different kinds of approaches to what change might be going on in the bread and wine at Mass. Paul VI actually condemned in an encyclical the ideas of "transfiguration" and "transfinalization" as explanations of what happens at Mass, but they would speculate about it at the seminary: Did the bread and wine really change, or were they only "changed" in the sense that they came to have a new meaning for the people? Another difficult issue was the point in time when the change occurs, whatever the change may be. There were those who said that it occurs in the context of the whole Canon—so that you couldn't say that it occurs in the words of institution, "This is My Body; This is My Blood." Of course, that is completely unacceptable! We've simply got different views than theirs.

They pointed out that, yes, there were those, like St. Thomas, who say that the change happens when the "words of institution" are spoken, but that there are others who say that it happens, somehow, within the context of the whole Canon. Again, there was never any answer given! The idea was that there were various speculations about these things, and, of course, the implication was that we were to choose whichever one was the most convenient to us personally.

Another issue that was never really clarified in the seminary was this: What is the role of the community and the role of the priest in the Mass, and how are those two roles distinct? For example, does anything happen at all if the community is not there at Mass? Is it the faith of the community that brings about whatever change happens? Or is it the words of the priest which make the Holy Eucharist? They didn't deny that the words of the priest were necessary, but they pointed out there was another way of looking at it! Maybe whatever happened, happened because of the assembly of the community and their expression of faith!

We were given a number of different ways of looking at the Mass, but, interestingly enough, the views of the Fathers of the Church, Eastern and Western, were basically ignored, unless they were mentioned in history class! Papal and Conciliar documents were all ignored, except, of course, for those of Vatican II!

You got the impression that the Church actually began sometime around 1965. It was as if there were this utopian "Apostolic Church," which, at least, by the early part of the second century (which is pretty darned early!), became infected by Greek and Roman philosophy, so the Holy Spirit took a kind of sabbatical. Then, there was this whole period, from, say, the second to the twentieth centuries, during which everything was wrong. (Of course, the absolute nadir was the Middle Ages!) Finally, of course, the Holy Spirit awoke at the Second Vatican Council and brought us back to this utopian "Apostolic Church" about which, in fact, very little is known. But that didn't matter, because, what they didn't know about it, they constructed according to their own view-point.

What did you think of the New Mass, even abstracting from all the aberrations which you have described?

FR. Y.: My position on the New Mass has always been that it's fundamentally an accommodation to Ecumenism. I don't think it is formally and positively heretical, and I think that, if the official text is followed, it's valid, because it does have the epiclesis, and the words of consecration are there, at least in the Latin text. No matter how minimally they are cast, the basic requirements for validity are present in the New Mass.

Some people call into question the validity of the changed formula of consecration, but *"Quod pro vobis tradetur"* (Which will be given up for you) is in the scriptural account of the Last Supper, and it does not change the meaning of the formula, so it avoids invalidating it. The displacement of *"Mysterium fidei"* (the Mystery of Faith) to a position after the consecration is not a problem for validity, either. Now, the translation of *"pro multis"* (for many) into English as "for all" may present a problem, because that seems to suggest a different theology of the Mass, or it could, at least, suggest a different theology. But, of course, in the Latin edition, it's still *"pro multis."*

Then how is the New Mass deficient?

FR. Y.: I think that it's mostly by way of omission—elements that are specifically Catholic have been either down-played or, in some cases, just omitted. If you look at the Collects, the "prayers over the gifts," and the Post-communion prayers, it's easy to see this.

Interestingly, in the Latin edition, the "prayer over the gifts" is called the *"Oratio super Oblata"* (the Prayer over the Things to be Sacrificed). Nowhere do you find the word *"dona"* (gifts)! It's interesting that we've got a "translation" into English that is not a translation at all! The "translation" of the only Canon we have in the New Mass, the Roman Canon, is not a translation either! There are many phrases in that "translation" that have no Latin equivalent whatsoever. "A sacrifice in spirit and in truth," for example, is not to be found in the Latin text at all. I won't say the New Mass in English because of that.

But, abstracting from the "translations" of the text of the New Mass, you can really see the changes in doctrine, at least the implied changes in doctrine, when you look at the Collects, Secrets, and Post-communions, because a very small percentage of the old ones were retained. You notice that there's no longer any mention of the devil or hell. The notion of the intercession of the saints is also radically down-played. We do speak of the saints praying for us, but the notion of "intercession" is radically down-played—the idea now is that we may imitate their deeds. The notion of merit is radically down-played. The saints can merit for us, and we can merit for each other—that's the classic idea of the Communion of Saints. Why would they want to de-emphasize that? They did it because, again, it's something that the Protestants would object to!

The role of the Blessed Virgin Mary has also been subtly denigrated. When I was in the seminary, she was presented as "the first disciple." But, you know, the curious thing is that I can't find any basis for that in Scripture! Where is she ever presented as a "disciple"? You can see in the New Mass that there's a subtle down-playing of her splendor, her grandeur, her magnificence, the unique and absolutely unparalleled position she has in "salvation history."

But the worst feature of the New Mass is the funeral rite. I think that there is one prayer that talks about the forgiveness of sins, but I don't think that there's any prayer at all that talks about the remission of the temporal punishment due for sins! Another problem is that there's no reference to the particular judgment, to the soul as about to be judged—it's all pointing to the resurrection! You will never find, in those prayers, the notion of a particular judgment of a separated soul existing in heaven, hell, or purgatory awaiting the resurrection. So you may get the notion, by reading only those prayers, that there is a kind of suspension of the soul's existence between the moment of death and the moment of the resurrection.

There's no mention of hell in the funeral rite either, nor is there any mention of protection from the devil. Of course, they've dropped the beautiful prayers asking God to "Spare us from the dreaded sentence" or "From the fires of hell, deliver them, O Lord!" That's all gone! I find that absolutely objectionable.

One day in the seminary, I asked why these prayers had been cut. One of my professors said, "Well, I suppose that these things are still part of our "*lex credendi*," (law of belief), but they're no longer part of our "*lex orandi*" (law of prayer)." He meant that they're still part of what we believe, but they're no longer of part of what we preach, because liturgy is meant to make people feel good!

If these things are no longer part of our prayer, will they continue to be part of our belief for very long?

FR. Y.: No, not for very long, because the way we pray expresses our belief. I can tell you from my personal experience that these things are no longer part of the belief of many Catholics.

Along those same lines, we were taught in the seminary that it's virtually impossible to commit a mortal sin. Now, nobody said that it's *absolutely* impossible, but they talked about the "fundamental option" of morality, and they said that a human being could scarcely be capable of the level of malice which would be required to commit a mortal sin. That notion underlies the whole theory of the New Mass. Original Sin was down-played but, of course, never formally denied! Other explanations were offered, other ways of interpreting it.

They pointed out that the text of Genesis didn't mean what it appeared to mean—it didn't contain the doctrine of Original Sin. Of course, St. Paul's Epistles are part of Holy Scripture, too, and the way St. Paul refers to Genesis points out that Genesis refers to Original Sin, but they didn't worry about **that** too much!

How is the implicit denial of Original Sin central to the idea of the New Mass?

FR. Y.: If you're going to be ambivalent about Original Sin, your whole notion of what the Redemption means is going to change fundamentally, and if you're going to change the notion of Redemption, then the value of Christ's sacrifice is going to have to be totally reinterpreted. Finally, if you're going to reinterpret the value of Christ's sacrifice, then the Mass is going to have to be reinterpreted too! We never heard mention of the idea of a propitiatory sacrifice with reference to the Mass, but all the other possible positions were given to us, and we were encouraged to honor them according to their "respective values." Pluralism was the big thing in those days, but, now that the Liberals have absolute and total control, Pluralism is forgotten. The one position which is absolutely untenable today is that of the Traditionalists!

For all their talk about "respective values," do the Liberals seem to value truth?

FR. Y.: That's another thing! Epistemology, the basic theory of knowledge and truth, is going to have a radical effect on whether dogmas make sense or not. *If we are not capable of the knowledge of truth, or if truth can't be expressed conceptually or verbally, then what in heaven's name are dogmas?* It was often suggested to us that a dogma was the best way of stating a position at the time the statement was made. Those who made the statements were "historically conditioned," they said, but, of course, everything is "historically conditioned"–that has nothing to do with anything!

The idea was that these dogmas had to be looked upon as "historically conditioned" and, therefore, relative. What may have been an ideal way of presenting, say, the union of two natures in Christ in the third century might not be the best way of presenting it today! There were a few of our professors who were involved in "process theology"–Jesus was born just as a man. God was not a Trinity from the beginning, but when Jesus was born as a man, he was taken up into the Godhead, and, then, from the inter-relationship between the Father and the Son, the Holy Spirit emerged. All of this was a "process," and we are in the "process" of being taken up into the Godhead as well, so that what happened to Christ is going to happen to us, too!

Thinking as a Catholic, how did you survive in a seminary where the professors were saying such things?

FR. Y.: Because I had had such a good formation before. I avoided getting kicked out only because I maintained a relatively low profile, and, at that time, nobody on the staff had their act together. Many of my professors and many of the administrators have subsequently left the priesthood. The seminary was in such turmoil, such disarray–it was constantly in the process of changing–that a trained monkey could probably have made it through in those days!

One man was actually asked to leave, and that was because he was filthy. His room looked like some of those photos of bombed-out London during the Second World War. If you ever got down wind of him, you'd get sick–he was a total mess. He was the only one during the years I was there who was asked to leave! We had another man who joined the police department, and he missed class constantly. He brought a python into his room. He would drive around the quadrangle and shine the lights of his police car in people's windows at night. He was not asked to leave–he finally quit and decided to become a full-time policeman, but he was not asked to leave! There was another man who was living off-campus, and I remember the rector saying, "You know, I'm really not too comfortable with that," but he wasn't thrown out.

Would it be fair to say that, with people like that around, you just "slipped through the cracks"?

FR. Y.: Well, I must say that there was a certain honest liberalism among the professors. I would always bring up the teachings of Aquinas on whatever they were presenting to us, and they respected that as one possible way of looking at the question. There were some real Liberals, in the sense that they really were tolerant, and they really had some sense of "Pluralism." My views were accepted as another way of looking at things. So, in all my papers I would deal with the subjects from the Thomistic perspective, and that was accepted as one possible way to go. Of course, I was very careful about criticizing the new way of thinking. I would do it implicitly by saying, "This is the mind of Aquinas on this point," and I didn't always bring out the consequences.

You get a feel for how far you can go with different professors. You pick your fights. What are you going to go to the barricades for, and what are you not going to go to the barricades for? We didn't have grades–we either passed or failed, and the mark had to be accompanied by a written evaluation. Mine were always very good, so I didn't really have any trouble getting through the seminary. They knew where I was coming from, but that was accepted as one possible way to go.

When you were ordained, how long was it before you began to say the traditional Mass?

FR. Y.: Well, let's see. My first assignment was under a now-deceased pastor, and he was like a feudal warlord over me. I said the New Mass for all of that year, and then I was moved because I was having nothing but trouble there. They had put me in charge of the CCD classes, and you know, it was just nonsense! You're just talking about "love," and you make the children go out and take different magazines and make a montage of pictures suggesting "love"! They don't know the Hail Mary, and they're making montages about "love"! So, I got into difficulties over that, and, of course, we had teachers who were totally untrained—they didn't know anything. And the children just ignored me. It was a very bad scene there.

And so, after one year I was moved to a place where we had two of the most liberal nuns imaginable—bachelor women, you know. They didn't live in a convent, but they called it a convent. They didn't live a regular religious life, didn't wear any habit at all. And I started getting into arguments with them.

At that point, I began to substitute English translations of the old Collects, Post-communions, and Secrets into the New Mass. It became very clear on comparison that the New Missal was very defective theologically—that's not the same thing as saying it's heretical; it's just saying that it's theologically defective. I was always in conflict about the New Mass, because I became more and more acutely aware of its deficiencies. As I became more aware of those deficiencies, it became more difficult to say it. Why would you "make do" with something from Woolworth's if you had available something from Gump's, or another really high-class store? I became more and more uncomfortable with the New Mass as a mediocre composition—let's put it that way—and I didn't want to use it, especially when it came to funerals.

So I turned to the old books more and more, because the theology that was being expressed in the new ones was foreign to me, not in the sense that I didn't know about it, because I spent years in the seminary. (I was certainly exposed to the New Theology, and it's a good thing to know your enemy!) But it's a different thing to treat the New Theology academically and to use it to minister to people. It looks quite different when you're actually performing the new rites! Using these new rites, I wasn't expressing what I really believed, so I went back more and more to the old ones.

Was there any reaction from the archdiocese when you first began returning to the old rites?

FR. Y.: One priest called me and said, "Why are you Latinizing the Mass?" I got in a big fight with the liturgy committee, because they wanted to move the tabernacle. I mentioned in a sermon that, if the liturgy committee had their way, the tabernacle would be out in the corridor where nobody would be able to see it. (And I wouldn't sit in front of it, either. This business of theirs of just sitting in front of the tabernacle is incredibly insulting! They ignore the Blessed Sacrament!)

And so, I just kept moving away from the new rites. When I had been in my second assignment for only one year, I was moved again, and then I started a doctoral program on the comparison of medieval Indian thought with medieval Christian thought. (I never finished the thesis, because I got sick.)

After the third year of my priesthood, I gradually abandoned the new rite, and by four years after ordination, I was pretty much saying Mass exclusively according to the old rite. At first, I would say more and more of the New Mass in Latin, and then, gradually, I would use the old Offertory, and so on. (I know we are not supposed to mix the rites, but I was doing it!)

I have come back to that same practice recently, in order to preserve my position. Most of the Masses I say are traditional, but we have just lost a priest, and I am the only priest assigned to the place right now. So, I have to say some of the major Masses in the main chapel, and those are Latin *Novus Ordo* Masses with the traditional Collects, Secrets, and Post-communions. I bring up my little 1962 *Missale Romanum* and take the Collects, Post-communions, and Secrets from it, because I will not accept the new prayers. There is no obligation to accept the new prayers, because they are not issued and promulgated as infallible truth. And I personally find them repugnant.

What about the Offertory of the New Mass?

FR. Y.: There isn't any.

The so-called "presentation of the gifts," then.

FR. Y.: Isn't it the adaptation of a Jewish prayer before meals? I don't think it invalidates the Mass, and I'll say it, but it's not an Offertory! But, again, I hate it because, if we are going to say a prayer before meals before we begin the Eucharistic Prayer, then it suggests that the Eucharist is principally a meal. Otherwise, why on earth would we do it? (I'm sorry to be getting hot under the collar, but I get angry when I think about these things!)

In a way, of course, the Mass is a sacrificial meal, but the structure of the New Mass deliberately down-plays the element of sacrifice. I think that in most of the Eucharistic Prayers, the word *sacrifice*–or even the word *victim*– occurs somewhere, but now, many people don't realize that the word *host* is derived from the Latin word *hostia*, which means *victim*.

Do you use the new Prefaces?

FR. Y.: The Prefaces are hideous! If you want to see a classic example of barbarism, just look at the Latin Preface of the Holy Trinity. It was one of the most concise and perfect statements of the Trinitarian doctrine, and look at what they did to it! They took all the metaphysics out, all the references to Substance and to Person–all that's gone. It basically comes down to this statement: "We worship you all equally." It's an absolute massacre! Then, of course, you get Prefaces like the one for Thanksgiving Day, which I only remember because it is such an atrocity. And how about the Preface for a patriotic celebration, which goes on and on and on—the whole page is scarcely big enough to accommodate it! They way they talk, you'd think that all of the founders of this country were basically saints, and that they came here to found a Christian community! Well, that's absolutely wrong! Most of our Founding Fathers were Deists, and some of them were atheists!

How did you learn the ceremonies of the traditional Mass?

FR. Y.: I had a Traditionalist priest friend, Fr. Smith, who was retired, and he tutored me through the rubrics. It was some job! The old Mass is immensely more complicated than the New, and everything is spelled out. There is no room for improvisation, as you know. We did a number of practice Masses, and it took me a while before I felt really comfortable that I was rubrically correct. After that, I didn't say the *Novus Ordo* Mass.

How did you end up in your current assignment?

FR. Y.: We had a meeting, and they said that a rest home was ideal for me: "Here we have this wonderful place, which is a combination rest-home and insane asylum, and it's just right for you!" I guess they thought that the residents are so old that the amount of "damage" I could do could be relatively contained there. I've been there since 1984, and it's wonderful—I love it!

How did you manage to remain in good standing with the Archdiocese?

FR. Y.: You have to be careful these days. I have never done anything to incur any canonical penalty. I've "pulled my punches" only in the sense that I'm not going to make trouble. For example, here I am in this parish house, right in the middle of San Francisco, but I have nothing to do with this parish. I'm not running up and down the streets saying, "Homosexuals go to hell!" I maintain a low profile. To that extent, you might say that I compromise myself, but that's the only compromise I've had to make. If I were asked to preach here, I would preach what the Church teaches, but I am not allowed to preach here, and I don't say Mass here. I have no ministry here at all, and I don't go out of my way to make trouble.

You mentioned that, in the traditional Mass, everything is spelled out in detail, with no room being left for improvisation. Is it fair to say that this Mass is the safest and the best expression of the unchanging Catholic Faith precisely because it leaves nothing to the whim of the celebrant?

FR. Y.: I think so, absolutely! Even in the Hindu rituals, when they are worshipping, everything is spelled out. There's a whole body of literature that deals with the proper way to conduct sacrifices in honor of the gods. Everything is spelled out; there is no room for improvisation at all. Everything has to be done absolutely as written, and the slightest mistake will vitiate the entire thing. In fact, they think that you'll get exactly the opposite of what you're asking for if everything's not done exactly according to the book.

In all cultures, in my limited experience of comparative religion, when people are dealing with something sacred, their rituals are spelled out in the most minute detail, and improvisation is terrible even to think of.

The old Mass grew organically. Of course, it was changed from time to time, but they were organic changes, and the whole thing is seen as one consistent development. But the New Mass is literally a new creation, invented by Paul VI and obviously influenced by his Protestant *periti* (experts). I think that it's an accommodation to Ecumenism, and that they tried to keep it valid–they tried, I think, to keep some semblance of Tradition–but, at the same time, they tried to accommodate the Protestants. They tried to make it a ritual that virtually any Christian could celebrate, and I think that the Anglican and Lutheran rituals are now incredibly close to the New Mass. In fact, I know Lutheran ministers who will use the *Novus Ordo* Mass, especially "Eucharistic Prayer II." (Everybody likes to use "Eucharistic Prayer II," because it's short, and it's alleged to be the "Canon of Hippolytus," which it doesn't resemble at all!)

So, even the Hindus realize that religion is something important enough that they want to make sure to get it right?

FR. Y.: Yes, and they don't leave anything to chance, because they think they're doing the most important, the most sacred, the most holy things imaginable. However they understand the gods, they are placing themselves into relation with the transcendent, and they want to do it properly–there is a set way to do it. They are also very concerned with maintaining the ancient traditions. You know, Vedic Sanskrit is used as the liturgical language. They want to keep in constant contact with how their religion was in its beginnings. It evolved in a way that was always consistent with its beginnings. How do we fit Cardinal Mahoney's new warehouse into that picture?

What effect does saying the old Mass –as opposed to the New–have on the life of the priest?

FR. Y.: The traditional Mass has a tremendously different effect on me, at least. It reminds me constantly of what the priesthood really is, and it calls me very forcefully to pray and to try to live up to that ideal. The old Mass reinforces all of the traditional ideas of the priesthood, because they are all expressly presented.

In the New Mass, on the other hand, the priest is the leader of congregational prayer–he's a presider. He is not necessarily a sacred person; he is simply one taken from the assembly and anointed by the assembly to lead the assembly in prayer. I think that the way the New Mass is celebrated tends to take away the priest's role as a sacred person; hence, the priest's identification with Christ–the emphasis on the priest as an *alter Christus*–is taken away. It is a more democratic approach, in which the priest simply becomes one of the people. This comes from the way the New Mass is celebrated; it's not necessarily built into the text.

The old Mass constantly emphasizes the sacredness of the priesthood and the unique mediatorial role of the priest. It has the sense of the sacred, the transcendent, the holy, the luminous, the other-than-ordinary, and so it calls upon the priest to try to be other-than-ordinary, to live up to the ideals of the priesthood. And it constantly reminds the priest that he is praying for the people, that he has been called and anointed by God–not by the people, but by God! I think that the traditional Mass constantly imposes upon the priest the necessity to focus upon his priestly obligations. When you say the old Mass, you know that you are appointed to be a mediator, to pray and offers sacrifices to God for the people. And you are surrounded by an incredible sense of holiness.

It's almost as if the New Mass emphasizes the ordinary, the banal–it has a certain aspect of the secular about it; whereas the old Mass emphasizes the sacred, the transcendent. When the priest celebrates Mass, he should want to create an experience that is not continuous with people's ordinary experience. The solemnity of the old Mass comes from that idea. The priest is meant to live on earth the life of heaven, and I think that the old Mass constantly reinforces that; whereas the New Mass is earthbound–it doesn't reinforce that ideal.

Could you give an example?

FR. Y.: In the New Mass, you're facing the people, so you're like an "M.C." I have seen priests who don't ever let go of the microphone. One priest even said, "This is My Body," while holding the microphone! He never put that microphone down for one minute, and that was a spectacle. He was an "M.C." (Actually, if they want to make the Mass egalitarian, let's all face the same way–let's all face east! Let's all face God! It makes no sense to say Mass facing the people. It just makes the Mass a show. I can't think of one theological reason for facing the people.)

But the priest is now an "M.C."–he's an entertainer, and some of them are quite amusing, actually. He's given the option to do a certain amount of improvisation, which, of course, makes for even greater entertainment if the man's talented and clever. But some of them are neither talented nor clever. Contrast the "M.C." idea of the priest with the traditional concept–the difference between these two ideas of the priesthood is immense.

Do you think that there is necessarily a built-in conflict for a priest who wants to be an *alter Christus*, a sacrificing priest, but who says the New Mass?

FR. Y.: That's difficult. I think that the New Mass will never promote or generate that kind of response in a priest as effectively as the old. Inasmuch as the New Mass is said properly, it's valid, and, if it's really the Mass, then it must be an infinite source of grace. But I think that (again, I speak from my own experience) the New Mass just doesn't have the capacity to generate that real response in a priest. The priest is always going to be somewhat limited if he says the New Mass, I would say. It's true that the priest can be the *alter Christus* and act in the Person of Christ in the New Mass, but, it seems to me, he will never come to as full a realization of those ideals as he would if he said the traditional Mass. For many priests who first come to the celebration of the old Mass, it is a really transforming experience. I have talked to other priests who have had this experience. The old Mass produces a different response–it's like entering into a new universe!

Do you think it is fair to blame the new ideas about the priesthood, at least partially, for the current scandals among the clergy?

FR. Y.: Yes, I think that these scandals are the inevitable consequences of changes made in the Catholic universities, and especially in the seminaries. That's where these priests come from–they're the product of the seminaries! I know better than you do what went on during those years. I was teaching during much of that time, and I was constantly fighting all of those ideas. The Liberals just gained control overnight.

Given the changes that were made in the seminaries from about 1965 onward, and, given the climate that existed throughout, at least, the second half of the sixties, through the seventies, the eighties, and into the nineties, what would you expect? At least in my experience, celibacy and chastity were ignored in the seminary. The real reasons–the theological basis–for clerical celibacy were never addressed. The history of clerical celibacy in the Church was never addressed.

Even chastity was kind of glossed over! The "Sexual Ethics" course was another case of ambivalence. "Masturbation? Well, it's a 'phase-specific behavior,' you know! It's not necessarily wrong!"

And you know what's happening with the Church's attitude towards homosexuality these days. "It's a viable alternative, as long as the relationship is loving!" In my seminary days, they were talking about this as well. Given that kind of teaching in the seminaries (at least in my own experience), and, given the virtually non-existent formation in chastity–let alone in celibacy!–I'm really not a bit surprised at what's happening. This is exactly what you would expect.

Why should a man have to sacrifice his "human sexuality," which is a part of his "human dignity," to become a community facilitator?

FR. Y.: I know priests who have that attitude. The notion was presented very often in the sixties and seventies (not so much now, perhaps) that you couldn't be "authentically human" if you were not "sexually active." You were somehow less than human, and, of course, you couldn't be "authentically masculine" (or feminine!) if you were not "sexually active." All of these ideas were floating around.

Of course, such "authentically human" behavior was seen as perfectly legitimate as long as it's done with genuine love. I talked to a priest once who had had an affair with a woman. I said, "How did you manage to justify that?" "It was an expression of love–it was beautiful!" he said, "It was a way of communicating, and God couldn't possibly object to that!" I mean, come on! "It was beautiful, and it was just love!" So, if you're relating to somebody in a genital way, and you see this simply as a way of expressing love, "God couldn't possibly object"!?! Given what went on before, this attitude should come as no surprise.

Many priests are afraid that they will be guilty of disobedience if they begin saying the traditional Mass. How would you reassure them?

FR. Y.: You know, that's a most difficult issue. My personal view is that there is a strong theological opinion to the effect that Paul VI had a right to create an alternative Mass, but that he did not have a right to forbid the celebration of the organically-developed traditional Roman rite, that he could not just cancel it out after virtually two thousand years of existence. There is also the opinion that he didn't, in fact, ever forbid it, because the word that he used in the Apostolic Constitution *Missale Romanum* (which promulgated the New Mass) is the Latin for "wish" rather than for "command" or "mandate." My impression is that a good argument can be made that he never did explicitly and formally forbid the celebration of the traditional Mass, and, even if he did, it can be questioned whether he had the authority to do so. And so, it seems to me, that, if the prohibition of saying the old Mass is doubtful, then it has not been adequately promulgated, and it doesn't bind in conscience.

From my point of view, it is not a matter of disobedience to say the traditional Mass, because the only proper authority has not actually forbidden it, and he may not have had the competence to do it, even if he wanted to. It seems to me that those who say that it is forbidden are expressing an opinion and working on the level of an assumption.

What about the question of the Indult Mass? Does that presuppose the previous abrogation of the "former rite"?

FR. Y.: It is possible to argue that the Pope is implying that the old Mass was forbidden by the fact that he gives an indult—that's only an implication. But it does not, in fact, express that the old Mass is forbidden without the indult! Frankly, in my view, I don't think that a bishop would have the competence to say that the celebration of the traditional Mass is absolutely excluded from his diocese. So, if I'm being disobedient, I'm being disobedient only in the respect that I'm not bound in conscience to obey. That would be my approach to the question of disobedience.

How can a young priest who has had no formation at all in Tradition escape the new ideas about the priesthood which were instilled in him in the seminary?

FR. Y.: That's very difficult. What can he do? There's no other way but to go back and start reading. I would suggest that he go back and look at the Fathers of the Church and examine what they were saying. He should look at Aquinas and the great Doctors of the Church. Of course, he should read the papal documents on the Eucharist–Pius XII's *Mediator Dei*, for example. Those things will probably be a revelation to him, but he has to go to the authentic sources–the Popes, the great Councils, and the Fathers of the Church (when they're unanimous on some point that pertains to the Deposit of Faith).

Is such a program feasible for a busy young priest?

FR. Y.: I don't know of any short-cut, do you? He has to go back to where the material is, and then he has to look at the old Mass in that context. He can certainly look at it in English translations, many of which are wonderful. But if he doesn't go back to the sources and "do the homework," he won't get far. And he can't depend upon the current theology books–he's got to go back to the authoritative sources that really express the official mind of the Church. There's no other way to go, in my opinion.

Could you recommend some specific texts?

FR. Y.: *The Faith of the Early Fathers*, edited by Jurgens, is an excellent source. The works of Aquinas have been translated into English, as have most of the major encyclicals. Of course, there are good English versions of the Canons and Decrees of the Council of Trent. These things are available, but he's got to go to them. He's not going to do that unless he wants to!

But he'll find that it's going to be worth his trouble. He's going to be going against the present trend, and the moment he does that, he's going to be running into opposition! But, you know, opposition can be a lot of fun! It generates a certain amount of electricity that gets you going. I find it very stimulating! When you start meeting with opposition, that really fires you up, and you're forced to clarify your position. You really have to get your position clear.

Can such a priest get his position clear just by reading books? Where would he be able to find a mentor to help him along?

FR. Y.: I would certainly be willing to help anybody who wanted to do that. For example, every Tuesday night we have a seminar on St. Thomas Aquinas here. No one from the parish is particularly traditional, to my knowledge, but we are analyzing some of the basic metaphysical and theological concepts of Aquinas. I think that those of us who are traditional and have the advantage of being well trained, really immersed, in Tradition have an obligation to offer whatever help we can to people who simply have not had that formation.

To contact Fr. Young:

Rev. Fr. William Young
100 Diamond Street
San Francisco, CA 94114
Phone: (415) 863-6260

FR. STEPHEN ZIGRANG

EDITED TRANSCRIPT

FR. ZIGRANG: I was ordained April 21, 1978, in Houston, Texas, having been born in St. Louis, Missouri, in 1950. My seminary was St. Mary's, Queen of the Clergy, in Houston, from 1971 to my ordination in 1978. Even before we moved to Texas in 1964, I had already made up my mind to be a priest. I got my vocation, I am sure, as an altar boy. In fact, it was in 1964 that we first went to Sunday Mass in Houston after having moved from St. Louis—the Mass had already changed. There was a mixture of English and Latin, and the priest already faced the congregation. It was quite shocking. My mother asked, "Is this a Protestant church?"

How did you react to those changes?

FR. Z.: I was only about thirteen. I naturally wanted to continue serving Mass, since I had been an altar boy for a long time. But I told my mother, "There's nothing to do, you just sit there." We were quite confounded because, in the move to Houston in July of 1964, it all changed—overnight. My mother called her sister saying, "Did anything change up in St. Louis?" My aunt said, "No, not at all." So St. Louis was a more conservative Catholic town. Houston was known for being avant-garde.

So you managed to struggle through with it...

FR. Z.: Yes, I continued to serve a little bit, but then I went off to high school and lost interest somewhere along the way. I remember more about being an altar boy in Missouri than in Texas, even though I was much younger at the time. By the time I graduated from high school, my mind wasn't on serving or on the Mass anymore. I was going to the University of Houston and majoring in geology, and I stopped thinking about being a priest. I don't think I considered the changes at all by that time.

Yet you still decided to enter the seminary?

FR. Z.: I went to the University for two years, then I went to the seminary in 1971. I remember thinking that it was not very pious. We had prayers, but it was not like I thought it should be, and my uneasiness about this eventually led me to leave the seminary after about two years. I went to Christ in the Desert Monastery near Albuquerque, New Mexico. But it was kind of kookie there, too.

Can you elaborate on the "kookiness" you observed there?

FR. Z.: They had a rigorous monastic schedule–waking up early for Matins, for instance, but they started to introduce things that were strange–drums, *etc.* I had trouble getting along with the monks there. I wanted things to be strict, but they did not. I left less than a year after I had arrived.

You went back to the seminary?

FR. Z.: No, they wouldn't let me come back. I had gone to the bishop saying that I wanted to be a monk, and he had argued against it, but then he said that, since it was a higher calling, he had to let me go. So when I came back he said, "Well, I told you so." I got a job and worked for a while in the world. I still tried to get back into the seminary, though, and with the help of some recommendation letters, they let me back in. At that time I was already in theology, with about two years left. They had already suppressed the minor orders and subdiaconate. I witnessed the last tonsure.

What were the Masses like in the seminary?

FR. Z.: As I recall, I was horrified because they, of course, had the "table" altar there already. The seminary in Houston is a very beautiful place. It's a Romanesque church on fifty acres of beautiful grounds; it has a quadrangle with old style arches like a cloister. Of course, none of that was used any more. The chapel has side altars in an ambulatory behind, so there were about seven altars–beautiful, with mosaics of St. Thomas Aquinas, St. Gregory the Great, St. Jerome, St. John Chrysostom–and beautiful wood painted panels. It was in these little chapels that priests said their private masses in the old days. When I first entered, there were still occasionally some visiting priests saying private Masses, and I got to serve, but, after abandoning the project of removing the altars (which were permanent and difficult to wreck), they converted the chapels into office and storage space. The high altar had a gold crucifix on a chain–which disappeared. The beautiful baldachino, altar, and tabernacle are still there, but they just sit there unused, and there are no adornments. It's very bare. They have a baby grand piano now, near the "table" altar. It's just ruined! It was disturbing to me even then. Even worse, they made a loose-leaf binder "altar missal." I remember how the priest saying Mass would open the binder like he was in class and take out a page–it was very stressful. It was not even the official text of the Mass–they were still using an experimental liturgy...but it was not, as far as I can recall, the 1969 liturgy.

How was your theological formation?

FR. Z.: It was terrible, even though I did not know why at the time! I was always arguing with the professors of moral theology, doctrine, and scripture. I remember how the Scripture professor, who was also the rector, would simply teach out of the *Jerome Bible Commentary*, which had the work of Raymond Brown and such people in it. All of it was form-critical interpretation, so Scripture was all myth–all of it. I asked once, "Well, if it's all myth, then do we still believe in the Eucharist, in the Real Presence?" The professor answered, "Some things aren't myth." "So, how do you determine which is which?" I asked. They couldn't answer that question. That was one of the reasons I went to the monastery. The seminary was a joke. Some professors were dating–they had girl friends! They *had* confessionals but never used them–except for storage! We never had a publicly recited Rosary. In class they once made fun of St. Louis Marie de Montfort. I distinctly remember that because, when I heard the name, I went to the library to see what he had written! There were some older professors who didn't seem to be joining in on all of the nonsense, but they were relegated to the sidelines. They must have suffered a lot, but I never really spoke to them to find out.

What did they teach you in moral theology?

FR. Z.: It was situation ethics–a lot of Charles Curran. There was no solid formation. God will always be nice and merciful.

What about dogma?

FR. Z.: I'm not quite sure how to characterize it. The course was taught by one of the older professors who kept to himself. I think he still kept the Faith. So I don't recall anything specifically wrong there. We did have a Lutheran professor for New Testament and Greek. We did argue with him when he denied the physical resurrection of Christ. We could not convince him, like St. Paul said, that if there wasn't any resurrection, then all this is stupid, foolish.

Did you ever study St. Thomas?

FR. Z.: When I entered, just out of my third year at the University of Houston, they sandwiched everything together–I had ancient and modern philosophy, but no medieval. I had Aristotle in ancient philosophy, but no medieval philosophy at all. I had no St. Thomas at all–neither in philosophy nor in theology. I asked, "When am I going to get St. Thomas?" "Well, you're already past that, so you don't need it," they said. So I had Kierkegaard and all the modern guys, but I never saw the *Summa*.

Did you study Latin?

Fr. Z.: Oh yes, but interestingly, only in the college level and not the theologate. It was classical, not ecclesiastical Latin. We read Catullus–Wheelock was the text.

What did they teach you about the priesthood?

Fr. Z.: They used current books on the problem of the priesthood, the problem of celibacy–we didn't have anything like St. Alphonsus to help us with formation. All of that was purposely avoided. We used modern viewpoints from priests who were in crisis–having trouble with their vocation and trouble with celibacy. We rarely spoke of the priesthood in any other way. It's amazing that anyone actually got ordained after all that. The priest was seen as appointed by the community. If they didn't say it specifically, it was implied. We were told that priests were the servants of the people. Whatever they wanted, we were there to help them and to serve them. We were not there to tell them not to use contraceptives, because that was their choice. I remember distinctly being told that if a couple already had children we were to tell them that it was OK to use contraceptives since they already had their children. Regarding *Humanae Vitae*, our professors were open dissenters and proud of it.

Did anybody ever get expelled from your seminary?

Fr. Z.: There were a few guys who insisted on wearing the cassock to class, and they were kicked out, but none of the liberals was ever harassed. Generally we wore a white shirt with black slacks, but on Mondays we got to wear our cassocks for Mass, the Office, and dinner. That was it. We could never wear our cassocks in a parish (if we were going there to teach). Those who insisted on wearing the cassock were scrutinized, then sidelined, and eventually we never saw them again. You would hear things like, "He was immature." "He was old-fashioned."

Why was Monday "cassock day"?

Fr. Z.: Monday was called "pre-eminence day." Why, I'm not sure. I was disturbed by all of this from the get-go.

How did you survive until ordination?

Fr. Z.: They didn't want to ordain me, but I had some people who went to bat for me. I really don't know why or even who they were, but they did, and I got myself ordained deacon. Then I went into a parish. They used deacons as interns. I was ordained a year later. I kept on questioning things, but they said, "Just go ahead and get ordained." I got exempted from some liberation theology stuff in San Antonio. I told them that I didn't want it and they said, "Okay," but normally they made everyone do it. For some reason, they let me off the hook. It didn't seem like I was a troublemaker back then. I was pretty dutiful; I just asked a lot of questions. But I got surly over the years because I started to mimic the answers. When I realized the bad stuff going on I took to keeping silent, so I earned the nickname, "Run silent, run deep."

What was your first assignment?

FR. Z.: It was a parish that actually had three priests. I replaced one, so I was the second assistant. The first assistant was a priest from Paraguay. I had studied some Spanish in the seminary and college level, so when he went on vacation I filled in for him, saying the Spanish Mass. This parish had a novena to Our Lady of Perpetual Help. It was a traditional-style church. The pastor was the vicar general of the diocese and a jolly old guy. So I had a pretty good time, but I didn't stay there long because I was assigned to work at the chancery in the marriage tribunal.

You must have had an affinity for canon law?

FR. Z.: My canon law professor was the one that got me hired at the marriage tribunal. He was also the *officialis*. He said I had a flair for it! He had a doctorate in canon law from Catholic University, and I followed him there, receiving a license, after which they told me to go home. I had applied to the doctoral program, but I didn't get accepted.

I entered Catholic University after having been a priest for only four years. At that time, we had to learn the old code. Then when we came back from the Christmas break, there was the new code of 1983. We knew it was coming, but we didn't know exactly when. Then we had to study both codes. I remember the guys who finished in '83 had to know both and we were told that we needed to know both for the comprehensive exams. As it turned out, we only had to know the new one, since none of the exam questions dealt with the old. Unless, of course, you had a real stickler for a professor, and then you got questions from the old code.

How did working on the tribunal affect your priesthood?

FR. Z.: First of all, I was not dressing like a cleric, since it was fashionable to dress in slacks and a nice shirt. At first I lived in the parish, but then it was too much of a commute, so they put me up in a room at the chancery. I lived there from 1980 to 1997–seventeen years in the chancery! On the weekends

I filled in for priests at their parishes when they were sick or on vacation. That was my life for all that time. Of course, for two of those years I was at Catholic University–from '82 to '84. When I would come home for the summer, I would do the same thing that I was doing while living at the tribunal.

Another effect the tribunal had on my priesthood was what I had to do to try to avoid even the appearance of a conflict of interest. I knew that I should not involve myself with certain people because of possible effects on my decisions, so I became a loner. I never really mingled with any people. I tried to tell them that I really couldn't "do lunch" and other things because they might one day present a case which I would have to judge–then what? But the new theology requires the priest and the bishop to be popular, to wine and dine, to be able to entertain and be like a bachelor.

How did you react to the sheer volume of the annulment cases?

FR. Z.: At first, I just went with the flow. But the most "convincing" point made in many of the petitions was that "These people want to get back to the sacraments. We have to help them." So we would always try to get a favorable decision for their cases. Then, as I went up through the ranks and eventually became the chief judge of the tribunal, I began to see that this was wrong, especially when people started coming back for a second and even a third annulment! You can't do that! Actually, Pope John Paul II, in one of his allocutions to the Rota, said that it's an act of charity to say, "No!" in some of these cases. That statement had quite an effect on me. I said, "Yeah, that's true, because in the long run, their souls are much more important than their annulments!" So I began to look at the cases in that vein and then, Boy! did I get into all kinds of trouble, because these pastors were going to bat–they were the advocates for these parishioners who were contributing financially in a big way–some were richer than others! So when they complained about a negative decision on their case, they went to the bishop, who hates complaints. Priests started opposing me and reporting me to the bishop because I was too harsh, too strict, too rigid.

How did the bishop react to these complaints?

FR. Z.: For some reason, he took their side, and he said that maybe we could look at these cases again. I told the bishop, "It's judged; it's finished! It has to go to appeal." So we would argue about things like that, about having too many cases to hear, *etc.* By the late '80's or early '90's, we started having arguments at the lunch table about different issues in the Church. So, eventually, the bishop began to look for my replacement, because he knew I wasn't going to change.

Do you think that this is an indication of a sort of real lawlessness?

FR. Z.: Oh, yes! I worked in the tribunal for years, and I could see the trends. On the national level the clergy on the tribunals were very, very liberal. Their view was, "Find grounds to get people back to the sacraments." But there was little questioning going on about whether the things the people were doing were immoral. They were living with their next "spouse," waiting for the case to go through–things like that. The bishop finally warned me by word of mouth that he was looking for someone else to take my place, because our arguments got pretty heated at times, even at the lunch table in front of other priests. It was getting pretty bad.

What were the purported grounds of most of these annulments?

FR. Z.: All canon 1095, paragraph 2 [lack of due discretion–*Ed.*]. We tried to use the old grounds, but eventually those were found too difficult to press. We had this saying that everything was "1095, §2." In fact, as a joke, we made lists of all the categories of 1095, paragraph 2. It was kind of a mockery of the system. We had about forty-five scenarios from cases–from real cases–it was actually hilarious! But I had very few helpers, and I was doing all the work myself. Even worse, Rome was starting to sniff around and look at sample cases, and they were not happy with our jurisprudence. I told the bishop that Rome wanted some case examples and that I knew they were not going to like what they saw. He said, "Just ignore it." So that's what we did. I always knew that wasn't right.

Didn't you teach in the diocesan seminary as well?

FR. Z.: Yes. I taught canon law from 1986 to 2000–for fourteen years. During that time, when we came to the canon about Latin as the language of the Church, I would bring up Archbishop Lefebvre. I had read everything I could get on the subject, and I would tell the students what was going on. So, when 1988 came and the excommunication was declared, I brought a copy of the bull to class, and I said, "Do you see this? This hardly happens at all now. But look, this man, this Archbishop, was excommunicated along with the ones he consecrated because all they did was want the old Mass." These seminarians were too young to understand, but they were kind of shocked.

What was it like coming back to pastoral life after so many years?

FR. Z.: It was very nice, at the beginning, to get my feet wet, to be the boss of the parish. This particular place had always been a small one-priest parish, attended mainly by Hispanic people.

What was it that moved you to take the now-famous step that you took on June 29th of this year [2003–*Ed.*]?

FR. Z.: I have tried to think what it could be that was really the catalyst, but I can't think of anything specific. My mother passed away the year after I got to the parish, in 1998, and it was toward the end of the year that I began to say the New Mass in Latin.

What made you do that?

FR. Z.: Well, there were days when there was not a scheduled Mass, like on a Monday–that's usually the priest's "day off." In one-man parishes they don't have anyone to say Mass that day. If I were there on Fridays I would say the *Novus Ordo* Mass in Latin. People heard about it, and they wanted to come–it wasn't even the Tridentine Mass!

Why did they want even the New Mass in Latin?

FR. Z.: Well, it could have been a novelty to them. I noticed that, after a while, they stopped coming.

So what was it that appealed to you and made you want to do this?

FR. Z.: Well, I think I had always wanted to say the old Mass, because I had served it as a boy. If a lay person asked, "How about the old Mass?" I said, "Well, the altar is not big enough." (We had such a very small altar, like a butcher block, in the chapel.) But that comment made me think. And in the meantime, probably through the aid of the conservative lay people, who were looking for priests that were of like mind, my interest was kindled. They worked on me because they heard that I was conservative in other ways, and that's how it started. They put me in touch with the Fraternity of St. Peter, from which I got a video and some literature, and I went on from there.

You taught yourself to say the traditional Mass through their video and books?

FR. Z.: Right, and by remembering from the past, and just reading the missal, having studied Latin. Luckily, when I was in the seminary we still studied it, but they don't do it now.

When you began, how often did you say the traditional Mass?

FR. Z.: I started to say it once a week on Fridays. Then I began a discussion with some of the teachers for the catechism in Spanish. They wanted another Spanish Mass on Sunday, and I said, "No, but I have an idea. Let's have the old Latin Mass early in the morning," and they liked the idea. They didn't follow up, though they came to see it, but since they didn't understand it, they didn't come back. And, of course, there were problems with not having the proper materials. We got some Spanish-Latin and English-Latin missals, but it never went off too well with the Spanish speakers.

But we continued. I started a Sunday morning Mass at 7 o'clock in the church, a Tridentine Mass. And that went on for almost a year before the bishop stopped it. He called me and said, "Are you saying the Tridentine Mass?" And I said, "Yes." "In the church?" And I said, "Yes, Bishop." "With *people there?*" And I said, "Yes, Bishop, with people." And he said, "Well, we can't have that; you have to stop that. It is not permitted." And I said, "Well, no, I have the other Masses as well." He said, "No, no, no." So it got to be where I could only say that Mass in the rectory. He meant for me to celebrate Mass with no one there, not even a server, as far as I could tell from what he said. But of course people started coming to the rectory, and I had a little chapel made in one of the rooms in the office. It worked out. I had about five people per day on average, so I started to say Mass every day at 6:30 in the morning.

You didn't think you needed any permission?

FR. Z.: I knew he wouldn't give permission; I just did it. I knew he wouldn't give it because of the conversations we had had before.

But you still felt justified in doing it?

FR. Z.: Oh, yes. I thought that he either didn't know that I really could do it without his permission, or he didn't want to know. In fact, I told him, "I think you know, but you just don't want to pursue the matter. You just don't like it. So I know I don't have to obey you in this because you are just being cantankerous or something."

He never said, "I forbid you to do it"?

FR. Z.: At first, he would circumvent the question; he would not really pin himself down to "forbidding" it. But then eventually, in letters, he forbade me. In fact, he called me once and said he had heard that I was going to put up a communion rail. I said that I was just talking to people about it, that I had no plans specifically, but that it would be easier for people to kneel for communion, since it is hard to push off the floor to get back up. We had a step there, but still, for the older people a rail would have helped. He didn't want kneeling for communion; he said that it was not appropriate, that he had new guidelines. He always made a point of saying that everything was approved by the highest authority in the Church. Now all the new things were permitted by the highest authority in the Church. For me to deny that was to be going "against the pope," you know! Yet he feels that allowing only one indult Mass for the whole diocese was sufficient to say that he was going along with the Pope! Because "Nobody wants the Latin Mass anyway!" He kept saying, "Nobody wants it." He always says to me, "Why are people wanting this? What is the problem?" Again, it was incredible. But I notice that other bishops do that, too. They just pretend–even Cardinal Arinze. I saw a statement of his recently asking, "Why do people want the old Mass? Why don't they like new?" Either they really don't see the answer, or they pretend they don't.

Did you ever make recourse to Rome?

FR. Z.: I wrote to Cardinal Castrillon-Hoyos, and he replied through Msgr. Perl. He wouldn't give me a *celebret*. He couldn't figure out why I couldn't say both Masses. He said that would be very good, because I could see and help both kinds of people. He did know, at least, that there were a lot of people wanting the old Mass, but he said that I should still say the New Mass to go along with the regime. That was how it panned out. But you know what? You can't do it! You cannot continue saying both Masses because after a while when you're saying the old Mass, you can't stand the New Mass. It is so obviously wrong that you can't do it! I can't do it, and I don't see how the Indult guys can do it.

So you were saying the Mass every day in the rectory, drawing only four or five people, but finally this fateful day of June 29, 2003, approached. Can you tell us a little bit about what led up to that during the last months?

FR. Z.: Well, of course, it was getting so bad I couldn't go to the chancery office and functions, or priests' meetings. It was just too horrible. What was said there was always inaccurate and not in accord with the Catholic Faith. Certainly concelebrating Masses and giving Communion in the hand caused me much more difficulty. I just couldn't do it! I would get mad at people. I said, "No, this is a Catholic church, and you don't receive in the hand."

And besides, I had had contact with the Society of Saint Pius X here in Dickinson [Texas]. I would come to the bookstore, come to lunch. One or two of the priests and I began to have conversations, on and off. I knew I was going to do something–I just didn't know how or when. I had gone to an *Una Voce* talk in New York, and then I had talked with Fr. A. from the Fraternity of Saint Peter. I actually stayed a night at their place in Pennsylvania. They didn't seem too interested in what I had to say. In fact, I didn't get to talk to Father at all while I was there; one of the deacons talked to me.

As time wore on, it was becoming less and less tolerable saying the *Novus Ordo*, especially on the weekends, with all the strange and irreverent things that were going on, and the way people dressed.

Did your increasing conservatism irritate the faithful?

FR. Z.: Just a few, actually. Many liked it and felt refreshed, I was told. There were some significant detractors who got a lot of people upset and wrote letters to the bishop. So I was getting calls and letters from the chancery saying that I needed to stop telling people that they couldn't receive Communion in the hand because it was their right to do so. I replied, "No it is not. The priest decides, since he is the custodian of the Eucharist." I cut out Communion under both species, and I wouldn't let any lay people give out Communion. Some of them felt that their rights as Catholics were being taken away; they thought that they could not "participate" in the Mass. But the majority felt good about the changes. In fact, many times I had already said the old Mass in the Church on significant feast days. They still had the other Masses, but I had the old Mass on the schedule, too. They were getting very used to it.

What did you feel happening to your priesthood, when you began saying the traditional Mass?

FR. Z.: I felt like a priest. I told the bishop this. I said, "You know, when I first said the old Mass, I feel like a priest."

What was the difference?

FR. Z.: There are no distractions with the old Mass as compared to the New Mass; in the New Mass they are continuous! It's like you are up on a stage, and you are looking out, and the people are looking to you for a prompt—for you to give them a little joke or something. Whereas, in the old Mass, you have a nice crucifix. You look up and then back down to the altar. I said, "This is really how it is supposed to be!" I knew that, having been reading a lot of things about the Mass, its history, and the problems in the Church, and, of course, from having taught at the seminary, and having seen all the changes in progress. Comparing the New Mass with the Protestant service, I could see that something was very badly wrong. When I read about the history of the Second Vatican Council, how the original schemata were changed and how many of the important figures in the Council (the advisors, the *periti*) were some of the very people who had been condemned by Pope

Pius XII, I knew something was wrong. I also knew that it would be danger-ous to leave the normal structure of the Church, but I knew that the structure was not right. Even though the hierarchy had the titles and the real estate, theirs was not the Catholic religion. I was convincing other people of that, and they were able to see it, too.

What were some of the more important books that you read?

FR. Z.: Well, Michael Davies's books, and *The Rhine Flows into the Tiber*, those kinds of books. And then Msgr. Klaus Gamber and *Iota Unum* come to mind, but there were a lot of things. I read a lot about Archbishop Lefebvre. It was fascinating.

Now, let's touch on what has been seen all over the news, the day when you decided to celebrate only the traditional Mass there in the parish.

FR. Z.: I decided to do it the week before June 29th. I was thinking about making the retreat up at Winona in August, and I was trying to get more in-formation when I called Dickinson to talk to Fr. B., but I got Fr. C.! He asked me if I was still saying "That poisonous Mass, that New Mass." I said, "Yes, but as soon as I can..."

He asked, "Well, when's 'soon'? You can say that for a long time; it could go on for years!" He was putting the screws on!

You have to remember that I am in my early fifties. I have seen no prog-ress from all the promised changes in the Church, which would purportedly make the New Mass better. I finally came to the conclusion that you cannot fix the New Mass because it is not the right Mass. It is totally people-oriented and not God-oriented. So, when Fr. C. put it to me like that, I said, "You know, Father, I think I am going to make the switch this weekend, because it happens to be the Feast of the Holy Apostles Peter and Paul."

Before that, saying both Masses, I always had to prepare for two calen-dars, and I had noticed that the Epistle and the Gospel were identical in both Masses. I said, "You know, I could do this, because they could still use their new missals for the Epistle and the Gospel!" And I had a lot of Latin-English booklet missals anyway.

That is when I made the decision to do it. Things had really come to a head with some of the people. Basically, they were not being Catholic at Mass, and I was tired of having to keep telling them. I said that I was long-ing to go to a place where people knelt to receive Communion without any controversy. I felt sure I would run into problems, and I didn't know how it would pan out when I finally made the switch. But the people who had known me over the years and talked with me about how things were tending knew that something was going to happen.

What was the difference? You had said the old Mass on feast days before, and you had said it every day in the rectory. Why did everything come to a head with that one Feast Day Mass?

FR. Z.: I don't know. I think they could tolerate my saying the old Mass occasionally, but not exclusively. Once they heard that I intended no longer to say the New Mass, that caused some problems. But again, there were many who were willing to try it! They were willing to have hand-missals. And I told them, "We'll find the proper missals, and we'll be able to do it! And we'll get some singing going, some Gregorian chant." They were just upset that this was going to be the only Mass I would say. No more Mitch Miller-type music! That kind of got to them.

What happened on the following Monday morning, after you had dropped your bomb-shell during the Sunday Masses?

FR. Z.: After the Sunday Masses, which I thought went very well, I knew there was some anger, especially among people who were leaders in the parish. They were the most angry of all. But almost all of the people went along on the Sunday. Nobody put out his hand for Communion; they all knelt if they could. It was beautiful. I was really moved by all of those Masses, even though the people in the different choirs, the staff people, and the deacons were pretty much all angry at me. They just couldn't understand it, even though I explained what was going on (and why) in all of the sermons that weekend. I explained that this Mass was the Mass of their patron saints. All of their patron saints went to this Mass, exactly as they saw it that morning. I pointed out the silence: this is a Mass where you can really get down and pray without having to listen to the priest chattering all the time.

It went smoothly that day, and things were okay afterwards. Everybody went home, but I think the calls started going to the chancery pretty quickly! Of course there was no one there, since it was Sunday afternoon. I started to get calls on Monday, but I had just decided not to take them, because traditionally, you know, Monday is the pastor's "day off." I decided to be unavailable, even though I knew the Chancery would be calling.

So I just left, and when I got back the vice-chancellor was waiting for me. He had driven; I don't know how long he had been waiting there to talk to me. We talked for four hours! He just couldn't see it, and I told him, "You know, you are going to follow me in five years, because you are not going to be able to handle it, because this New Mass is not the real thing. You keep pretending. You keep agreeing with me about Communion in the hand, but that practice is not going to change, because they are now making it the law that the people can decide how to give Communion, not the priest. It is actually getting worse, instead of better!"

But then he used the humanistic motives, like "What about your salary? What about your insurance?" Security! And I said, "My security is sanctifying grace–trying to get to heaven! Who cares about money? Somebody'll donate something; I don't care." He said, "The bishop's not going to like it." It was a pretty long four hours! A couple of times I had to go back to the church to check on things, because we were having adoration that Monday evening, but he still stayed there waiting until I finally kicked him out.

Did he threaten you?

FR. Z.: No, he just said that he was going to recommend that I needed psychiatric treatment.

On what grounds?

FR. Z.: Because I shouldn't be acting so melodramatically. So I said, "Come on now, Father, like St. Thomas, 'Let us go and die with Him.' You want to do this too! You're just following the bishop because you don't want to lose your job in the chancery. But you keep complaining about your job in the chancery. Just tell the truth, and you'll see what happens!"

I said that there's nothing wrong with the old Mass, and that that can be proved by the Commission of Cardinals. The fact that it is not admitted publicly or written as a policy now doesn't keep their conclusions from being true. They said that the old Mass has never been abrogated and that no bishop can keep a priest from celebrating it.

What reaction did you get from the bishop?

FR. Z.: Well, I called him Tuesday morning after my 6:30 A.M. Mass, and he said that he would see me immediately. I told him that I had an emergency Communion call for a man who was dying, and that I would stop by the chancery after that. As it turned out, because of the traffic, I had to go and see the bishop first. It was a little difficult, since I had the pyx on my neck. He realized that right away. I said, "I couldn't make it to my Communion call, and I didn't want to be late."

It was actually a good meeting in the sense that we talked, and nobody got angry or yelled. I told him where I was coming from, that there are no good fruits coming from the New Mass. I said, "You know that the old Mass draws men; it doesn't turn them away." I told him that I felt like a priest when I said the old Mass, but he just looked at me. It was like it meant nothing to him, but he said, "Well, what are you going to do? You won't have any salary. How are you going to support yourself? And your insurance?" He said all the same things that the vice-chancellor had said.

It was a foregone conclusion that I would not be able to operate in the diocese without saying the New Mass because the bishop was not going to allow it, you see. I told him that this has been done in other dioceses, and that there is nothing wrong. I said, "Let's try it for the sake of vocations. It can't hurt anything. Besides, you'll have the people there still within the diocese, and you'll still have the normal tax from the parish, the little mission, or whatever we want to call it. Even if you don't let me do it, I can't stand the New Mass, and I am not going to say it any more anyway. That's that!"

"And," I said, "You can't make me say it, because Pope Pius V, who was a saint, covered his bases when he codified the Mass. He gave an indult and a privilege for every priest to say this Mass forever." St. Pius V meant that the Mass was to stay in that form because it was perfect, nearly as perfect as possible. The reason he did that was to ward off the errors which came right back and attacked the Church in the Second Vatican Council, and the errors won when we let down our defenses. The Mass was the main defense, and we let it down, took it away, and then we were overrun by all the errors and the immoralities. I said, "Bishop, I am feeling that I am being overrun in the New Mass."

How did he react to your determination that you were not going to say the New Mass at all?

FR. Z.: He was incredulous. He said, "This is the Mass of the Church. The Holy Father, the highest authority would be against what you're doing." I said, "No, in fact there are several fraternities and institutes who won't say the New Mass, and they are not going against the pope! That can't be. Bishop, this was the Mass of your ordination. What is wrong with it?"

Sometimes he couldn't answer; he just stared at me. For a long time, I did all the talking. It was amazing. Maybe it was because of the presence of the Blessed Sacrament. I am almost sure that he would have really gotten angry with me, as he had done before on occasion.

I concluded at that meeting that he had already abandoned the Catholic religion that he was raised in, because, when we got on the question of Jews and religious liberty, he said that the Jews have a separate covenant from ours. I said, "Bishop, you can't really mean that. You are just saying that. You don't have to say it to me, because there are not political issues between you and me. There are no Jews around for you to insult by saying that they can't get to heaven." He actually asked me, "Do you really think that they are going to go to hell?" I said, "Well, what do you think? How can they get to heaven without Christ?"

What was his answer?

FR. Z.: He had no answer. The only thing he said was, "Well, God wouldn't do that." I said, "Well, then what's the reason for being Catholic? Why are you a bishop? What is the Church for, if people can get to heaven on natural goodness alone?" That is what he had determined: that God only asks for natural goodness. I said, "Well, what about baptism?" He answered, "Well, that is only for those whose tradition is to be baptized." I was really amazed!

He seemed convinced that Vatican II had changed everything. Nothing I could tell him about it availed–that it was not a doctrinal Council, the Holy Father John XXIII said that we were not here to condemn error. I said, "Bishop, when you don't condemn error, it means that you agree with it. You can't be neutral with error." Then I gave him an epistemology test! "Truth plus error equals what?" He answered, "Well, truth...truths!" "No," I insisted, "the answer is error. You can't have error and truth together. They don't mix." That is what we are seeing now. We have some truth here and truth plus error there, and what happens? It is a disaster.

We now have Cardinal Kasper telling people that they don't have to convert to the Catholic religion. It is not necessary, he says, because as long as you believe, that is the essential thing. And that leads to the question of Faith in the Eucharist. I said, "Bishop, I don't see how you can let people handle the Eucharist if you believe that that's really God. If it's only a symbol of God, I would have no problem with that–you can receive it any way you want! But, if we really believe that it is God, then we have to insist on kneeling and reception on the tongue. The Sacrament is too important to mess with like that."

There are too many sacrileges, but the bishop doesn't see it that way, because, again, "God is love," and if people rough Him up a bit, He likes it even more! He is not saying it quite so bluntly, but that is the ethos of the new way. The new way says, "Thank God people are at Mass! Who cares what they actually do at Mass as long as they laugh, and clap, and are active and smiling?" That is what is important–that people smile and let a couple of giggles slip out here and there. That is a successful Mass!

What was his final verdict?

FR. Z.: Well, I asked for his blessing and kissed his ring, and then he said, "I am going to call you tomorrow. I want you to think about it tonight and pray hard." I said I would think about it. He did say, "You realize that you could be suspended." I replied, "Bishop, you just do what you think you have to do." Of course, I wouldn't agree with such a move. What I have done is not sufficient grounds to be suspended. An offense has to be more weighty to warrant that penalty. He even showed me a suspension letter all typed up and ready to be signed. He had me read it, and I said, "It has some canonical mistakes, and you didn't show any of the relevant canons. To be suspended, I must have committed some delicts, but you don't refer to any. There has to be a reason; you can't just say it like that. Why don't you give this back to Father and have him try to rework it?" He gave it back to me–he wouldn't take it back, so I took it home. That is the one, I think, that went on the Internet.

When he called the next morning, I said, "Yes, Bishop, I did think about it." Nothing had changed. He told me to take a two-month leave and to go on retreat. I said, "Well, you know, I was going to go on retreat any way! I'm glad you said that." And that was that.

Where did you go?

FR. Z.: I went home to my father's house. He was extremely angry because of all that had gone on. I stayed there until I went on retreat. I went up to Kansas City, and then on to Winona from there. From Winona, I came back here to Queen of Angels just to see where I would be staying and to see whether it would work out. Everybody here was very gracious. "You're welcome here if you want, but if you can't come for some reason, don't worry."

Meanwhile I stayed at my father's and said Mass in homes where people have chapels–at the houses of home-schooling families whom I have known over the years. They supported me. It was during this time that all the correspondence started coming in from everywhere. Everything was going to my father's house, and he was fielding calls, talking to strangers.

Because of the publicity from *The Remnant* and *Seattle Catholic*?

FR. Z.: Yes. Actually, the story was on *Seattle Catholic* first: "Bishop Cans Priest for Saying the Old Mass," or something like that. I can just hear the reactions: "Hey, honey, look at this. This is not something that we've heard before. The old Mass...." It made people question and say, "Hey, you mean the old Mass is still around? We'd like to check that out." The publicity of my situation generated a lot of interest.

But it's funny that, the more the Bishop publicized the case by putting it in his Catholic paper, the more it spread in the public papers, starting with the Houston paper. They ran a truly amazing article. The diocese distanced themselves from it and said that it was all wrong, but it was actually pretty good.

What did you do during this storm of publicity?

FR. Z.: I came to Queen of Angels and got to work right away in the school. It was August 10th when I came, so we had about two weeks left before school started. I was just getting adjusted. I started off saying Mass here and then at the North Houston chapel. That has been pretty much the routine since then.

What was your first impression of living in a situation where you could say the Mass and people would kneel for Communion?

FR. Z.: Oh, it was beautiful! I am still very moved, especially with the children at the school Mass. It is so quiet, so reverent, so beautiful. I used to preach at my former parish that, when you put out your tongue for communion, you are actually more beautiful. You don't realize that the priest sees you and that he is much more moved than when you put out your hand as if you were equal to God. It was psychologically much better here.

How have you fared with the traditional liturgy from a ceremonial standpoint?

FR. Z.: I am still being trained in the Mass of course. They tell me different things, give little corrections–nuts and bolts. That will be part of the experience of just about any priest who starts saying the old Mass, especially the ones who haven't even looked at the missal. It may be interesting at times! For me, having already said the Mass for four years, maybe it was easier. It would be a bit more tricky to just start cold, but, you know, where there's a will there's a way.

Tell us about the end of your two months' "leave of discernment."

FR. Z.: When I got back from the retreat, the bishop wanted to see me right after Labor Day, and he did call me, but I couldn't go see him right away. Do you know why? Because I had class, and he was a bit surprised that

I couldn't just drop everything. I said, "Well, I have students; I can't leave a classroom full of children." He seemed to see that, so he arranged a meeting for the following Wednesday, which was a half-day for the school. So that is when I went down to see him, and I brought along some of the Dickinson clergy. They just sat in the foyer, but the Bishop did come out at one point.

I talked to the bishop about my two months off and told him that I had made a decision–that the Society was the answer, and there was nothing wrong with them. "They do pray for you, Bishop," I said. (He had been under the impression that they were not praying for him in the canon of the Mass, so he was kind of surprised about how things really were.) He did not tell me that I couldn't stay with them; he did not say any of those things I expected to hear. Then, he sent a letter a week later saying that I had to leave here and stop associating with the priests here. So the letter was quite different from the meeting, but, by then all of the publicity had gotten out about my being "allowed" to stay here.

Do you think he was more or less willing to let sleeping dogs lie until the arrangement got so public?

FR. Z.: He might have done that. In fact, even now, he hasn't acted. He gave me a deadline of October 1st to move out, but that has come and gone, and he hasn't acted. He published that warning in the Houston Catholic paper: "Stay away from the Society!" But, actually, this stand of his is giving more publicity to the situation. People are inquiring about the Society. Queen of Angels is totally full! I am seeing *Novus Ordo* people here now. I can tell, because when I give them communion, they say, "Amen." They are coming–or at least they are checking it out.

What sanction did the bishop use to back up his warning? Did he suspend you?

FR. Z.: No, he still is extending it, *de facto.* You see, this time he has listened to his canonists. The canon he referred to this time says that, if I disobey a precept, I can be punished with a just punishment up to and including suspension, but which precept am I disobeying? I don't know which precept he is referring to! He has, as yet, given me no precept to disobey. I mean, it is not a precept to say that I can't say the old Mass. I think he knows he can't say that, because that matter is above him, you see. How can he forbid that? But he still could come out with something real. But, the longer he drags it out, the more negative publicity he is going to get, and he is getting some really tough letters. I know that because people have been showing me the letters they have sent him, and they are really rough!

Of course, the numbers, again are relatively small, because hardly any-body reads *The Remnant*. The letters I get from priests and religious in the diocese are all against me, but, of course, they haven't read anything! They don't read the *Remnant* or *Seattle Catholic* or anything like that. All they know is that I "disobeyed the Pope" and that I am thus equivalent to Martin Luther. In their minds, that's that. I am now Protestant. That is exactly what they think, and they say that I only want something from the past which "doesn't work anymore." To them, the old Mass "doesn't work for modern people."

How do they respond to the allegation that the New Mass "doesn't work for modern people"?

FR. Z.: Well, they say that it really does, but that there are still problems because we haven't tried it long enough. They say, "A Council takes a long time to kick in!" I reply, "Well, how long did Trent take?" Right after Trent did they have, all of a sudden no priests, no nuns, no missionaries? Did every-body go cuckoo? Or after Vatican I, did anything comparable happen? But you see, they don't have any answer, and they don't even want to discuss it because I am evil, or I am sick. Something is wrong with me.

But, really, something is wrong with **them**! They've got to go through all the mistakes in the New Mass and the new ways until they finally figure out that, "Hey, this is not working!" But it is going to take all these people's dying first, because their pride won't let them go back. They have too much invested in the new ways–way too much. They always say that the people like it. Even the Holy Father says that he sees "vibrant faith"–faith is vibrant and active! But obviously the ones who say this are not hearing confessions, because, if they did, they would know how little things have changed. Spiritual life is still a wreck, and that's in the few people who still go to confession! That was an-other contention I had in the parish: people weren't confessing. I said, "How is it that all of you are coming up here to communion, even though I didn't have much of a line for the confessional today? That seems odd with all the temptations out there–the TV and the movies and the way people dressed! Some of you come up here dressed like prostitutes!" In fact, I refused com-munion to some of them because they were dressed horribly.

If the bishop were to suspend you, would that suspension have any value?

FR. Z.: Not in my eyes. As we say around here jokingly, he only means to suspend me from saying the New Mass!

What about this objection, raised (no doubt) by many who may read this: "It's a real suspension, and you're flouting it; therefore you're lawless!"

FR. Z.: I'm not flouting it. I'm not saying he can't suspend me. I'm saying that it isn't correct for him to suspend me. He certainly has the episcopal authority to suspend canonically, but he has to have an adequate reason to do so. "Disobedience" is not enough. He really could nail me on the assignment question–that I failed to take an assignment, but even that seems overly harsh. Suspension, you have to remember, is a very harsh penalty and must be used as a last resort. What would the weighty reason be in my case?

You've asked for an assignment, have you not?

FR. Z.: I proposed something to him, but I did say that I could not say the New Mass ever again, so you have to take that into consideration. To his mind, that is impossible, and he won't let it happen. He is allowing only one indult Mass, and when that priest is retired, as far as he is concerned, that is the end of the indult! Here is one priest that has agreed to say it, and even though I had asked him in the past, he said "No," because I was too young. I used to joke with him when I would see him over the years: "You know, I'm getting older," but he is not a one for pleasantries. He is not a person that takes jokes well. He just doesn't get it. Humor is not a part of him, as far as I know.

Maybe reactionaries drain the humor completely away?

FR. Z.: I have no clue. He bounced from a pretty solicitous view when we all went down there to a really harsh letter with canons and threats. I said, "Boy, is this the Church of love and peace and ecumenism?" This is sick. In their view, we're the only enemy left on the planet. Not even the Muslims, or the atheists, or anyone like that, can be such a threat to them! We're worse than the Masons. To them, Masons are nothing. Masons and Knights of Columbus are equivalent in the eyes of the bishop. We are the enemy today.

It's true, isn't it, in a way, because the truth is going to be perpetually at war with error.

FR. Z.: The truth for them is, "You follow the Pope. If the Pope decides you can have Communion in the hand, that's the truth." So to those who say, "No, that's not a good deal," then they shout, "Hey, you're against the Pope!" It is an extreme situation. Look, the same people who went against the Pope before on *Humanae Vitae* are the very ones who are now appealing to the Pope against the old Mass. It is the exact same ones, because I still know the old dogs from the past, from 1968. They were the ones who said, "It's horrible. The Pope's in the bedroom now, and that has never happened before. Jesus wouldn't get involved in the bedroom!" These are the same ones who now say, "You have to obey the Pope. The Pope says you've got to have Communion in the hand and altar girls. Who are you to go against the Pope." They make no distinctions. And these people have Ph.D.'s and S.T.D.'s!

Will any of the Romans in charge ever realize what the modernists have done and stand up against it?

FR. Z.: They'll have to eventually, because the Lord promised, and His promises are true! Our Lady says the same thing. We are in a trial and a war. I don't know how long it will take, but still we know, as I try to explain to people, that there are certain things that you just can't change: number one, Jesus Christ. To be saved you've got to believe in Him. You've got to benefit from His crucifixion through the sacraments. You can't get to heaven just by being nice, because if that were the case, He would not have come on earth. Moses himself couldn't get into heaven without Christ. John the Baptist was in limbo.

When I ask, "What about all that?" they answer in a Rahnerian way, by saying that everybody is really a Catholic or a Christian. They don't know it, but, as soon as God became flesh, all flesh after that was divinized. And so, the main thing with religion is just to realize the blessings that God has given by sending us His Son. No matter what faith you have, if you realize that fact and are nice to people, you'll be all right. Basically, that is the religion of today.

So the fact of getting all these religions together is something that they look forward to, because it will help end wars, and end starvation, and hunger, and diseases if we work together. This is a higher good for them than believing in a certain dogma. The humanistic religion is the top story of today.

Do you think it is fair to say that the New Mass is a logical result of this new religion?

FR. Z.: That is hard to say, but the New Mass certainly *aids* the new religion and the new way of thinking that God is not a judge, that there is no retribution, that the Bible has to be nuanced, and all those things in the law about condemnation and fire are really just to get the people to wake up. There were no miracles—of course there were miracles of sharing and caring and Jesus had a touch about Him that could heal people, just like some people today can do. And of course, the Eucharist is a memorial, the Mass is a memorial of the great thing that the Lord did, just like when He fed the five thousand people on the side of the mountain when they were hungry,.

So the logical question to them becomes, "If the Eucharist is just a memory, why can't I remember it with the traditional Mass while you remember it with the New Mass?

FR. Z.: I think the true liberals don't have any problem with people wanting the old Mass if that turns them on. It's these other ones who think that makes a difference, like the "neo-conservatives." The old Mass has to be jettisoned to get on with the program of the new evangelization. I think that they are more dangerous than the real liberals. The real liberals allow everything: Wicca, old Mass, whatever. The true liberal should have no problem with anything.

If you had to advise a priest who was vacillating a little bit and wanting to do something better for his priesthood, who was perhaps a little bit scared of trying the old Mass, what would you tell him?

FR. Z.: It depends where he's at. I noticed that when I was teaching the young guys when they first entered the seminary, that they were very open to Tradition, but it didn't take long for them to start to question things because of the other courses and professors. Then they would look at me like I was a bit "off," that maybe I actually believed all that stuff in the Bible. So, if this hypothetical priest got through the seminary somehow and still maintained some traditional sense, probably the best thing for him to do would be to start reading some good books, like St. Alphonsus de Liguori. Get his sermons for the year. Those had a great effect on me. He should read good books like that and lives of the saints–about the martyrs in England, for example. Also, all of Michael Davies's books are good because they trace what happened from the 1960's through the 1970's, from what we used to have to the current mess. He should try to see some videos, too, especially videos of the Mass if he can't get to the Mass in person. That was very helpful for me, too, very inspiring.

What should our hypothetical priest do, especially if he's never had any proper studies, or never studied any Latin?

FR. Z.: Well, the Latin should be no problem. If St. John Vianney did it, anybody can do it! It is easier–to pronounce at least–than many languages. He can work on it, and after a while he'll really get the hang of it. I don't think that the lack of previous Latin studies should be a worry to him, although it is a setback.

The thought of learning Latin and the ceremonies does scare some priests, but with practice, they'll just love to say the Mass. When you start off the Mass and you bend over to the *Confiteor*, it is right then you know you are doing the right thing. You are not telling the people, "How y'all doin'? Guess what happened to me yesterday when I was at the airport?" That's not Mass! We know better, but these priests who are already inquiring have come part of the way out of the mess, and God is helping them. It is not just that we are trying to persuade them. They're doing most of the work anyway.

He should also get the Douay-Rheims Bible, and just start reading it. So many of the *Novus Ordo* priests are angry about the new translations. I say, "Well, just junk it and use the Douay-Rheims. Get rid of the modern translations with the 'she' and the 'it' instead of 'God,' because you know that's not right."

What would you tell a priest who was worried about his future support if he starts saying the traditional Mass and the bishop pulls out the rug from under him?

FR. Z.: People will come to the rescue. Besides, it's either God or Mammon! It finally comes down to that choice. When you have less, you feel better about your Faith. If this hypothetical priest is any good at all, and yet he's living his priesthood in the lap of luxury compared to the people, that situation should bother him. If he sees that things are being taken away from him, he should actually feel better. Ask him if he's there for the money. He'll say, "Oh, Father, of course not." Well, capitalize on that and say, "Then, you know, the Holy Ghost will help, and you'll be provided for." The Lord promises that we will be provided with everything we need. "Seek ye first the Kingdom of God, and all the rest shall be given unto you." All the rest! Popcorn, and Cokes, and everything! Now, not TV of course, but you can still have the popcorn and Cokes!

To contact Fr. Zigrang

Rev. Fr. Stephen Zigrang
4100 Highway 3
Dickinson, TX 77539
(281) 337-2508